In Pursuit of the Nez Perces
The Nez Perce War of 1877

In Pursuit of the Nez Perces
The Nez Perce War of 1877

as reported by
Gen. O. O. Howard
Duncan McDonald
Chief Joseph

compiled by Linwood Laughy
● ● ●
Mountain Meadow Press

In Pursuit of the Nez Perces
The Nez Perce War of 1877

as reported by

General O. O. Howard
Duncan McDonald
Chief Joseph

Compiled by Linwood Laughy

Published by Mountain Meadow Press
P. O. Box 1170
Wrangell AK 99929

Printed in the United States of America
First printing 1993

Copyright 1993 by Mountain Meadow Press

Library of Congress Catalog Card Number 93-077621
ISBN 0-945519-13-3

Foreward

All history is fiction of varying degrees of plausibility.

Voltaire

Many perspectives have helped weave the historical fabric of the American West. Threaded through this tapestry is the thirteen-hundred mile trail of the non-treaty Nez Perces driven from their homelands in Eastern Oregon and North Central Idaho during the Nez Perce War of 1877. This book brings together three different descriptions of this historical saga, each prepared while the scars of battle remained fresh on the landscape.

In Part I, *From the General's Pen*, General Oliver O. Howard, the principal U.S. military leader during the war, describes both the activities that preceded the military engagements and the actual U.S. Army campaign against the non-treaty Nez Perces. In 1881, in an effort to justify the decisions he made while in pursuit of the Nez Perces, General Howard published his account of the war under the title *Nez Perce Joseph: An Account of His Ancestors, His Lands, His Confederates, His Enemies, His Murders, His War, His Pursuit and Capture.*

In Part II, *Through Nez Perce Eyes*, Duncan McDonald, son of Hudson Bay Fur Company manager Angus McDonald, presents a much different view. Duncan McDonald's mother was the sister of Eagle-of-the-Light, chief of the Nez Perce band later led by White Bird. McDonald was fluent in English and Nez Perce and was known personally by many of the approximately two hundred ninety Nez Perces who fled to "Grandmother's Land," Canada, from the Bear Paw Battlefield where the Nez Perce War ended. MacDonald interviewed these refugees shortly after the war and in 1878 published a series of articles in

The New North-West, a Deer Lodge, Montana, newspaper. The newspaper's editor specifically requested that McDonald provide "the Nez Perces' version of their troubles and of their remarkable campaign," an unusual condition in that time of anti-Indian sentiment among most white miners and settlers in Montana.

In Part III, *In-mut-too-yah-lat-lat Speaks,* Chief Joseph provides a brief history of his people, explains the causes of the Nez Perce War, and states the conditions that would lead to a meaningful peace for Native Americans throughout North America. Historians surmise that Joseph's translator was Ad Chapman, who had lived on Idaho's Camas Prairie before the war, participated with the U.S. Army throughout the Nez Perce campaign, and later served as translator for Chief Joseph during his trips to Washington, D. C. Joseph's statement appeared in the *North American Review* in 1879 under the title "An Indian's View of Indian Affairs."

These three historical records inform, intrigue, entertain, and guide readers traveling their own trail *in pursuit of the Nez Perces.*

Linwood Laughy

Without the presence of troops it is impossible to enforce the laws of the United States on this [the Nez Perce] reserve. The town of "Lewiston" will be built despite the laws and proclamations of officers. The rivers and streams will be cut up with ferries. Squatters will settle down on every patch of arable land. The fences of the Indians will be burned for fire wood by travelers—their horses and cattle will be stolen without redress—whiskey is and will be sold to them without an effort at concealment, and the Indians will be overreached, plundered and destroyed.

Charles Hutchins
Nez Perce Indian Agent
January, 1862

When I am gone, think of your country. You [young Joseph] are the chief of these people. They look to you to guide them. Always remember that your father never sold his country. You must stop your ears whenever you are asked to sign a treaty selling your home. A few years more, and the white men will be all around you. They have their eyes on this land. My son, never forget my dying words. This country holds your father's body. Never sell the bones of your father and your mother.

Old Joseph
1871

Suppose a white man should come to me and say, "Joseph, I like your horses, and I want to buy them." I say to him, "No, my horses suit me, I will not sell them." Then he goes to my neighbor and says to him: "Joseph has some good horses. I want to buy them, but he refuses to sell." My neighbor answers, "Pay me the money, and I will sell you Joseph's horses." The white man returns to me and says, "Joseph, I have bought your horses, and you must let me have them." If we sold our lands to the Government, this is the way they were bought.

Chief Joseph
1879

Credits

Cover (and title page) photo "War Poles," (#63-221.18) reprinted with permission of the Idaho State Historical Society, Boise, Idaho.

"From the General' s Pen" reprinted from the original account entitled *Nez Perce Joseph: An Account of His Ancestors, His Lands, His Confederates, His Enemies, His Murders, His War, His Pursuite and Capture, by Gen. O. O. Howard*, published by Lee and Shepard Publishers of Boston in 1881.

"Through Nez Perce Eyes" reprinted from the original series entitled *The Nez Perces: The History of Their Troubles and the Campaign of 1877* by Duncan McDonald, published in *The New North-West*, Deer Lodge, Montana, in 1878.

"In-mut-too-yah-lat-lat-Speaks" reprinted from the original entitled *An Indian's Views of Indian Affairs*, published in the *North American Review* in 1879.

Table of Contents

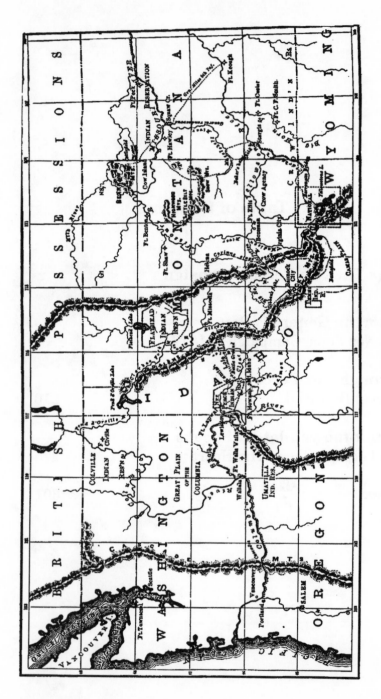

Map to illustrate GEN'L HOWARD'S NEZ-PERCÉ CAMPAIGN 1877.

Part I

From the General's Pen
The Nez Perce Campaign of 1877

by
General Oliver Otis Howard

Introduction

A military hero of the Civil War, General Oliver Otis Howard suffered serious financial difficulties during the 1870's stemming from legal problems he faced as the postwar head of the Bureau of Refugees, Freedmen, and Abandoned Lands. Howard turned to writing as a means of supplementing his income, and following the conclusion of his term in the Nez Perce War of 1877, he published a series of magazine articles describing this campaign. In 1881, these articles and additional material were published in book form under the title *Nez Perce Joseph: An Account of His Ancestors, His Lands, His Confederates, His Enemies, His Murders, His War, His Pursuit and Capture.*

During the Nez Perce campaign Howard had endured continuous assaults by the press upon his military capabilities, particularly regarding the slowness of his pursuit of the hostiles. Citizen volunteers who joined the military march as it passed through their home territories added to this public clamor by abandoning the pursuit and citing Howard's inability to catch the Indians as their reason. The warring Nez Perces themselves referred to Howard as "General Day-After-Tomorrow" because of his failure to follow up his advantage after the Battle of the Clearwater. Over three months in the field pursuing a group of Indians that included more old people and children than warriors likely added to Howard's public relations difficulties, especially in light of his several predictions of imminent success. Even the final victory report, given to the press by General Miles, failed to credit Howard and his forces for their role in the long campaign. In view of these criticisms, Howard no doubt wrote his 1881 book not only as an interpretive account from a military perspective, but also to explain and justify the decisions he had made as the commander in charge of the war effort.

Nez Perce Joseph reflects as well Howard's apparent ambivalence toward the non-treaty Nez Perces. He recognized the unfair treatment long afforded the Indians by white miners and settlers, yet condemned the Indians' eventual response. Often referred to as "The Praying General," Howard's deep religious convictions placed the non-treaties in the realm of heathens needing God's love and care—yet he attempted to destroy those who did not respond to the missionaries' message. His was the role of the stern but loving father—backing up his demands for obedience with force, yet not truly wishing to harm those whom he tried to control. Perhaps this ambivalence contributed to Howard's pursuing but never catching with his own command this frustrating but lovable enemy.

Returning once more to the original title of Howard's book, one can speculate that Chief Joseph's veneration in the press and numerous circles in Washington, D. C., may have itself contributed to Howard's motivation to tell his side of this western epic. He was, after all, the general who had played a significant role in the capture of this Indian chief who was fast becoming a legend.

Chapter I

Near the confluence of two mountain torrents, which unite and flow into the Snake River some twenty-five miles above the town of Lewiston, Idaho, is a rough valley which bears the euphonious name of Imnaha. This valley, small and narrow as it is and environed by the rugged hills of the Snake country, was formerly the home of a branch of the Nez Perces—that tribe of Indians which is now so well known in America—a tribe remarkable for presenting some of the best and some of the worst features of Indian life and character.

The old chief, who figures in the early times of Oregon and in the accounts of the celebrated Hudson Bay Company, was called Joseph, and later "Old Joseph." Indeed, Joseph appears to have been the name of a dynasty rather than of an individual. Here in Imnaha, in a nook sheltered from the storms of winter, old Joseph set up his lodge. He was acknowledged to be the hereditary chief of the remnant of the "Lower" Nez Perces. He was a sturdy old Indian, strongly knit in frame, and with a face usually mild, but exhibiting the signs of an iron will.

The old chief, as well as certain of his tribe, entered into some agreements with Governor Stevens, of Washington Territory; but to the white man's improvements and encroachments he usually maintained a sour and persistent opposition. He married a wife among the fierce and treacherous Cayuses. These are the people who thirty years ago figured largely in the history of Eastern Oregon, and who used to embroil with themselves the voyageurs of the great Fur Company and later, the Catholic and Protestant missionaries, and who finally capped the climax of their diabolism by the Whitman Massacre in 1847.

Two boys were the fruit of the old chief's marriage. They were nearly of the same age. Some neighboring white men regarded them as twins. The one who took the name of the old chief was called "Joseph," "Little Joseph," or "Young Joseph;" the other, "Ollicut."

When I first saw them they were already young men. Their father had died a year before, in 1873.

Though Young Joseph succeeded to the chieftainship, Ollicut generally participated in all affairs of government. The former was noticeable for the peculiar expression of his face. It appeared to partake of the mild obstinacy of his father and the treacherous slyness of his mother's people. He was about six feet in height and finely formed. His brother's countenance was in complete contrast. Ollicut was considerably taller, lithe and active; he appeared frank, open-hearted, and generous. Joseph wore a somber look and seldom smiled. Ollicut was full of fun and laughter.

Before proceeding with the narrative in which these Indian youths bear a prominent part, it may be interesting to recount some facts concerning the tribe to which they belong.

In these times of hurried work and hasty reading not one man in ten will stop to look up the data of geography; yet the tenth man may be curious enough to do so. The ordinary atlas gives only the most general notion. Even a tract of a hundred miles, which it takes four days of the fastest foot-marching to get over, and which contains hills, mountains, valleys, and streams of every variety, is represented by a bit of blank space as clean and objectless as were the unknown parts of Africa on the maps of our early days. The newspaper editors would be more patient with Indian chasers if they could be made to realize how deceptive the small-scale atlases are.

I notice that Irving, in *Bonneville's Adventures*, refers to the Nez Perces, for the first time, as not far from his camp on the "upper waters of the Salmon River." This is a little indefinite, for there are numerous branches of the upper waters of the Salmon. But as Bonneville speaks also of the Horse Prairie as being in that vicinity, "a plain to the north of his cantonment," this fixes the locality pretty well. Find Bannock City on the map of Montana, let your eye pass a little to the south, and you will see "Horse Prairie" in very fine print even on the largest maps; close by is the Rocky Mountain Divide. From Horse Prairie, cross this divide by either of the rough trails and you soon strike the head waters of the Salmon. Here was probably Captain Bonneville's camp in the winter of 1832-1833. By the route our troops lately pursued, from Lewiston, Idaho, to Horse Prairie, the distance is in the neighborhood of three hundred and twenty miles; and to cross the "mountain divide" to Bonneville's cantonment would be about twenty or twenty-five miles further.

It was there where the hunters came galloping back, making signals to the camp, and crying "Indians! Indians!" Captain Bonneville immediately struck into a skirt of wood and prepared for action. The savages were seen trooping forward in great numbers. One of them left the main body and came forward making signals of peace. He announced them as a band of Nez Perces, or pierced-nose Indians, friendly to the whites, whereupon an invitation was returned by Captain Bonneville for them to come and encamp with him. After arraying their persons and horses, painting their faces, etc, "they arranged themselves in martial style, the chiefs leading the van, the braves following in a long line, painted and decorated, and topped off with fluttering plumes. In this way they advanced, shouting and singing, firing off their fuses, and clashing their shields. The two parties encamped hard by each other. The Nez Perces were on a hunting expedition, but had been almost famished on their march."

This account indicates the region over which the Nez Perces roamed and hunted game. The Salmon River and its tributaries furnished an immense territory for them. The paths made by them in their expeditions after buffalo, antelope, and other game are even now clear and well defined— five or six, and sometimes as many as ten or twelve, distinct horse trails, parallel and as near to each other as horses can walk with ease. These trails constitute some of the peculiar signs of these Indian tribes. They often make a side hill look as if terraced, and are as graceful in their windings as if made by a skillful engineer. Sometimes called "the great Nez Perce trails," they extend for hundreds of miles. The more permanent home of the Nez Perces, or more accurately that portion of them usually designated as "the lower Nez Perces," was then, as now, nearer where the Salmon, the Clearwater, and the Grande Ronde flow into that almost endless and peculiar river, so well named "The Snake."

When Mr. Spalding, a remarkable Protestant missionary whose name is today a household word with the Christians of the tribe, came in 1836 to the Nez Perces, Old Joseph and his band were induced to settle for a time near Lapwai Creek, to cultivate a small farm there and send their children to Mrs. Spalding's school. The sudden massacre of Dr. Whitman and his family by the Cayuses in 1847 caused the Spaldings to leave the country in haste.

At that time a rival chief, Big Thunder, succeeded in displacing Old Joseph's band by the usual cry, "This is not your country. Go back to Imnaha and Wallowa, where you belong." Thereupon the old man, doubtless chagrined by the selfish conduct of the other bands and disappointed by the sudden departure of the white people whom he had trusted, returned to the Wallowa region. Thenceforth his band seems to have resumed with a will all the old superstitions of the tribe and added new ones. The counsel he gave his children was, "Be at peace if you can, but never trust the white men nor their red friends. Raise ponies, eat things that grow of themselves, and go and come as you please."

The main tribe, the "Upper Nez Perces," occupied the Lapwai. With these the government has had most to do in times past. With these Governor Stevens made his celebrated treaty of 1855, to which Old Joseph gave his assent; and well he might assent to this the first treaty, for it embraced in its established boundaries all his lands, and allowed him and his people to live in the same place, and in the same manner, as the Lower Nez Perces had lived for generations. Therefore we are not surprised to find his name appended to an instrument which in itself was not inequitable, but which was preliminary to the usual course of dispossessing the Indians of the property rights which they claimed.

Chapter II

The missionary Mr. Spalding was a brave man, and his excellent wife was the embodiment of Christian sweetness, self-sacrifice, and devotion.

He planted his mission among the Nez Perces on the Lapwai in 1836, and he remained there for eleven years, more than a hundred miles from the nearest settlements and cut off from all association with white men.

The Indians trusted him, loved him, and even now the old men never tire of talking of his instruction and of the messages he sent them just before his death.

At one of my visits to Lapwai an old Indian, dim-eyed and shrivelled in appearance, sat on a box in the back office of the agent and through the interpreter talked to me for an hour of these early times. He was the father-in-law of Young Joseph. He said in substance, "I was a wild boy, like the boys of the Dreamers. My father hunted the buffalo far away. The squaws planted the little patches, the boys fished for salmon in the rivers and rode the ponies; we were all just like the other wild Indians. Sometimes we were fighting the Blackfeet and the Snakes. Mr. Spalding came. He made the men work. We said, 'You make squaws of us!' A few Indians used the hoe, then more and more. His klootchman (Mrs. Spalding) had a big school—many, many tilicums (grown people) went. It was not a little school like that one there (pointing to the school building). There were many children. Old Joseph's band was here then. His children went to the school."

"But Young Joseph and Ollicut would be too young!" I suggested.

"Yes, they were little, but they went to the school."

Allowing Young Joseph to have been thirty-seven at the time of the war, he would have been seven years of age at the time of Old Joseph's return to Imnaha from Lapwai.

From this it will appear that the boys learned very little from books. Neither spoke more than a few words of English when I met them, though I believe they understood English much better than they pretended.

The missionary's letters give us a few openings through which we may obtain glimpses—the shadows of these faithful workers in this beautiful Lapwai Valley, toiling on, planting much, and seeing little fruit from the seeds of knowledge which they scattered in this untoward soil. Spalding wrote, "I was located at this place on the Clearwater or Koos-koos-ky River." The Lapwai is a small stream that flows westward and empties into the Clearwater. In 1839, besides this station, where was the school of Mrs. Spalding, there was another, about sixty-five miles distant, among the Nez Perces at Kamiah.

In 1844 Spalding writes, "The assembly on the Sabbath at Lapwai varies at different seasons of the year and must continue to do so until the people find a substitute in the fruits of the earth and herds, for their roots, game and fish necessarily require much wandering. I am happy to say that they are very generally turning their attention, with apparent eagerness, to cultivating the soil and raising hogs and cattle, and find a much more abundant and agreeable source of subsistence in the hoe than in their bows and their sticks for digging roots."

In another place an exhibit is given of the Nez Perces' nomadic ways. "For a few weeks in the fall, after the people return from their buffalo hunts, and then again in the spring, the congregation numbers from one to two thousand. Through the winter it numbers from two to eight hundred. From July to the first of October it varies from two to five hundred."

This gathering, as well as school attendance, increased every winter, as the quantity of provisions raised in this vicinity also increased.

"Last season about one hundred and forty cultivated from one-fourth of an acre to four or five acres each. ... One chief raised one hundred and seventy-six bushels of peas, one hundred of corn, and four hundred of potatoes. Another, one hundred and fifty of peas, one hundred and sixty of corn, a large quantity of potatoes, vegetables, etc. Ellis, I believe, raised more than either of the above mentioned. Some forty other individuals raised from twenty to one hundred bushels of grain. Eight individuals are furnished with ploughs. Thirty-two head of cattle are possessed by thirteen individuals; ten sheep by four."

In spite of the non-fulfillment of our treaty obligations to give the Nez Perces land that they could rely upon as their own, and to protect them in their occupation and title; in spite of the hurricane brought upon them by the Cayuse and other wars, and the withdrawal of aid and instruction for years; in spite of the plunderings of men who, among other knaveries, drew five thousand dollars from the government to build them a schoolhouse and built them one worth less than three hundred; in spite of our shrewd Yankee ability, which has found mines of gold and silver within their boundaries, and has cut down their territory to one-sixth of the generous limits marked out by Governor Stevens; in spite of all this hardship and of this wrong-doing to a people just beginning to bear the ignominy (to them) of manual labor—still they have kept on in the path in which they were started by the worthy, self-sacrificing missionary. I mean here, of course, the Christian, friendly Nez Perces, comprising two-thirds and more of these Indians, now and all these years remaining contentedly on their present reserve.

It was amid these influences that Joseph and Ollicut spent the first few years of their lives. They also made frequent visits to Lapwai afterwards; and in later years they sometimes helped their father-in-law on his farm, so that, though they had imbibed the spirit of their mother and were doubtless much affected by the recital of the wrongs of their father, and subsequently had been deeply influenced by Indian dreamings and superstition, still it is evident that the remarkable knowledge they afterwards displayed had here its abundant source.

In following the subsequent career of these young men, wicked and disastrous as it was, one cannot help thinking about "what might have been"—about the grand possibilities in these superior natures. But the rule is as fixed as the stars, that the sins of the fathers shall be visited upon the children unto the third and fourth generations of the men who hate God.

Smart as these youths were, their tendency to evil was undoubtedly inherited. While we abhor their crimes and shudder at the horrid outrages which their people have committed, we nevertheless admire their wild courage and cannot help wondering at their native ability. With them, it meant war. It was hate and destruction in every form. The refinements of war they had never learned. Perhaps, with General Sherman, Joseph might say, "War is cruel, and it is difficult to refine it." Certainly the Indians' attempts to do so were very few.

Chapter III

It is difficult to explain the almost uniform injustice which the American people have practiced toward the Indians. I do not believe that we are worse than the French, the Spanish, or our English neighbors in British Columbia in our dealings with the red men. I am inclined to believe the jar to be in our unadjustable system which, like a machine built upon a springy soil, is perpetually out of gear. Our fathers, finding the Indians here and being disposed to peace, first recognized in them the right of occupancy of the lands. This recognized right the Indians have always misunderstood. They have believed it to mean much more than simple occupancy.

As our new settlements have rapidly extended we have entered into, and recorded, solemn treaties by which we have made of the numerous small tribes so many nations.

Soon the national and local laws, which are constantly in conflict with the laws of these independent nations, go into active, and often antagonistic, operation. For example, the settler, in carrying out the homestead law, plants his stakes on the Indian's farm. A petty contest results. An Indian or a white man is killed. Close upon this follows a horrid Indian war—a war so outrageous that *bona fide* forgiveness, anywhere in the neighborhood of the remembered crimes, seldom if ever succeeds. This is substantially the history of a portion of the Nez Perces.

Governor Stevens came to them in 1855 and settled the grand and liberal treaty which bears his name and which was confirmed by the United States Senate. It prescribed for them limits, but limits so ample that even Old Joseph, who was always tenacious of Indian rights, agreed to the stipulations. It included all the country that they occupied when Captain Bonneville found them in 1833, embracing the Lapwai, the Imnaha, the Wallowa, and the Grande

Ronde country. Was it possible to preserve these extended limits in face of the constant flood of immigration? Certainly it was not done. In 1863, the negotiation of another treaty had to be attempted. The new treaty finally agreed upon excluded the Wallowa and vast regions besides. It did much more than simply reduce the limits of the reserve. It made a breach in the tribe that was never to be closed. It divided the Indians who had sent delegates across the continent to visit our fathers and to solicit an increase of knowledge, into two great and hostile factions. One party agreed to all the terms of the instrument and stayed within the boundaries fixed and have always called themselves "treaty Indians." The other persistently refused to accept the new limits and were denominated the "non-treaties." All the dissenting bands, except that of the sub-chief Looking Glass, have pitched their lodges outside the present Lapwai reservation.

We have already noticed the home of Old Joseph and his band. Now it is important to fix in mind the other bands of non-treaties who became the confederates of Joseph's band, in peace and in war, to resist efforts of the white man to displace them or change their mode of life.

The principal non-treaty chief, who often disputed with Joseph the command of the united forces, was White Bird. He and his band roamed over that rough, mountainous territory along the Salmon River and its tributaries. They had no permanent abiding place. One deep valley, now well known from the terrible battle fought there, is named the White Bird Canyon. The small stream that flows through it and empties into the foaming Salmon is also named White Bird.

There was also a band which roamed between the Salmon and the Snake, over that wild country that became Joseph's hiding place during the war. The chief of this band, since my acquaintance with it, was Too-hul-hul-sote. He was a cross-grained growler, a sort of sub-chief to White Bird, and a Dreamer drummer called by the Indians a *Too-at* [shaman].

South of the Snake, not far above the mouth of the Grande Ronde, is Ashotin Creek. Here too was a small band which always acted in concert with Joseph's people.

The remaining bands of malcontents were situated to the westward and hunted through the region south of Lewiston. They acknowledged Hush-hush-cute as leader, a wily chieftain about the age of Young Joseph. It could be said of him, in the words of Scripture, his heart was deceitful above all things and desperately wicked.

There were at this time on the present reservation a large number of friendly Nez Perces, most of whom remained true throughout all changes and some of whom helped us during the conflict; namely, the present head-chief, James Lawyer, and his people, mainly located at Kamiah on the Clearwater seventy miles from Lewiston; the sub-chief Jonah; James Reuben, the son of the late head-chief, and their people, located on the Lapwai near the Nez Perce agency; also Catholic Indians, situated eight miles from the agency on the Little Mission Creek, who dwell habitually in their small log village near their church. The whole number of these friendly Indians has been rated from two to three thousand. A recent census lessens the number. But the count, which was attempted during the war, could hardly be reliable. The Indians at times were much afraid that Joseph and his warriors would suddenly return and exterminate them; therefore, they indulged their wandering propensities. Some went away among the Coeur d'Alenes, the Spokanes, Cayuses, and other neighboring tribes. Many others doubtless took up new camping grounds where they thought they would be safe from distrustful white men as well as from the hostile bands who might beat the troops and suddenly return to do them mischief. Probably there are in existence at least two thousand friendly Nez Perces.

The non-treaties, after they were finally separated from the others and arrayed against us as enemies, numbered about seven hundred men, women and children. Perhaps more. There were at least three hundred twenty-five warriors at the battle of the Clearwater.

During the campaign many well-sketched pictures of scenes connected with these Indians were sent to illustrated papers, but as published the appearance of the Indians themselves was misrepresented. They were depicted with hair flying in all directions, in the ordinary wild Indian style, with meagre attire, and with long lances poised above their heads. They do not so appear in fact. They carry rifles, not lances. The friendly Nez Perces now for the most part are dressed as white men; the hair, especially of those at Kamiah, is cut short. This gives them much the appearance of the Mexican ranchers who live along our southern border. The women invariably wear long skirts and usually crop their straight, jetty hair by a square cut at the neck. The shawl is habitually drawn up over the head, so that one has to be in front to see a woman's face. I have noticed on church, council, and gala days that bright handkerchiefs often took the place of bonnets, shawls, or hats as head gear. The children are dressed much as among the whites, and though often in some fanciful attire, they are for the most part plainly clad.

An old account mentioning the "Pierced Noses" and "Flat Heads" as early as 1811, says, "They do not go naked, but both sexes wear habits made of dressed deer skin, which they take care to rub with chalk to keep them clean and white."

The Nez Perces of today take pains with their personal attire, as they did forty years ago. The Christian portion at Lapwai and Kamiah, as they gather inside and outside their church buildings on Sundays, present a fine appearance.

The men average in height five feet eight inches, are strongly built, and always show grace in their movements. They are so constantly on horseback that they seem to be almost part of the animal. You can tell them at great distances by the ease and grace of the arms as, in Indian style, they carry the whip up and down. This is quite in contrast with the angular, jerky motions of our white couriers and hardy frontiersmen.

Their women are usually short of stature, but have bright, intelligent faces and a healthy appearance. They ride as well as the men, but are generally perched at the top of a load, and usually each has a child in arms or one clinging behind.

Chapter IV

It is sometimes amusing, and sometimes extremely vexatious, to find statements which have been many times refuted reappearing in important publications.

With regard to the Nez Perces, there are two parties who are responsible for untruthful statement, the enemies and the would-be friends. The enemies of the Nez Perces, who are, *per se*, the enemies of all Indians, desired greatly to make it appear that the treaty and the non-treaty, the Protestant, the Catholic, and the Dreamers, were all alike bad. They argued that all should be treated as hostile, that the worst treachery lurked behind the friendliest looks. The cogent reason given for this opinion was that *Indians are Indians!*

The would-be friends, with a view of defending a people who have always been reputed as friendly, have striven to represent all these Indians—friends and foes, the farmers of Lapwai and the murderers of Camas Prairie—as aggressors whose conduct was justified in a general war. So it is constantly asked, "How is it possible that Indians, always so well disposed as the Nez Perces, could go to war?" Or, the statement is made, "When *we* visited the Nez Perces a few years ago, they were far advanced in civilization. It must have required great provocation to induce them to go to war." May I ask the reader, then, to bear in mind the facts? The Christian Nez Perces, including all treaty Indians, both Catholic and Protestant, constituting a large majority of the entire people, have always been, are now, and probably will continue to be, friends of the government. The non-treaty Indians—Joseph, with his band and his confederates, whom I have already described—regarded the Nez Perce people proper as their bitter foes.

A year after the death of Old Joseph, the war with the Modoc Indians occurred, including the treacherous massacre of General Canby by this tribe. As is always the case in Indian wars, all Indians, far and near, were agitated by this outbreak. The non-treaties, now led by the ambitious young chief, Joseph, became suspiciously restless. In the summer of 1874, a delegation of citizens came to Lapwai from a hundred miles distant to meet the then department commander, General Davis, who had just closed the Modoc campaign. The delegation alleged "That the Indians, including the non-treaties, had assembled in large numbers in Paradise and Hog-Heaven Valleys, ostensibly for the purpose of digging roots, hunting, and fishing, and that they were talking very saucily to the settlers, and had committed various trespasses upon the farmers of the country." The troops were sent thither. This, for a time, put an end to the troubles and probably prevented bloodshed.

General Davis thought the moving cause of the restlessness and sauciness was that these beautiful and fertile valleys were being rapidly occupied by an industrious and thrifty class of white farmers and stock-raisers. In his investigations he could discover no other cause.

About this time several non-treaty Nez Perces had assumed an attitude of insolence toward the Indian agent at Lapwai, Mr. John Monteith, and toward the other employees of the government, which foreboded evil if not actual hostilities.

A large gathering of Indians was soon to take place, about the fourth of July, at the Wee-ipe [Weippe], situated east of Kamiah. It is a small grassy prairie, surrounded by forests of huge firs, whose somber shadows are often deepened by contrast with successive sunny glades.

Here had been an annual assemblage of the non-treaties. Many other Indians came to participate in horse races, or to win or lose in gambling horses, furs, and other Indian property.

This year the notice circulated was for a talk, and the agent was curious and wished to be present, but he thought the Indians would prevent him unless defended by troops. Therefore, the troops, Colonel David Perry and his company, marched some two hundred miles from Fort Walla Walla and were there with the agent for a few days.

Monteith reasoned that if the Indians met for pastime and enjoyment, the troops in the vicinity would not hinder, but if for evil purposes, they would serve as the ounce of prevention.

Colonel Perry and agent Monteith found the Indians assembled as anticipated at the Wee-ipe. The talk took place, but it was annoyed and constrained by the presence of armed men. It proved but a brief council. General dissatisfaction seemed to prevail among the non-treaty Nez Perces. This was particularly the case with Joseph's band, the claimants of Wallowa Valley.

There was evidently some mischief hatching in the neighborhood of Joseph's lodge. The young man was yet hardly in the saddle as chief. The sentiment of his followers and of his neighbors was divided. The wary, cautious malcontents of the tribe thought they would lose by a war. They counselled a persistent but peaceful opposition to the army of settlers now approaching, no longer from the East but from the West—from the Pacific. The young men, with Ollicut at their head, were for war. During the same year, in the fall of 1874, Colonel John Green, an officer of prudence and experience in Indian matters, was sent to Wallowa with two cavalry companies to keep the peace. The troops did keep the peace as long as these Indians were roaming in that valley and then withdrew to their posts.

A summary of the views of the Governor of Oregon, the Hon. L. F. Grover, expressed in a letter to the United States government in July 1873, gives the opinion and the temper of the majority of intelligent citizens of this state.

Grover first opposes the withdrawal of citizens from Wallowa for the purpose of securing the same to Joseph's band. He recites the stipulations of Governor Stevens' treaty of 1855, which includes Wallowa, to which Old Joseph assented.

Grover then quotes the supplementary treaty of 1863, to which the majority of the Nez Perces assent, but which the minority of bands refuse to sign. The new treaty gives Wallowa back to the United States. Old Joseph and all the non-treaties protest against this action. After Old Joseph's death, his sons, Joseph and Ollicut, lay claim to the same

Wallowa, saying that the Nez Perce bands are independent and not bound by a majority of other bands. Grover argues that they must be so bound, according to all law and precedents.

The Governor continues by citing the Act of Congress of May 28, 1867, by which the lands of Wallowa went to Oregon and were opened for settlement. Eleven townships were thus formed. Eighty-seven farms are entered or occupied already. The government ought now to consider the Indian title extinct, argues Grover. If the government yields to the claim of Joseph, it will be obliged to yield to a core more of just such claims in this neighborhood.

Grover then begs for the uniform policy of the United States, namely, "of removing as expeditiously as circumstances would permit, *all Indians* from the confines of the new states." Pointing out that the country to which Wallowa Valley is the key is greater in area than Massachusetts, he argues that its restoration to the aboriginal character would give a serious check to frontier civilization.

As a final argument, Grover states that there is room enough for the malcontents on the Lapwai reserve. Joseph himself is reported as not averse to this, suggests the Governor, but those about him want to roam and will not give up their nomadic ways. They simply want the Wallowa Valley to gratify a wild, roaming disposition.

Grover's letter ends with an urgent plea on behalf of the settlers and the state of Oregon that the preliminary steps just taken by the government in the interest of the Indians—for the white settlers to vacate the Wallowa country—be rescinded.

So much for our ideas of justice. First we acknowledge and confirm by treaty to Indians a sort of title to vast regions. Afterward we continue, in a strictly legal manner, to do away with both the substance and the shadow of title. Wiser heads than Joseph's have been puzzled by this manner of balancing the scales.

Chapter V

My first personal interview with the young chieftain was in 1875. I had, the previous September, succeeded to the command of the Geographical Department which included within its limits the Nez Perces.

To better acquaint myself with my command, I soon visited the military posts and the different Indian agencies. While conversing with the sprightly Frenchman in charge of the Umatilla Agency in Eastern Oregon, a Cayuse Indian came in, accompanied by the stout interpreter McBean. The latter said, "Here is a messenger from Joseph. He and ten of his Indians are at Young Chief's camp. Joseph and his tilicums want to have a talk with the agent and with the new commander."

I had already heard of this band and so expressed a desire for the interview. The messenger then left.

In the course of half an hour the eleven strangers made their appearance. They were all quite carefully dressed in Indian costume. They were noticeably tall and stout for Indians. I was out of doors at the time with the agent, looking at his buildings. The Indians first approached in single file, Young Joseph ahead. One after another took the agent's hand and then mine in the most solemn manner. Joseph put his large black eyes on my face and maintained a fixed look for some time. It did not appear to me as an audacious stare, but I thought he was trying to open the windows of his heart to me and at the same time endeavoring to read my disposition and character.

An Indian is usually a shrewd physiognomist. I think Joseph and I became then quite good friends. There was at the time little appearance of that distrust and deceit which some time afterward very strongly marked his face, especially while listening to white men in council. He said through the interpreter, "I heard that Washington had

21

some message for me. I came to visit my friends among the Cayuses. Young Chief told me to speak to the agent. That is all."

We answered, "There is no word from Washington. We are glad to see you and shake you by the hand."

The Nez Perces then formally took their leave and retired in company with other Indians of the Umatilla reservation.

After becoming more familiar with the situation of affairs with the Nez Perces, I appreciated the drift of this visit and of the question concerning news from Washington. For already, General Davis had reported his belief that there would be trouble with Joseph, that there was restlessness, that his dissatisfaction and that of others arose because these beautiful valleys were being filled up by industrious settlers.

The governor of Oregon had, moreover, succeeded in getting his petition heard, and by the President's order the disputed grounds had once more ceased to be a reserve for Joseph. Joseph and his band, and his non-treaty confederates, were then still clinging to the old habits and haunts. They were pasturing their numerous ponies and herds on the plains of Wallowa and along the ridges of the tributaries to the Salmon. Meanwhile the white men were crowding into the Wallowa and Salmon Valleys, erecting their white cottages and stretching out their crooked fences in plain sight of the wandering Indian herders.

While admitting the injustice of the United States and of Oregon towards this band, when contrasted with the rights and privileges extended to citizens, still I do not think the real cause of the Indian war with the nontreaties came from the reduction of the reserve, nor from the immediate contact with immigrants and the quarrels that sprung therefrom. These, without doubt, aggravated the difficulty.

The main cause lies back of ideas of rightful ownership, back of savage habits and instincts; it lies in the natural and persistent resistance of independent nations to the authority of other nations. Indian Joseph and his malcontents denied the jurisdiction of the United States over them. They were offered everything they wanted, if they would simply submit to the authority and government of the United States agents. "No! no! no! We will go where we please, and when we please, and do as we please! Who gave Washington rule over me?" asked the growler of growlers, old Too-hul-hul-sote, Joseph's most influential confederate.

My first report was made in 1875. On this subject of "inherited causes" of trouble are the following paragraphs:

> Early in July the Indian agent at Lapwai reported the receipt of an executive order opening Wallowa Valley, in northeastern Oregon, to settlement by whites. He expressed fear of trouble between the whites and Joseph's band of the Nez Perces—especially in the Indians' annual visit to the valley for purposes of fishing and grazing their ponies, of which they have large herds, wherein consists their principal wealth.

> Two cavalry companies were accordingly sent for the mutual protection of the citizens and Indians in the valley, and for the preservation of the peace. These returned as soon as their need there ceased.

> The troubles at Lapwai, and at Wallowa Valley, have not thus far resulted in bloodshed; but it has been prevented by great carefulness on the part of government agents. The courts will have to settle the former trouble, and Congress the latter. I think it a great mistake to take from Joseph and his band of Nez Perce Indians that valley; ...and possibly Congress can be induced to let these really peaceable Indians have this poor valley for their own.

Now we can see how much expense in blood and treasure would most probably have been saved if this course had been pursued—for this was before an Indian had been killed—yet, with the idea of absolute independence in their brains, I now doubt if Wallowa would have satisfied them. It certainly would have contributed nothing whatever to quieting White Bird, Looking Glass, Hush-hush-cute, and other malcontents outside of Joseph's people.

In my report in 1876 concerning Joseph's people, I said, "An Indian was killed by a white man in a dispute concerning some stock...and I renew my recommendation of a commission to hear and settle the whole matter before war is even thought of." The commission was at last ordered, but it was not till after blood had been shed, nor till after the Indians had stood up in battle array against armed citizens in Wallowa and only stopped resistance at the intervention of troops. The commission came and held its memorable sessions at Lapwai in November of 1876, and labored long and earnestly to get the consent of Joseph and Ollicut and of other disaffected non-treaty Indians to some measures of adjustment.

At one time during their meetings Joseph was almost persuaded to yield, and Ollicut appeared to catch the spirit of peace, but the old Dreamers, the *Too-ats*, talked to them earnestly and prevailed against the commission. The commission stated the matter clearly and plainly:

> The Dreamers, among other pernicious doctrines, teach that the earth, being created by God complete, should not be disturbed by man, and that any cultivation of the soil, or other improvements, to interfere with its natural productions—any improvements in the way of schools, churches, etc.—are crimes from which they shrink.

> This fanaticism is kept alive by the superstition of these "drummers," who industriously teach that if they continue steadfast in their present belief, a leader will be raised up in the east who will restore all the dead Indians to life, who will unite with them in expelling the whites from their country, when they will again enter upon and repossess the lands of their ancestors.

> Influenced by such a belief, Joseph and his band firmly declined to enter into any negotiations, or make any arrangements, that looked to a final settlement of the questions pending between him and the government. While the commission give all due respect to the precedents and authorities in the

government dealing with Indians, and to the decisions of the Supreme Court of the United States, which recognizes an undefined right of occupancy by Indians to large sections of the country, yet in view of the fact that these Indians do not claim simply this, but set up an *absolute title to the lands*, an *absolute and independent sovereignty*, and refuse even to be limited in their claim and control—necessity, humanity, and good sense constrain the government to set metes and bounds, and give regulations to these non-treaty Indians. ... And if the principle usually applied by the government—of holding that the Indians with whom they have treaties are bound by the majority—is here applied, Joseph should be required to live within the limits of the present reservation....

If these Indians overrun lands belonging to the whites and commit depredations on their property, disturb the peace by threats or otherwise, or commit any other overt acts of hostility, we recommend the employment of sufficient force to bring them into subjection and to place them upon the Nez Perce reservation.

The Indian agent at Lapwai should be fully instructed to carry into execution these suggestions, relying at all times upon the department commander for aid when necessary.

The doings of the commission, approved at Washington, resulted in all the preliminary acts of the government that preceded the outbreak. Every possible effort of the agent was exerted to carry out the recommendations of the commission without provoking hostilities. But as a time comes when an ulcer will break, so the time came when the Indian sore had to come to the surface.

Chapter VI

The Department of the Interior at Washington issued its ominous instructions to carry out the recommendations of the November Commission to its agent at Lapwai early in January, 1877. Copies of these instructions were sent to me, directing me to occupy Wallowa Valley, as had really been done for three years, "in the interests of peace," and to cooperate with and aid the Indian agent. The agent was Mr. J. B. Monteith. He was a tall, well built young man, apparently about thirty-five years of age. His health had not been good, yet he had been unsparing of himself in his journeys over his reservation and beyond, sometimes having ridden his horse for sixty or seventy miles in a day.

Monteith sent friendly Indians to Joseph and the non-treaty Indians and did all in his power to induce them to do what they told the commission they would not do; that is, come on the Lapwai reservation. These Indians were already on the alert. They, in preparation for war, were sending small delegations to other tribes.

Some time in March, Mr. Cornoyer, the Indian agent of the Umatillas, was in Portland, Oregon, and paid me a visit. He said Joseph had sent him word through his, Cornoyer's, head chief, that he and a few of his principal men wanted to come down to the Umatilla and have a talk. Joseph did not think the interpreters at Lapwai had told the commission truly what he had said and wished. I replied, "Mr. Cornoyer, encourage them to come; and I will send my aide-de-camp, Lieutenant Boyle, who is a judicious officer and has had long experience with Indians, to represent me there and to hear and report what they have to say."

Lieutenant Boyle accordingly accompanied Cornoyer on his return to the agency and met the Indians, several from Joseph's band having come one hundred and twenty miles to Umatilla. Joseph himself did not come, but was represented by his brother, Ollicut, who was frequently called "Young Joseph." Ollicut was over six feet tall and perfectly formed. He had small hands and feet, was very intelligent, and had made quite good maps of the country about Wallowa. He was very quick and graceful in his motions, and when he spoke in council his brother always made his speech or promise his own. I think that in private Ollicut always urged Joseph to war measures and took the side of the reckless young men, who would rather than not have a fight with the white men—the prospective excitement of the battle over-topping any fears of remote consequences.

At his first interview with Ollicut, Lieutenant Boyle mistook this fine-looking, warlike, impulsive Indian representative for the chief and telegraphed me accordingly to Portland. After the lieutenant had made his way from this meeting to Fort Walla Walla, April 11th, these words came over the wires, "It is Joseph's understanding that General Howard was to have another interview with him this spring. He will be at Walla Walla with his people on the 20th inst." To this promise I assented and made all my arrangements to go to Walla Walla and meet this appointment, hoping that, as the Indians had sought the interview, some permanent and satisfactory settlement of the grievous troubles could then and there be effected.

Now comes a preliminary campaign. Lieutenant Wilkinson accompanied me. The journal gives this brief notice: "Left Portland, Oregon, Monday morning, April 16th, 1877, for settlement of Indian Joseph's difficulties. Remained overnight at the Dalles." It does not say anything of the waking at four o'clock in the morning, the prompt departure at five, the filling out lost sleep on the long cabin seat to the music of the tread of the walkers and the talkers, the monotonous sounds from the engine, and the dripping drive-wheel always rolling and splashing, half in and half out of the water. Then there was the breakfast after passing Fort Vancouver. Good coffee, good salmon, always good steak and potatoes, and unfailing good company when Captain Wolf, with manly manners and voice, sits 'y you. How can any one go from western Oregon to the Dalles without thinking of the unsurpassed scenery; the grand woods, valleys, hills; the mountains of two thousand feet; the wild cascades; then the five-mile railway over rough scenes, beside torrents and falls; then a cheery, light-painted steamboat; the table set with white cloth, at the head of which sits a captain full of goodness and humor! Forty miles past Wind Mountain, which looks like a pictorial wild Indian's head in battle, past Hood River settlement, through diminishing mountains and hills to the Dalles where the high-water mark on the hotel is five feet above your head, where the Columbia, tired of a monotonous boiling, undertook to rise, and mercilessly toppled over all the poor, small shops on Water Street!

"Over night at the Dalles." It reminds one of the dark morning of steady knocks from door to door along the upper passageway of the Umatilla House before break of day, while clear sonorous tones, following each knock, were saying, "Four o'clock! Four o'clock!" We were off at five in the morning among as cheerless and silent a set of passengers as are West Point cadets on the way to and from reveille. The first fifteen miles were by railway. Sit without fail upon the left side of the car, as you are on the south bank of the great river, going east. If this be your first trip, you will see, close at hand, the Columbia, which is more than a mile wide at Vancouver, here so set up on edge that you can throw a stone across it, pressing along with the quietude and stillness of great depth. You will notice the banks of sand in the river bends that have all the shape of drifting snowbanks of the east. Graceful lines and curves are formed, and are ever forming, ever changing in the restless breezes that sweep up and down or over the hills to give new touches to the pliable heaps. Then you pass under frowning precipices, so high above you that it requires a trip to the rear platform to take in their lofty heads.

The steamboat Almota, built for business, waits at Celilo. About fifty miles below Umatilla a cylinder-head to one of the engines blew out, which delayed the steamer from about noon until midnight. Captain Baughman returned with a boat's crew to Celilo for another steamer, with which he arrived about dark, when baggage and freight were transferred to the steamer Tenino.

Having enjoyed the exhilaration and excitement of ascending the several rapids of the Columbia, rapids like those of the St. Lawrence, which demand of the pilot a quick eye and steady nerves at the wheel, at last, on the 18th of April, we arrived at Wallula.

Wallula is situated where the old Fort Walla Walla, built by the Hudson's Bay Company, was located. Its crumbling walls are still there, surrounded by the houses and sheds of the present hamlet.

Wallula is a sweet name that one loves to speak. Its sweetness, however, stops with its name. Pebbles, sand, a constant wind, and a few old buildings in a row, with straggling suburbs and withered grass or flowers—such is Wallula, forlorn indeed! Still it is an important place, being at the head of navigation and the river terminus of the railway which runs to the town of Walla Walla. Indian Smohollie, who has grouped around him a band of renegades, who is the high priest of Dreamer-drummers, is on the opposite side of the Columbia. He sends his messenger, who encounters us as we step ashore. "Smohollie wants to have a talk with General Howard."

He is answered, "All right. General Howard has no communication for him from Washington. He must obey his Indian agent and go upon some reservation."

Afterwards I left an appointment for a meeting with him and his Indians, to take place on the 24th of April at Wallula during my return trip from Walla Walla.

I have been particular to mention this man because of his history. His followers have been embraced in a score of tribes, and his deleterious influence has been sadly productive of suffering. He is a large-headed, hump-shouldered, odd little wizard of an Indian and exhibits a strange mixture of timidity and daring, of superstition and intelligence.

There is another small band of natives who are fast disappearing by disease and destitution. They are usually located about a mile above the hamlet, and appear to enjoy their flinty beds among the millions of small stones which the overflow of the Columbia has strewn upon the hereditary sand, rather than the fertile lands of the Umatilla, where other Indians dispute their title and the Catholic agent insists upon the sufficiency of one wife for their fat chieftain. This chieftain, old Homily, lately found even Washington city inferior to the wastes around Wallula. "Oh!" he said on his return home, as he shook his fat sides with laughter. "You, General Howard, may think more of Washington, but I wasn't happy there. The gravel stones and sand of Wallula make me happy. My tilicums are there."

Homily, too, begged for a talk. An odd little train of cars has been waiting while I have interviewed the messengers and thus inspected the town. With a shrill whistle that sets ponies to dancing and numerous dogs to barking, we are off at a rate that, as yet, even old Homily on his white cayuse can rival.

Chapter VII

It was dark when we reached Fort Walla Walla on April 19th. A welcome spring wagon took us to the quarters of the commanding officer. How pleasant, after a tiresome journey, is a cordial welcome, a warm fire, a hot cup of tea, and a cheerful, restful chamber for the night.

Ollicut put in an appearance about six p.m. Young chief and several other prominent Indians accompanied him. Among them was an old medicine man who, seven months later, surrendered to us north of the Missouri with a wounded, broken, almost putrid right arm. These Indians came to the western gate of the fort, and Ollicut gave an excuse in the most gentlemanly manner for not having been at the fort sooner. He stated that the chief, his brother Joseph, was not at that time well, otherwise he would have been there himself to meet me. The next day was fixed upon for a talk, and the Indians sought a place to encamp for the night. Colonel Grover arranged the band room for our purpose on the morrow.

Talk commenced about 10 a.m. We gathered in the long, low room at a large table, Indians on benches on one side—officers, citizens, and a few ladies opposite, on straight benches and chairs or peeping in curiously at the doors.

The council talk amounts to little. The Indians are very polite, as a few at a five-company post would be likely to be. The wishes of the government are explained to them, but they are only delegates and can make no "binding promises." They beg for another interview with me for the whole band and for the Salmon River non-treaty Indians, in fact for the various companies of malcontents. I grant the petition and agree to meet Joseph and the others at Lapwai in twelve days. The old medicine man looks happy, and Ollicut believes we shall have no trouble. Young Chief, the Umatilla friend and advocate, wishes some new lands in

Wallowa that will hold them all in fellowship (Cayuses, Walla Wallas, Umatillas, and non-treaty Nez Perces). Matters did not look much like war, except perhaps the sly and thorough observation of the Indians of the strength, or rather weakness, of this post, whose companies were so reduced in numbers as to appear more like corporals' drill-squads than like captains' proper commands.

At this visit I took a good look at the gatling guns. We tried them at two hundred, three hundred, five hundred, and eight hundred yards. The rapidity of fire—at least two discharges per second—and the wonderful accuracy of aim, made one think that warfare was coming to its best and quickest results. But, alas! How many conditions are not thought of on trial occasions, such as wide intervening rivers, wooded buttes, and precipitous ravines, conditions of which Indians take advantage against even the best gatlings.

When I came to this "Geographical Department" three years before, there was no public conveyance except a stage coach or army spring-wagon provided for the occasion, to take me from Wallula to Walla Walla. Enterprising citizens, not content with the desert lands on the Columbia for the establishment of new homes, had gone straight inland to Dr. Whitman's ground of Wait-waiilatpu-pu and farther along the valley of the little Walla Walla to the vicinity of the magnificent rolling wheat country and the neighborhood of the foothills of the Blue Ridge. Here there was for them plenty of wood, water, sunshine, grass, and fertile soil.

But, oh what a stage or spring-wagon road! You ate, drank, and breathed in but not out, the finest and most abundant of dry alkaline dirt, and you bumped up and down on the roughest and most uneven of roadbeds, which lies beneath the ten inches of deceitful dust. So you may judge of the delight with which we now, with plenty of good company and only a moderate amount of alkali, pass over the same thirty miles of country in two and a half hours by rail. But this time the enjoyment of quick communication, good society, and the modicum of disagreeables was foregone in order to visit Waiilatpu, where the Whitman mission had been planted and where, by the treacherous Cayuses with their aiders and abettors, the Whitmans were massacred. We reached Wallula, on the Columbia, at 6 p.m. on the 23rd of April.

How can a public house at a small hamlet, which is a junction of water-steam with land-steam, compete with city hotels which are daily thronged with passengers at four and five dollars per head? Our host and my lady of the Wallula House were very industrious and hospitable and made the stay of my friends and myself just as pleasant as they could. They have toiled on the frontiers from Kansas to the Touchet and finally have set themselves down at Wallula, replete in personal experience and primed with the overland stories of remarkable character, incidents of danger, of exposure, of plenty, and of want. Here we spent the night and will remember the occasion longer than the last visit to the Ebbitt House of Washington, notwithstanding its rich table, restful elevators, and other contrasts of comfort.

The work of this day was the beginning of a series of measures that kept the "Columbia River renegades" from joining the non-treaty Nez Perces of Joseph.

In accordance with my promise, a message was sent to Smohollie, the leader of the Indian spiritists who is in camp across and up the Columbia. Smohollie, through a messenger, requests General Howard to come to his camp and is informed by the general that he came to Wallula to meet him by an appointment of his own seeking, and he (General Howard) is not anxious to see him. If Smohollie has anything to say to General Howard he must come to Wallula to say it. And after Smohollie's remonstrance, by a second messenger, he is again informed that General Howard has nothing to communicate to Smohollie and does not really care whether he sees him or not. This was rather ungracious, but I suspected treachery. There was no excuse for the shrewd Dreamer's attempt to draw me across the river. All of our party regarded it then as meaning mischief. A little after noon, Smohollie, having given up his first designs, crossed the river just above the village and mustered all his people, including women and children. They were bedecked with much paint and feathers, and with all the pomp and circumstance possible came into town "to meet the General who, by previous arrangement and promise, had with him

Indian Agent Cornoyer." The talk was held in a large store-house. Some two hundred and fifty Indian men and about fifty women and children gathered in and about this build-ing. The regular interpreter, McBean, was taken ill enroute and could not reach us at Wallula. Having no interpreter except a few bystanders who made a feeble attempt at translating in the Chinook jargon, the council adjourned until the arrival of Mr. Pambrun. He was a good interpreter who spoke the Walla Walla tongue, now the language com-mon to the Cayuses, Umatillas, and Walla Wallas.

At half past seven Mr. Pambrun arrived. He was twenty miles away when our mounted messenger found him. A lit-tle school room had been prepared. Upon notification, Smohollie—with some of his principal men, Young Chief, Homily, and Thomas—reassembled. Talk ceased between ten and eleven.

These Indians had the same statements to make as the non-treaty Nez Perces. They want peace, but they wish to roam at large whenever and wherever they please. They really belong on various reservations, and the word "rene-gades" describes them well. I think they were meditating resistance at that time and were only waiting and parley-ing to ascertain first what the non-treaty Nez Perces would do. Should they then, and alone, precipitate war, they knew well enough they would soon be swallowed up. The wishes of the government were carefully explained to them by Mr. Cornoyer, and they were earnestly exhorted by him to run to the shelter of the reservations. I explained to them the wishes of the government, as contained in the instructions from Washington, and endorsed the statements of Mr. Cornoyer. With apparent good feeling except on the part of old Thomas, who lived on the Snake near some of the non-treaty Nez Perces and who was tremblingly fierce to know why we were sending troops to Wallowa, the Indians shook our hands and left the town before midnight. After the adjournment, old Thomas' people rushed northward for a hundred miles, beating the steamboat, where they crossed their hands and stated that we were going to put them into the "Skookum-house," meaning the military prison or guard-house. Father Wilbur, as the agent at Yakima is called, had previously brought us an insubordinate Indian, and we had confined him at Fort Vancouver. Thomas' Indians, although two hundred miles further inland, had heard of this and had pleaded with me for the imprisoned Indian's release. Thus connected are the renegades in common feeling and sympathy against all white men, even where they quarrel and fight with one another.

April 25th and 26th we spent in ascending the Columbia and Snake Rivers from Wallula to Lewiston, Idaho.

At 6 p.m. we arrived at Lewiston. This town of a few hundred inhabitants, three hundred miles east of Portland, Oregon, was to be the main depot of my operations in the upper country after war began. It well represents the world in miniature. It has an enterprising newspaper and many fair merchants, but yet thus far enjoys but few of the comforts and luxuries of existence. At this time I met by appointment Colonel Perry, commanding officer at Fort Lapwai, and Indian Agent Monteith. To them I read carefully my full instructions from the Honorable Secretary of War, General Sherman, and the commanding general, Military Division of the Pacific, especially in relation to the part the military was to have in placing the Indians upon the reservations.

The particular object of this visit was to avoid a long correspondence and to concert measures of cooperation. The interview which Joseph and Ollicut had solicited with the non-treaty Nez Perces was arranged for the third of the ensuing month. Then I returned by steamboat the next day to Wallula, where I could have the telegraph to conduct the affairs of my department. I wish also particularly to meet officers coming to me from Portland and to provide for the withdrawal of our troops from the territory of Alaska. The recall of these troops had just been determined upon by the War Department and was indeed a fortunate circumstance, as it enabled me to catch these forces on the wing and turn them quickly towards Lewiston as soon as the terrible storm of Indian outrages had begun.

Chapter VIII

It seemed to Eastern people a few years ago, when the son of Bishop Kip of California wrote from Walla Walla some interesting articles concerning the Indians, that he had gone pretty near to the world's extremity. But here now is Walla Walla, a thriving, growing, enterprising city. A railroad train from its suburbs connects daily at Wallula with the passing steamers that at least twice a week penetrate to the very heart of Idaho. Daily stages start from this railway terminus for east, and north, and south, and the busy telegraph keeps the newsmen and merchants in perpetual contact and business sympathy with San Francisco and New York.

The journey through the rich and beautiful valleys, threading our way among the hills and over the spur of the Blue Ridge, brought us back to Lewiston and then twelve miles further to Fort Lapwai. A lady, the wife of an army officer, said about this latter place: "You don't know how I do love Fort Lapwai, and with what regret I left the place." It is the bright sunshine, the beautiful rolling hills and gorgeous mountains, and valleys of every shape and description, lighted up into attractive pictures; it is the excellent climate that invigorates while it does not freeze you; it is these, with good companionship, that make this most frontier of posts dwell pleasantly in the memory of those who have resided there. There is really no fort. There is a hollow square on the western side of the ravine. The Lapwai flows northerly, near the eastern slope of it. The usual officers' quarters are on the west, facing inwards; the barracks opposite; office on the south; guard-house, with its one sentinel walking up and down in front, on the north, and the parade between. The post trader's and laundress' houses are nearer the Lapwai, while the stables and other outbuildings are arranged a few paces outside the square and

up the valley. Behold any two-company army post prepared
for cavalry and you have caught the type.

The first council with young Joseph was held at Fort
Lapwai the 3rd of May 1877. Present were Agent Monteith
with his interpreter, Whitman, and Joseph and Ollicut with
about fifty of Joseph's band of Indians.

We had, by way of preparation for the council, a large
hospital tent pitched in front of that one walking sentinel
at the guard house and extended the tent by prolonging
and propping the ridge-pole and stretching over it the tent-
fly, with ropes well out and with sides of tent looped up.
This whole contrivance was to give all the shelter practicable from the sun and still open everything to the free circu-
lation of air and sight, not forgetting to be open to the
guard on the one hand and to the garrison of soldiers, who
were to remain at their barracks, on the other. "You were
already afraid of the Indians?" Oh, no, that is against the
soldiers' theory, but it is well to be prepared.

The non-treaty Nez Perces were arranged as usual, a
long rank of men, followed by women and children. The
men's faces were painted, the red paint extending back into
the partings of the hair—the men's hair braided and tied
up with showy strings—ornamented in dress, in hats, in
blankets with variegated colors, in leggings of buckskin,
and beaded and plain moccasins. The women wore bright
shawls or blankets and skirts to the ankle and "top moccasins." All were mounted on Indian ponies as various in
color as the dress of the riders. These picturesque people,
after keeping us waiting long enough for effect, came in
sight from up the valley, from the direction of their temporary camp just above the company gardens. They drew
near to the hollow square of the post in front of the small
company to be interviewed. Then they struck up their
song. They were not armed, except with a few tomahawk
pipes that could be smoked with the peaceful tobacco or
penetrate the skull-bone of an enemy at the will of the
holder. Yet somehow this wild sound produced a strange
effect. It made one feel glad that there were but fifty of
them and not five hundred. It was shrill and searching,
sad, like a wail, and yet defiant in its close. Our ladies,

thinking it a war song, asked with some show of trepidation, "Do you think Joseph means to fight?" The Indians swept around outside the fence and made the entire circuit, still keeping up the song as they rode. The buildings broke the refrain into irregular bubblings of sound till the ceremony was completed.

thinking it was long enough, added with some show of trepidation, "Do you think I knew it, point to fire?" The Indians
swept around one at the time and made the entire circuit, still keeping up the sonorous low to it. Then, beginning
from the criminal to the regular buildings or sound till the
ceremony was completed.

Chapter IX

The second Indian council was held at Fort Lapwai on May 4. It was a glorious day. The sun shone without a cloud, but its heat was relieved by a gentle breeze which was coursing through the valley and over the smooth hills, causing the abundant grasses and flowers to ripple and sparkle in long noiseless waves.

White Bird had marched into the valley with a part of his band. The remainder, he reported, were driving the ponies and fetching the lodges and provisions across the Craig Mountain. The Ashotins were present, and Too-hul-hul-sote and his followers were straggling in. The trails are still difficult at this season, often obstructed with deep drifts of snow which, being softened by the increasing warmth, are worse than at an earlier season, when they are stiffened by the frosts of winter.

The Indians gathered and formed in lines, as on the previous day. There was the same careful preparation, the same preliminary ride around the garrison, the song being louder and stronger and perhaps more defiant than before, the same back-door entrance and cordial hand-shaking. We were then seated. At my request, one of the most handsome and pleasant of the treaty Nez Perces, and one whom I had noticed as active and happy in the religious gatherings, called Alpowa Jim, was requested to conduct the opening service. He fervently prayed in his own language. Then Mr. Monteith repeated the reading of his Washington instructions, carefully explaining them as was done the day before. After a little delay Joseph made a brief speech. "This is White Bird. I spoke to you of him. This is the first time he has seen you, and you him. I want him and his Indians to understand what has been said to us."

Joseph, with his shining hair very carefully braided at the side and his face slightly rouged, sat on a low bench.

His tall brother half reclined on the ground before him. White Bird, with his followers massed behind him, squatted on the grass to the left of Ollicut.

White Bird was a demure-looking Indian, about five feet eight inches tall. His face assumed the condition of impassability, of rigid fixedness, while in council, and probably for fear that some passing event, some look or word, might surprise him into the betrayal of the slightest emotion, he kept his immense ceremonial hat on and placed a large eagle's wing in front of his eyes and nose.

In speaking earlier of the country occupied by the Indians, I mentioned the sub-chief who habitually encamped on the north side of the Snake River, Too-hul-hul-sote. He held, as we have seen, some of the country between Joseph's Wallowa and White Bird's Salmon River region. He was broad-shouldered, deep-chested, thick-necked, five feet ten in height with a heavy, guttural voice. He betrayed in every word a strong and settled hatred of all Caucasians. This man the Indians now put forward to speak for them, not, probably, that they had already decided to endorse his sentiments, but as he always counselled war, they evidently desired to see what effect his public utterance would produce upon us. He said, "There are always two parties to a dispute. The one that is right will come out ahead." This was introduced by plentiful flourish of words and illustrations, but with no attempt at conciliation even in manner. The old answer was repeated in substance: "We are all subjects, children of a common government and must obey its requirements." Too-hul-hul-sote replied, "I have heard about a bargain, a trade between some of these Indians [referring to the treaty Nez Perces] and the white men concerning their land; but I belong to the land out of which I came. The Earth is my mother."

We rejoined: "The Nez Perces did make such an agreement, and as the commission from Washington explained last fall, since the non-treaty Indians were in the minority in their opposition, they were bound by that agreement and must abide by it."

The old man, more surly than before, declared, "You have no right to compare us, grown men, to children.

44

Children do not think for themselves. Grown men do think for themselves. The government at Washington shall not think for us."

This method of talking, continuing for some time, was troublesome, and I saw that the Indians were evidently excited and tired. Further, from their manner I felt that it would be wise to have the troops that were already on the march in position; namely, the Wallowa force, about a hundred cavalrymen, as near us as the Grande Ronde; a new company at Walla Walla; and one of the cavalry companies from Walla Walla in our immediate vicinity.

Therefore, when Joseph asked for postponement, I proposed not to meet again till the following Monday. This arrangement seemed to please everybody. I remarked, as we were about to separate, "Let the Indians take time; let them wait till Monday morning and, meanwhile, talk fully among themselves." So, with pleasant faces and cordial handshaking, the second interview ended.

There was, however, great anxiety during the few days of intermission. The treaty Nez Perces betrayed symptoms of fear. The extravagant speeches of young Indians were circulated by the women. Gossips came to servants of the officers and told of the sayings and the threats of Joseph and White Bird.

For a time there were at the fort and at the agency, which is but three miles distant, much sleeplessness and terror lest there should burst out somewhere in our neighborhood a fire that no ordinary effort could quench.

The wild Indians were well armed with many breach-loading rifles and pistols. The friendly Nez Perces had nothing but shotguns. The former were constantly trained by their unceasing racings and firings, while the latter were cultivating their farms. The non-treaties had made themselves, like the irregular cossacks of Russia, the best skirmishers in the world. They are quick-sighted, superior marksmen, and subject to sufficient discipline when following their recognized chiefs to scatter, run to cover, and reassemble without disbanding.

Already there were hovering about our garrison at Lapwai this well-appointed force of Indians, greater in number than the two skeleton companies of United States soldiers stationed there and every hour brought them new accessions. Someone asked, "Did not General Canby trust the Modocs? And what was the result?" It must be confessed that my reflections were not altogether pleasant, nor such observations and questions very reassuring.

The interval of waiting was, however, relieved by the lively exercises of the Sabbath. At the agency chapel the Dreamers—men, women, and children—and the Christians filled the house, the steps, and the borders round about while their songs of praise could be heard for a long distance.

There is so much that is picturesque in the Indian costume that such an assembly presents a gay spectacle at any time. This Sunday was not an exception. The gloom and anxiety, which like a heavy cloud had previously settled upon the whites in the vicinity, seemed to drift away before the cheerful spirit of this occasion. Reuben, the chosen head-chief, James Reuben, the teacher, and Archie Lawyer, who read in English and preached in Nez Perce, all prophesied peace. By night the Indians in general were happy, and the whites in attendance became hopeful of a peaceful solution of disquieting questions. Yet, as I subsequently heard, Joseph held himself aloof from the Christian gathering, and stirred up many of his immediate followers by those interesting Dreamer ceremonial movements, drumming and song, which the following November at the prisoners' camp at Leavenworth, Kansas, brought together five thousand of our citizens to hear and see them.

Chapter X

The day for the third interview with the discontented Indians came. It was Monday, the seventh day of May, 1877. There had been many additions to their numbers. They had come to Lapwai from all directions. Hush-hush-cute, the oily, wily, bright-eyed young chief, who could be smooth-tongued or saucy as the mood seized him or as he thought would best serve a present purpose, had just arrived from the vicinity of the Palouse River with a number of followers. Messengers had come to Joseph from the mouth of the Grande Ronde declaring that soldiers were already in the Wallowa country.

The ceremonial display of the Indian bands, with greatly increased forces, evidently gave the Indians courage, and those disposed to war measures were bolder in their manner and in their demands. Mr. Monteith was very kind and conciliatory toward them, stating that they had evidently received a wrong impression with regard to the government requirement. There was no purpose to interfere with them in their religious rites and ceremonies, no restraint except when a Too-at or Dreamer, in his mistaken zeal, occasioned a disturbance of the peace. It was added that a bad teacher, who counselled disobedience of the clear instructions of the government, would certainly have to be punished.

Too-hul-hul-sote, the cross-grained growler, was again designated as the speaker and took up his parable. He was, if possible, crosser and more impudent in his abruptness of manner than before. He had the usual long preliminary discussion about the earth being his mother, that she should not be disturbed by hoe or plough, that men should subsist on what grows of itself, etc. He railed against the violence that would separate Indians from lands that were theirs by inheritance. He repeated his ideas concerning "chieftainship," chieftainship of the earth. Chieftainship cannot be sold, cannot be given away. Mr. Monteith and General Howard, he said, must speak the truth about this chieftainship of the earth.

He was answered: "We do not wish to interfere with your religion, but you must talk about practicable things. Twenty times over you repeat that the earth is your mother and about chieftainship from the earth. Let us hear it no more but come to business at once."

The old man replied in a very insolent tone: "What the treaty Indians talk about was born of today! It isn't true law at all. You white people get together, measure the earth and then divide it, so I want you to talk directly what *you* mean!" The agent then stated very pleasantly, "The law is, you must come to the reservation. The law is made in Washington. We don't make it."

To other similar remarks the old Dreamer replied fiercely, "We never have made any trade. Part of the Indians gave up their land. I never did. The earth is part of my body, and I never gave up the earth."

I replied, "You know very well that the government has set apart a reservation and that the Indians must go upon it. If an Indian becomes a citizen, like old Timothy of Alpowa, he can have land like any other citizen outside, but he has to leave his tribe and take land precisely as a white man does. The government has set apart this large reservation for you and your children that you may live in peace and prosper."

The rough old fellow, looking fiercely at me, said something in a short sentence in his most provoking tone.

The interpreter quickly said, "What person pretends to divide the land and put me on it?"

In the most decided voice I replied, "I am the man. I stand here for the President, and there is no spirit good or bad that will hinder me. My orders are plain, and they will be executed. I hoped that the Indians had good sense enough to make me their friend and not their enemy."

Signs of anger and bad blood began to appear. Looking Glass dropped his gentle style and answered me evasively. White Bird, from behind his eagle's wing, spoke mildly, but endorsed his aged spokesman. "If I had been taught from early life to be governed by the white men, I would be governed by the white men. The earth sustains [or rules] me."

I now perceived that the Indians were trying to see how saucy they could be through this Too-at, and I noticed that some of them had weapons. I perceived that I must somehow put in a wedge of separation and curb their unruly tendency. So I said to the old man, "Then you do not propose to comply with the orders of the government?" He answered, "So long as the earth keeps me, I want to be left alone. You are trifling with the law of the earth." I replied, "Our old friend does not seem to understand that the question is whether the Indians will come peaceably on the reservation, or do they want me, in compliance with my orders, to put them there by force?"

He declared, in substance, "I never gave the Indians authority to give away my lands." I asked, "Do you speak for yourself alone?" He answered with additional fierceness, "The Indians may do what they like, but I am not going on the reservation!"

Speaking as sternly as I could, I said, "This bad advice is what you give the Indians. On account of it you will have to be taken to the Indian territory. Joseph and White Bird seem to have good hearts, but yours is bad. I will send you there if it takes years and years. When I heard that you were coming, I feared that you would make trouble. You say you are not a medicine-man, but you talk for them. The Indians can see no good while you are their spokesman. You advise them to resist, to fight, to lose all their horses and cattle and have unending trouble." I then turned to the others and continued, "Will Joseph and White Bird and Looking Glass go with me to look after their land? The old man shall not go. He must stay with Colonel Perry."

The old Dreamer said, "Do you want to scare me with reference to my body?" I answered, "I will leave your body with Colonel Perry."

At this time I called for the messenger, but he being away, Colonel Perry and I led Too-hul-hul-sote out of the council. My conduct was summary, it is true, but I knew it was hopeless to get the Indians to agree to anything so long as they could keep this old Dreamer in the lead and defy the agents of the government, and I believed that the Modoc massacre would very soon be repeated if I gave time for concert of action. In fact, in dealing with Indians, my conviction is strong that the true policy is to demand obedience to the requirements of the government of the United States. The crisis had come when either this demand must be made or these wild Indians be allowed all the latitude and leisure that their hearts desired.

A far different spirit now prevailed among them. Their tones changed. They spoke pleasantly and readily agreed to go with me to examine the Lapwai, and afterward the valley of the Clearwater at more remote parts of the reservation, where there would be good ground to cultivate, fair grazing for their animals, and plenty of wood for the winter months.

With this satisfactory conclusion, the council again adjourned.

Chapter XI

Tuesday, May 8th, Joseph, White Bird, and Looking Glass rode with Wilkinson and me up the valley of the Lapwai. These chiefs were dressed in their best. Their swinging side-locks were braided with unusual care. Their faces were painted as usual with a line of red running back along the parting of the hair over the head. Well mounted on large-sized Indian ponies of diverse colors, with their rich blankets dropped from the shoulders to the saddle, they sat waiting for us near their lodges. They appeared hearty and cheerful, chatting with us and with each other as we rode along.

At Caldwell's, in the upper part of this valley, a lady very kindly gave us a lunch. Joseph looked over Mr. Caldwell's house with much apparent interest. I said to him, "Joseph, you prefer canvas houses; you don't like these wooden-frame houses?" He answered, "Oh no. When I come upon the Lapwai, I shall want a frame house." On our way back to the post we had quite a horse race. White Bird wished to try his snug-built roan and see if it could not out-run Captain Wilkinson's American bay. All laughed and talked in the most friendly way. On one occasion during the ride Looking Glass came to me and begged me to release the old man—Too-hul-hul-sote—from confinement. He said he would make him say that he was sorry for his crossness, and that he and White Bird would be responsible to me with their lives for his good behavior. It was, doubtless, with his promise to me in memory, that Looking Glass later became afraid to surrender and always said, "General Howard will surely hang us." And this promise also so affected White Bird that before the final surrender, he crept out between the lines rather than risk a meeting.

Looking Glass and White Bird were told, as we approached the fort on our return, that the old man would be kept under restraint until all the land matter should be arranged. The friendly sub-chief, Jonah, and Joe Robosko, the interpreter, went with us this day, and both remarked that "The non-treaties have now made up their minds fully to come on the reserve. Joseph and his band of Wallowa Indians apparently wanted the Lapwai from where the Sweetwater joins it to its source above Caldwell's ranch. White Bird wanted to go to Looking Glass' country on the Clearwater above Kamiah. Hush-hush-cute would go to the land along the Clearwater just above the agency." Joe Robosko was very happy about it. He said, "I didn't believe till today that they had decided to come." Of course all of us were very glad. Matters appeared to be taking a good turn. The beauty of the day, the exhilaration of this ride of fourteen miles, the effect of the fine lands presented to Joseph's eye, the sight of the nice house on the Lapwai that would be his, and the breaking of bread with us at lunch—all appeared to combine to soften the heart of the young chieftain and relieve him from the sinister undercurrent of his thought and purpose.

The next day was Wednesday, the 9th of May. We set out for Kamiah before the sun arose. I never can forget that lovely morning when the sun began to appear, touching the round hills with light and glorifying the mountain before us.

Looking Glass rode by my side and told of his father, long since dead, and of the old man's good advice, advice that he had not hitherto heeded, but that he now meant to follow. "What makes me feel like laughing this morning, General Howard?" he asked in pleasant thoughtfulness.

I answered, "There are three kinds of laughter—one from fun, another from deceit, and another from real joy!"

"Mine," he replied, "is from real joy. I shall never forget our ride along these paths." So we talked.

White Bird took to Captain Wilkinson for his amusement. His face lighted up and broke into smiles as he talked. I believed, as did all my staff who made this journey of sixty miles with us—and as did Mr. Monteith, the Indian agent, who went over the hills and mountains along the banks for sixteen miles above Kamiah the next day—that these leading Indians then really meant to conform to the wishes of the government and come on the reservation.

After the return to Lapwai the Indians came together for a final interview, Tuesday, May 14th. Captain Trimble's company of the 1st Cavalry had arrived at Lapwai and gone into camp. Special news had just come in that two other companies, Whipple's and Winter's, had reached the banks of the Grande Ronde not far from its mouth. This news created much excitement among the Indians. Word was brought to Joseph to hurry and make terms with me, for a thousand soldiers were near his old camping ground beyond the Snake River. Joseph had, in consequence, very early this morning run to my aide-de-camp and asked to have all matters speedily settled.

The white inhabitants from the Salmon River and Camas Prairie country, from the vicinity of Wallowa, and from the neighborhood of Hush-hush-cute's roaming places, had from time to time sent the Indian agent the most marked complaints of the unruly character of many of these Indians and forwarded earnest entreaties that they be made to go upon the reservation. A formal entreaty of this kind from Salmon River was received this very morning, of which the Indians were informed. It evidently strengthened their decision to come to the reservation, yet, as subsequent events proved, these remonstrances were treasured up in memory and made the excuse for murder and outrage.

All came together, Indians and white men, near the adjutant's office. Their petition to release the old Dreamer had been granted. Then they each entered into formal agreement with the agent and the army to be put on the Lapwai reservation in one month, that is, by June 14th. Joseph at last concluded that he would rather go to the Clearwater with the others. This favor was granted because it relieved us from the unpleasant necessity of disturbing two white men, who together held some seven hundred acres of the good land along the Lapwai Creek. And as there was seeming hostility even against the friendly reservation Indians at the town of Lewiston, twelve miles from them, it was deemed for this reason also a good thing to settle the new-comers seventy miles or more farther off.

Hush-hush-cute was given thirty-five days. He was the only Indian who at this time betrayed any symptoms of treachery. His protection papers were withheld on account of it and given to the agent, to be presented to him when the agent should be satisfied of his good intentions.

There was general rejoicing over the peaceful outcome of our councils and long rides to locate the Indians. Other Indian agencies were notified of the results. One reliable story came in, however, that a Columbia River renegade had burned his stuff and had gone on the warpath and that, according to his bitter threats, my life was in danger. This had a good foundation, but we supposed as soon as the news of peace should reach the runaway that he would return to his deserted wife, and surely one should never lie awake of nights from fear of personal harm.

The military aides and I now turned homeward. We had a quick and pleasant trip down the Snake and Columbia Rivers, and Saturday, May 19th, found us again with our families in Portland. The next time we set out, thanks to the enterprise of the redoubtable Joseph, we would not turn back till we had reached the Missouri River and looked into the eyes of our friends beyond, in St. Paul and Chicago.

Chapter XII

If you take your map of Oregon and look up Portland, you will find it one hundred and ten miles from the sea on the Willamet (sometimes called Willamette and sometimes Wollamet), but you may not realize the fact that this cosmopolitan city of twenty thousand people is really the center of all kinds of activities, military and civil—oceanward, up and down the gentle Pacific; southward, by rail and by river, to the broken mountain divides; northward, by rail and by stage, to western Washington Territory; and eastward, by the broad, grand old Columbia River, with its numerous and almost endless branches that mingle their fountain extremities with the millions of their kind which supply the brooklets, creeks and rivers of the Atlantic slope.

My companion and I came back with the feeling that a difficult task had been done. We felt almost sure that there would be no difficulties with the Nez Perces. All their history and their traditions favored this view. But we did forget, I think, that even in the veins of Joseph there was some of the Cayuse blood. The Cayuses had intermarried largely with the Nez Perces. It was, as we have seen, the Cayuses that accomplished the cowardly, treacherous, excuseless, and horrible massacre of Doctor Whitman and his helpers. Blood tells! Why ever forget it?

The days came and went in Portland much as usual. The streets were lively with the summer trade. The thousand children at the central school were coming out and going in with joyous, springing gait and an almost infinite variety of plumage. The rains had pretty nearly ceased, or had been replaced by brief showers that one enjoys as he does tears of gladness after a long sorrow. How many items of comfort in common, almost unnoticeable things, come back to the memory when the spell is over and the perpetual conflict is joined! So were we in comfort and peace and hope when Colonel E. C. Watkins, the Interior Department Inspector of Indian affairs, came into my office during this interval of rest.

Colonel Watkins was not only able and competent officially, ready as he was to take the lead in the work of gathering in the renegade Indians scattered along the Columbia, but he was also personally very pleasant company. He had served acceptably during the war of the rebellion and had, as we all must have, a fund of anecdotes relating thereto. He is a large, full-built, wholesome man, backed up with genuine courage in any dangerous position.

After much conversation and reflection upon the situation, Watkins and I agreed that if Joseph could secure allies among the numerous Columbia River tribes, he might yet change his mind, should he be inclined to treachery. It was certainly wise to anticipate him and if possible divert the bands that were roaming up and down the great river.

On the 31st of May, at the usual early hour of five in the morning, we set out for the Dalles. I little thought, as I took my small valise in hand and bade adieu to my drowsy family, that I should pass through an Indian war and be absent five months before I should look upon their faces again. Yet so it was to be.

What books would be written to fill the world if what is said and done on transport steamers and other vehicles were only jotted down! Colonel Watkins and Captain Wilkinson had a fund of stories, so that the day passed quickly as the palatial steamer ascended the Columbia.

Forty miles above the Cascades, the steamer was left. As travelers, we did not tire of the hills and mountains on the north bank opposite the Dalles, and the grand scenery as we turned our eyes from time to time to look at the valley of the Columbia, and the twice ten thousand hills, and the old mountains beyond them. Thither we wound our way, up, up, and over into the valley, and up and up to the top of the Simcoe range. Near there, with weather cold as in the Alps, we camped for the night.

By eleven the next day, June 2nd, we were at Father Wilbur's Indian agency on the Simcoe River. The Simcoe is a branch of the Yakima, which enters the Columbia above the mouth of the Snake. The Yakima gave the name to the most handsome Indian reservation of the Pacific coast. Mr. Wilbur was away when we arrived, at a remote part of his reserve branding cattle. That evening he and his wife returned. How strong he looked. Standing six feet in his slippers, a broad-shouldered, thick-chested, large-headed, full-voiced man. Yet he tires sometimes as age creeps on. Mrs. Wilbur said, "We had to stop by the way, and he lay down a while and took a sleep and rest." I do not wonder, for he had the care of a nation on his shoulders and was his own cabinet, legislature, and judiciary. He did have a prime minister, however, who was systematic and painstaking, and that was Mrs. Wilbur. The next day we looked in upon one of their churches, that one which was crowded to over-flowing with Indians and had the fences lined with their waiting saddle horses. That church was without a speck of dirt, even a tobacco stain!

Monday, messengers were sent out to Indians along the Columbia for hundreds of miles, and they asked the bands to meet at Fort Simcoe. While we were waiting for this important gathering, Colonel Watkins, Captain Wilkinson and I looked over this extensive and celebrated Indian reservation, so well known to benevolent people everywhere. We went even to the cattle ranch, twenty-six miles from the agency, and saw how the young cattle and calves were branded and did not wonder that Mr. Wilbur got weary when we saw the practical way in which he taught the Indians to mark a wild steer. The animal had to be thrown down and made to lie flat and still while the strong man applied the heavy and fearful branding iron. To catch, to throw, to fasten, to hold, to brand, then to sep-arate the public and the private, the Indian's and the white man's, was a trying ordeal, almost like a battle in its excitements.

While Colonel Watkins and his escort were waiting on the Yakima, the mail brought only good news. Joseph, Ollicut, and White Bird were gathering in their ponies and cattle, preparatory to settling down as they had promised. The newspapers, which are fond of sensational paragraphs, gave out good tidings. The favorable reports gladdened the hearts of the Yakimas also, for while there is an Indian war all the red men are more or less involved in suspicion and trouble.

Chapter XIII

I returned to Fort Simcoe in time to meet the renegade Indians, should they listen to the appeal of our messenger and come in.

This Fort Simcoe is located about sixty-five miles north of the Columbia. It is in the Yakima and Simcoe Valleys, lying close to the foothills of the Cascade range in a beautiful grove of oaks. It was built for two or three companies of infantry by Major Garnett, who was at one time the commander of the Military Academy and who afterwards fell in the Confederate service. He made picturesque quarters for his officers and good buildings generally and surrounded the gardens with handsome fences. The improvements were years ago transferred to the Indian Department and became the headquarters for the agency of the Yakima, or Simcoe, reservation. The great beauty and fertility of this valley, the complete success of civilizing influences under Agent Wilbur, the neat Indian houses and farms it contains, and the other evidences of progress have long been the subject of public record. I may here add that all this ground force was brought to bear by the agent, employees, head chief Joe Stwyre, and the friendly reservation Indians, to help Colonel Watkins in carrying out his instructions. These were to gather the renegades and wild roamers of the Columbia and start them on the road of civilization.

White people tried to hinder and frighten Joe Stwyre. "You'll be killed *sure*, if you go to Smohollie!" "No, no!" Smohollie received him gladly and hastened with his principal friends to set out for Simcoe. So, also, Moses from Priest's Rapids and the other nomads along the Big River Valley. Pambrun, the interpreter, the son of the Pambrun of the time of the Cayuse massacre, who spoke a language that all these understand, came from his home near Touchet. All the Indians, far and near, gathered in the neighborhood of Simcoe on Saturday, the 8th of June.

It was a hot, sunny day, so that the tent stretched in the grove afforded a very grateful shade. Behold the formal grouping! I never have experienced so much solemn formality, except at the first January examination at the Military Academy, where the superintendent and all officers of the army came and arranged themselves in dazzling order; so was it at an Indian council. First, Colonel Watkins, Agent Wilbur, our military selves, white men and ladies arranged; then facing these are the Indians on benches or chairs, in the first row, in order of their supposed rank, from right to left—Moses, Smohollie, One-eyed John, Calwash, Skemiah, Thomas, and others. Friendly Indians mingled with the newcomers. Renegades came in behind, sitting or gracefully crouching. The background was finely studded with women and children, with bright and contrasted colors, with straight black hair and flashing black eyes.

After the opening prayer, Colonel Watkins made the first speech. It was in substance: The government of the United States now requires you all to come on this or some other of its reservations. In every possible way of looking at this matter it is evidently better for you to come; the commander of the military forces will enforce this requirement.

Agent Wilbur talked mostly to the second proposition and strove to influence Smohollie particularly. Smohollie, the author of the Dreamer religion, is believed to be the cause of the restlessness of the Columbia River tribes, for it keeps alive the hope of supernatural aid to come through a general Indian resurrection. As it was late and the Indians were tired from their long journeys, after a few remarks of notice and welcome, the council was adjourned to Monday. All were invited to stay for the morrow's religious service at the grove where we were at the time assembled.

The next day's service cannot well be forgotten. All took part. Father Wilbur with his great spiritual power, and Colonel Watkins with his calm statements, and Captain Wilkinson with his nervous energy and moving pathos, were followed by Indians pleading for the cause of Christ in the Indian's own tongue. Smohollie and other wild ones answered these appeals with much apparent sincerity and feeling. The well-dressed and happy Indian school children cemented the whole in joyous demonstrations of sacred song.

The adjourned meeting reassembled at eight a.m., the 10th of June. I will simply introduce the Indians' speeches as I recorded them.

Moses, a handsome Indian, neat in his dress, full-built and muscular, his head held well up and back, his eyes red from inflammation—probably the effect of wind and alkali dust and Indian fires, "My Indians are scattered over a large country. I cannot say what they will do. I am ready to tread on any reservation. If it is better for me to go on some reservation other than this, all right. The Indians above the Spokane, several tribes, have invited me to become their chief and if they shall have a reservation I would like to go to them."

Smohollie, with his hunchback figure and big head, apparently fearing that Moses may get ahead of him, even in our favor, remarked at once, "Your law is my law. I say to you, yes. I will be on a reservation by September. I have but two or three hundred people."

The oldest chief, Thomas, bleary-eyed, spare, tall, full of trembling, says, "I have about fifty Indians in all. I will go to the Umatilla Reservation by the 1st of September." He kept the promise in November.

The others, Skemiah, One-eyed John, and Calwash, made similar promises, naming the number of Indians for whom they were responsible. These five Indians were chiefs of bands. They made their promises freely, and so far as joining others against the whites is concerned, none of them did so, and few of their people have since misbehaved.

That afternoon we bade our good, hospitable friends at the agency goodbye, feeling as if another peaceful work had been done, and well done. Surely at least five hundred warriors, apprised that Joseph and his discontented Indians had yielded to us, were themselves deterred from all preparations for war. If any of them afterwards meditated treachery, as people who doubt all Indians claim, it was too late. The military movements prevented reinforcements from this quarter without great hazard. And really I do not think such treachery was contemplated after this gathering.

In a spring wagon drawn by two good mules, our party followed the Yakima down its southeasterly course to near its mouth. The interpreter and many Indians on their ponies afforded the wagon a lively cavalcade. The heat and finally deep sand for several leagues prevented our arrival at Wallula the night of the 11th. We had at least twenty-five miles to go when it occurred to me that the Indians might take us down the Columbia in a canoe. We came to near the mouth of the Yakima just about sundown. Captain Wilkinson here became alarmingly ill, could eat nothing at the ranch nearby, and could hardly be induced to proceed. Still, we thought it very important to be at Wallula to catch the upriver boat to Lewiston. Colonel Watkins must go to Lapwai to inspect, and then together we were bound for the Spokane and beyond. So we went to the Columbia's bank and called loudly for the promised canoe. At last two of Smohollie's Indians pushed out in the darkness and paddled over a long dugout. The captain was carried and assisted to a comfortable, though narrow, bed midway. The Indians and Pambrun managed the boat. Colonel Watkins and I told stories and sang our songs, till Captain Wilkinson was soon sufficiently recovered to join us. Past the dark places, past the islands, past the Homely Rapids, frightful to our small craft by their roaring, past the mouth of the Snake—we shot along, wind, current, and Indian paddle all in our favor. It was two o'clock in the clear morning, the dawn just appearing in the east, when we pulled up at the little hamlet of Wallula. The gangplank was just about to be drawn in when the night travelers stepped upon it and hurried to the steamer's deck.

"Grant me fifteen minutes for messages below and eastward?" "Yes, yes; hurry," the captain answers. In less time we are off for Lewiston. Our sick friend now is all right, eating a hearty, early breakfast in the steamboat kitchen.

We again get good accounts of matters among the Nez Perces so that, worn out with the great fatigue of the journey and without anything to disturb our repose, we were soon fast asleep. The steamer toiled on, without our care or help, making slow headway against the powerful current of the Snake River.

Chapter XIV

The Snake River comes into the Columbia a few miles above Wallula. The scenery along the Snake is unique and striking. The banks are high and very broken with surfaces worn into all kinds of fantastic forms. The snows, the rains, the winds, and the extraordinary river risings when the freshets from the supplying mountains come tumbling down into this immense and crooked drain, shape the shores and mould into variegated forms the contiguous receding hills. It takes but little fancy to see, as you look left and right, sleeping giants, reclining beauties, or figures of the animal creation of all descriptions, each carved from the earth-masses and lying there covered with a grassy spread in everlasting repose. The scenery is wild, untamable, and in spite of immigration it will be so for a century. Here and there we find a landing where emigrants and prospectors are getting off the steamer.

A year ago Almota appeared pretty well out of the world. The son of the famous missionary, Mr. Spalding, had here but his one cottage and his lovely wife. Now there are many houses. His own house has become a hotel, and he is boarding at it. Almota has become a large supply depot for a backcountry fast settling. This and a few other landings make a slight impression on this large, grand, almost boundless country but they no more remove from the traveler's mind a feeling of the vastness of the expanse around him than do a few ships at sea as he paces, day-by-day, his steamer's deck.

By eight o'clock, June 14th, we came into view of the distant village. We say "village," for however large as a mining town Lewiston may have been, after the change of the mining interest to other centers of fortune hunting and gambling, the city of Lewiston has relapsed into its normal conditions of a frontier village. The hills behind this pretty

town, and close to it, look like regularly constructed fortifications. The line of the table land is just above the
chimneys and nearly horizontal, and the white fence of a
burying place on the top, in the distance, adds to the idea of
a constructed parapet. Lewiston has a mill, a newspaper,
and several well-to-do merchants.

As we neared the landing, the people of the village were
seen in waiting. As soon as our boat touched the shore,
Colonel Perry, Major Trimble, Lieutenant Bomus, and
Charlie Monteith, the brother of the Indian agent, sprang
on board and gave us a welcome. Colonel Perry was still in
command at Fort Lapwai. He has a prominent part in this
history and deserves special notice. His rank, not the
brevet, is that of Captain of Company F, First United
States Cavalry. He is a little over six feet in height and
very erect. He shows a clear Saxon eye and usually wears a
pleasant smile—pleasant, but with a reserve in it. One
hardly can command men and go into battle often and still
keep an altogether sunshiny face.

Major Trimble is another who has a brevet title. His
ground rank is that of Captain of Company C. His post
proper was Walla Walla. It will be remembered that he
came with his company to Lapwai, marching overland a
month before. He was first brought up to Lewiston to be
where he could strengthen Fort Lapwai or the troops near
Wallowa as need might require. But, as our councils with
Joseph were in progress, he was sent on to Fort Lapwai,
partly for the comfort of his men and partly that Joseph and
his Indians might see during the conference a larger force
than the ordinary garrison. With Trimble added, we had
about one hundred and twenty men to garrison the post.

Lieutenant Bomus was the post Quartermaster, afterwards to serve in a more important position at Lapwai and
Lewiston. Such were the friends who came to meet the
steamer at the landing.

"How is Joseph, Colonel?" I asked.

"All right, at last accounts. The Indians are, I think,
coming on the reservation without trouble."

Mrs. Perry was here to go down on the steamer to the
Dalles. Young Monteith, the clerk, had come to meet Colonel

Watkins. He told the same story, "All quiet at last accounts; Indians seem to be acting in good faith; guess they will make no trouble." Mr. Coburn, and a member of the firm of Loewenburg, and several of the other citizens of Lewiston united in similar testimony: "The Indians are all right." I said at first to Colonel Watkins that I saw no need of my going farther at this time toward Lapwai. Colonel Perry could now attend to all manners. I would wait at Lewiston for Watkins to finish his inspection at the Lapwai agency, and he could pick me up on his return. Then we would proceed to the Spokane and Colville country, obey our Washington instructions, fulfill our promises to the Columbia River renegades and settle the vexed questions of the upcountry.

But Perry said, "You had better go with me. It will be more pleasant for you to wait at the fort."

The Colonel's kind hospitality was at last accepted and, leaving Lewiston early in the afternoon, we rode the twelve miles together behind his spirited and handsome horses.

After the first considerable ascent, we sped away for six or seven miles on a beautiful tableland, over the finest of roads, even and hard, so that we made excellent time. Ahead were the usual rolling hills of the Snake region, to the left the Clearwater, and beyond the almost mountain ridge that hides the new town of Moscow. Behind was the Lewis River, or Snake proper, and all that vast succession of indescribable breakages of the earth's surface, with edges smoothed off and softened down, peaceful outdoor pictures, too numerous for the pencil but kaleidoscopic and pleasant to the eye.

Soon appeared the charming Lapwai Valley, always fresh and new in the sunlight. Down the long descent we whirled, then turned to the right, taking a half mile's survey of the tented post. In a few moments we were passing the gate, which had been opened by the quick courtesy of the guard. My former aide-de-camp, Lieutenant Boyle, had been promoted since we last saw him. He was here with his beautiful family, no longer Lieutenant, but Captain Boyle, in command of a Twenty-First Infantry company. He is a sturdy and loyal officer. No war cloud now, so the meeting

at the fort was most pleasant. Here was Trimble's lieutenant, a colonel by brevet, by "ground rank" Lieutenant
Parnell. Here also was Lieutenant Theller, a generous,
brave man with a warm heart. He had quarters near
Lapwai Creek, where he and his wife were wont to give
cheery hospitality to the Department's officers as they came
and went on duty. You could see him often trying the speed
of his stallion on the race course just west of the garrison.

On my arrival all seemed as peace-like and happy as
home, but toward evening there came a ripple, a slight
warning. A courier approached Colonel Perry and handed
him a letter from Mount Idaho. Here is a copy:

Mount Idaho, June 14, 1877.

Colonel Perry: – Dear Sir: Mr. Overman, who
resides at or near the head of Rocky Canyon eight
miles from here, came in today and brought his
friends. They are very much alarmed at the action of
the Indians who are gathered there. He says there
are about sixty lodges, composed of the Salmon River
Indians, Joseph and his band, with other non-
treaties, and that they are insolent and have but
little to say to the whites, and that all their actions
indicate trouble from them. Mr. Overman is regarded
as a very truthful man and confidence can be placed
in all his statements. Some of the other neighbors
have likewise moved over this way where there are
more people.

Yesterday the Indians had a grand parade.
About a hundred were mounted and well armed,
and went through the maneuvers of a fight—were
thus engaged for about two hours. They say, openly,
that they are going to fight the soldiers when they
come to put them on the reservation, and I understand that they expect them up on Friday next. A
good many were in town today and were trying to
obtain powder and other ammunition. Mr. Scott told
me today that they offered him two dollars and a
half for a can of powder. Up to this time, I think,
they have been buying all the arms, &c., that they

could get, but do not believe they can make any purchases now. They have a strong position at the head of the canyon, among the rocks, and should they make any resistance could give the troops much trouble. I do not feel any alarm, but thought it well to inform you of what was going on among them. Early this morning one Indian came here and wanted to know when General Howard was coming up. As the stage came up last night, they perhaps thought we might know when he would be up. They are evidently on the lookout for the soldiers. I believe it would be well for you to send up, as soon as you can, a sufficient force to handle them without gloves should they be disposed to resist. Sharp and prompt action will bring them to understand that they must comply with the orders of the government. We trust such action will be taken by you, so as to remove them from the neighborhood and quiet the feelings of the people.

I write this for your own information and at the suggestion of many settlers who are living in exposed localities.

Very respectfully yours,

L. P. Brown

Colonel Perry read the letter, then handed it to me. He in substance remarked, "Mr. Brown, who is a reliable man, is not greatly alarmed. I will send out a detachment to bring us information. That is best, is it not?"

I said, "Yes, do so by all means."

The town of Mount Idaho is situated at the further edge of an extensive camas prairie, near the mountain spurs that lie between the Salmon and the Clearwater rivers. Its distance from Fort Lapwai is sixty miles, in a direct southeast line. The Rocky Canyon where Joseph and the nontreaties were behaving so insolently, the same distance and nearer the Salmon. This canyon empties into that furious river. They were, in fact, near the borders of the reserve and apparently hesitating whether to go on peaceably or stay off and fight.

At dawn on the 15th the military detachment left the fort, accompanied by Joe Robosko, the half-breed interpreter who had just before the last interview at Lapwai helped in locating Joseph. The detachment moved, probably as fast as the horses could carry them, towards Mount Idaho. The place where the Indians were encamped was to the right of the Mount Idaho road after passing Norton's ranch. It was nineteen miles from Norton's ranch to Mount Idaho. Craig's mountain had to be passed before Norton's. Our detachment met two Indians somewhere near Craig's mountain and turned back with them. These Indians were much excited. They arrived at Lapwai about noon. The name of one was Pu-ton-ah-loo, and the other was an Indian lad of perhaps fourteen years. We heard their story, sifting it through Joe Robosko's interpretation. It was to the effect that some three or four Indians had committed a murder near Slate Creek, where there was a scattered settlement some forty miles beyond Mount Idaho. It was in some way connected with a citizen, Larry Ott, who had killed an Indian. Colonel Watkins had gone directly to the Indian agency on our arrival and had remained there. As was proper then, taking the messengers with us, Perry and I started immediately for the agency and had the Indian authorities examine the young men through Mr. Whitman, the official interpreter. Mr. Whitman confirmed the Larry Ott story. All believed that serious trouble was coming. The interpreter and the Indian agent thought it wise to send at once the acting head chief and Joseph's father-in-law, who still insisted that Joseph would not fight and who volunteered to go. This party rode off at full speed. They had not been gone very long when—I think it was half past four—the party came back, running their horses and bringing with them another communication from Mount Idaho, brought by the brother of Looking Glass and a half-breed citizen by the name of West.

The brother of Looking Glass was a stalwart Indian with a very intelligent and pleasant countenance. Mr. West was a man short of stature with long, black hair. He spoke English freely, so that we had an account of matters straight from his lips. Other Indians, friendly Nez Perces, came into Fort Lapwai about the same time, among them several who belonged to the Catholic mission and who had gone out with the non-treaty Indians to participate in their sports of gaming, lance throwing, running, and horse racing. As soon as they found that these malcontents meant war, they broke from them and rushed with their small herds toward their homes.

Chapter XV

The most intense feeling now existed at the fort and at the agency. A large group of people were on Colonel Perry's front porch—the officers, the ladies of the post, several principal friendly Indians. The newcomers gathered around the steps of the porch or were sitting upon them. The dispatch was instantly opened. One of the essential things in war-like operations is for the commanding officer to preserve his poise under all circumstances, but there are times when he is likely to be moved by the contagion of others' excitement. This was such an occasion, so I made an unusual effort to be perfectly cool and self-possessed while I read, first to myself, then to the officers, the following startling communications:

Mount Idaho, 7 a.m., Friday, June 15, '77
Commanding Officer Fort Lapwai:

Last night we started a messenger to you who reached Cottonwood House, where he was wounded and driven back by the Indians. The people of Cottonwood undertook to come here during the night; were interrupted, all wounded or killed. Parties this morning found some of them on the prairie. The wounded will be here shortly, when we will get full particulars. The whites are engaged, about forty of them, in getting the wounded. One thing is certain: we are in the midst of an Indian war. Every family is here, and we will have taken all the precautions we can, but are poorly armed. We want arms and ammunition and help at once. Don't delay a moment. We have a report that some whites were killed yesterday on the Salmon River. No later word from them; fear that the people are all killed, as a party of Indians were seen going that way last night. Send to Lewiston, and hasten up. You cannot imagine people in a worse condition than they are here. Mr. West has volunteered to go to Lapwai; rely on his statements.

Yours truly,

L. P. Brown

The next letter was received at the same time. It speaks for itself:

Mount Idaho, 8 a.m., June 15, '77
Commanding Officer Fort Lapwai:

I have just sent a dispatch by Mr. West. Since that was written the wounded have come in—Mr. Day mortally; Mrs. Norton with both legs broken; Moore shot through the hip; Norton killed and left in the road, six miles from here. Teams were attacked on the road and abandoned. The Indians have possession of the prairie and threaten Mount Idaho. All the people are here, and we will do the best we can. Lose no time in getting up with a force. Stop the stage and all through travelers. Give us relief, and arms and ammunition. Chapman has got this Indian [the messenger, Looking Glass' brother], hoping he may get through. I fear the people on Salmon have all been killed, as a party was seen going that way last night. We had a report last night that seven whites had been killed on Salmon. Notify the people of Lewiston. Hurry up; hurry! Rely on this Indian's statement; I have known him for a long time; he is with us.

L. P. Brown.

P.S. – Send a dispatch to town for the express not to start up unless heavily escorted. Give the bearer a fresh horse and send him back.

Chapman.

"Well, colonel, this means business!"
"Yes, sir."

"Are your men in readiness?"

"Everything but some transportation that must come from Lewiston."

"Captain Wilkinson, get ready to go to Walla Walla at once."

Lieutenant Bomus had his buggy at the door of his quarters in less than ten minutes.

During the few minutes of preparation, I examined Mr. West, who corroborated all the statements of the letters and gave the graphic accounts of an eyewitness of the murders and outrages which had been committed. Then immediately the messages and letters from Messrs. Brown and Chapman were sent to the Indian agency for the information of Colonel Watkins, the inspector, and Mr. Monteith, the agent, and the following letter was sent by Smith to Mount Idaho:

Fort Lapwai, I. T., June 15, '77, 5 p.m.
Mr. Brown:

Dear Sir: Your two dispatches are received. I have sent forward two companies of cavalry to your relief. They leave tonight. Other help will be enroute as soon as it can be brought up. I am glad you are so cool and ready. Cheer the people. Help shall be prompt and complete. Lewiston has been notified.

Yours truly,
O. O. Howard

Wilkinson and Bomus are ready to start. Wilkinson's memoranda:

I. Order through Colonel Grover, Captain Whipple's two cavalry companies from Wallowa to Lapwai by shortest route. (They march.)

II. Send Infantry from Walla Walla and vicinity to Lapwai. (By steamer.)

III. Forward dispatch to Colonel Wood at Portland for more troops and three months' supplies to be sent to Lewiston at once.

IV. Send dispatches to General McDowell, San Francisco, and request twenty-five scouts.

All the details of these memoranda were set in order and executed. To do it, Captain Wilkinson rode with Lieutenant Bomus to Lewiston and then got a special conveyance from the stage line and kept up the most rapid riding, making his one hundred and ten miles to Walla Walla by eight a.m. of the next morning. There he came upon a line of the telegraph and communicated accordingly. As the information then appeared, it was put into the dispatch to Division Headquarters: "Indians began by murdering a white man in revenge for a murder of his, killing three others at the same time." (This statement will have to be modified now, though there seems still to be some connection between the first murder and the death of the Indian previously killed by a white man in the Salmon River country.) "Since then they have begun war upon the people near Mount Idaho. Captain Perry started with two companies of cavalry for them. Other troops are being brought forward as fast as possible. Give me authority for twenty-five scouts. Think we will make short work of it."

The work did not appear short to the impatient country. Yet, as the history shows, a month's battling on fields wide apart, and three month's pursuing brought us through.

Lieutenant Theller had been added to Perry's command—four resolute young men, including Trimble and Parnell. They were all married. Mrs. Perry had just gone down the river and was sent by her husband's dispatch to Mrs. Howard at Portland. Mrs. Trimble and her children, and Mrs. Parnell, were at Walla Walla. Only Mrs. Theller was there to suffer the added trial of parting with her beloved husband for battle, or it might be for death. Perry and I stood there in the doorway of his hospitable home and looked into each other's faces. How tall, strong, and confident he appeared. He set out with one hundred cavalry men less ten—too few for the work ahead, but the best we could do. We cannot wait even a few days for reinforcements, for if we do the murders will continue. "Hurry, hurry!" is the citizens' watchword and earnest call. We could not send more from Fort Lapwai, for no smaller force than the twenty men of Captain Boyle would answer for defense of goods and home and agency and Lewiston. The best we could do, these ninety men!

"Goodbye, General!"

"Goodbye, Colonel. You must not get whipped."

"There is no danger of that, sir." And indeed, there did not then seem to be much danger of such a catastrophe, with trained and disciplined troops against these Indians as yet unused to war with white men.

When the husband buckles on his armor and sets out for war, it is the wife left behind who requires patience and fortitude. She busies her fingers to keep the blood in motion and keep it from stopping at the heart at every ring of the door bell. To her the ruthless newspapers are a terror, a cruelty.

It was my duty at this time to remain and wait for the soldiers to come together from distant places, to carry them forward should they be needed at the front, and to watch against other firebrands of dissatisfaction and outbreak among the thousands of savages apparently at peace. To remain behind and wait—it awakened in my heart unusual sympathy for other watchers, nay, a painful feeling hard to bear. So to busy myself and find relief for anxiety, I read and wrote, studied maps, counted days for the marches, paced my room, and watched every flying rumor.

Stoicism is properly condemned. Imperturbability is a suspicious accomplishment, akin to deadness of love. Still the exhibition of these qualities is very properly demanded of the soldier. They are not so hard of acquirement in danger, but to remain at home and wait amid the pulsations of extreme anxiety—who but woman is equal to the task?

Chapter XVI

Like an arrow shot into the air that may return and wound you, like a plunge to save life, which may cost you your own, such was the venture in the quick movement of Perry's command toward the hostile camp.

A fine body of men they appeared as they rode away that night. A few horses plunged and reared and bucked, but the men soon mounted and had them under control. They rode off into the darkness toward the Camas Prairie and Mount Idaho. While they toil along the muddy, hilly road for the seventy or eighty miles before reaching their enemy, let us look through subsequent glasses and see if we cannot make out and set down what had really been happening in that Salmon River country and on the extensive and fertile Camas Prairie.

Until very recently the testimony had been uniform that Young Joseph had nothing to do with the perpetration of the following chapter of horrors. Of late it is asserted by Arthur Chapman, the interpreter, that other Indians accuse Joseph himself of killing Mrs. Manuel with his own hand after others had left her wounded and entreating for her life. I believe that this charge is not true. Joseph's wife was ill and separated from the main camp. Joseph, it is proved by our own scouts, remained there with her, protesting, till he believed it too late—till he felt, like many who joined the great southern rebellion—that in a war already begun, he must identify himself with his own people.

The first day of March 1875, Larry Ott had a quarrel with an Indian which terminated in the death of the latter. Ott lived on the south side of Salmon River. The grand jury had the killing of this Indian by Ott under consideration and, being unable to find sufficient evidence of guilt, brought in no bill. Ott was not killed by the Indians, as reported, but is still alive.

In August 1875, Samuel Benedict, who then resided with his family at the mouth of White Bird Creek, killed an Indian. The circumstances under which the killing took place were as follows: Late at night, several intoxicated Indians came to Benedict's house and demanded admission. Upon being refused, they commenced breaking the doors and windows of his residence. Benedict's wife and her two children made their escape through a back window under cover of darkness, waded White Bird Creek, and found shelter in a neighboring house.

Benedict fired, killing one Indian and wounding one or two more. He is accused of previously having sold liquor to the Indians.

Another citizen, Harry Mason, whipped two Indians early in the spring. A council of arbitration met to decide who was in fault. Mr. Elfers, a white man whom I believe was chosen by the aggrieved Indians, was a member of that council. The decision of the council, as one might have predicted, was unfavorable to the Indians.

On or about the 1st of June 1877, the Salmon River Indians collected on White Bird Creek near Manuel's ranch. Soon after, Joseph and his band appeared on Camas Prairie ten miles west of Mount Idaho. The white settlers, who had never seen anything like an armed hostility on the part of the Indians except in a few individual cases, were not at first alarmed but supposed that the Indians were gathering preparatory to going on the reservation. About the 10th of June, however, the Indians made such warlike demonstrations as to seriously alarm Mr. Jarrett and others who lived near the Indian camp, and they took their families to Mount Idaho for safety.

The outbreak commenced on the afternoon of June 13th, by a small party of Indians killing Richard Divine, an old man who lived alone on Salmon River eight miles above Slate Creek. The next victims were Henry Elfers, Robert Bland, and Henry Beckroge, the killing of whom took place between the hours of six and seven o'clock the following morning. These Indians then mounted the horses of the murdered men and rode off down the Salmon River. They soon met Samuel Benedict, who was out looking for his cattle, and shot and wounded him. He managed to get on his horse and succeeded in reaching his home, where he was followed and put to death on the afternoon of the same day.

It is stated by the Indians that but three were engaged in the perpetration of the above murders, to wit, the killing of Divine, Elfers, Bland, Beckroge, and the wounding of Benedict—two of whom were Salmon River Indians named Mox-Mox and Wall-Tits. The other was a strange Indian said to belong to Joseph's band.

After the three Indians had wounded Benedict, they came up to Camas Prairie where Joseph's main band was encamped. The three Indians referred to were here joined by about seventeen more and immediately returned to Salmon River. On their way they shot and wounded J. J. Manuel and his little girl, killed James Baker, and upon arriving at Benedict's place, they discovered Benedict attempting to escape across White Bird Creek. They fired at him and he fell dead. At the same time they killed a Frenchman named August Bacon. On the following day, June 15th, they killed Mrs. Manuel, William Osborne, and Harry Mason. This is the time when Joseph is accused of participating.

June 14th, Mr. J. M. Crooks of Grangeville rode to Joseph's camp at Rocky Canyon and asked the Indians whether they intended to fight. They told Crooks that they would not fight the settlers provided they would not help the soldiers. The alarm about this time became general, and families came rushing from all directions into the village of Mount Idaho.

On the evening of the 14th, Arthur Chapman came to Mount Idaho from his home on Camas Prairie east of the Lewiston Road. His horse was covered with foam from hard riding, and he reported that an Indian boy had come to his place and informed him that the Salmon River Indians had commenced killing the settlers. Lew Day immediately volunteered to go to Fort Lapwai for military aid. He had proceeded on his way about twenty-five miles when he was fired upon by the Indians and slightly wounded. Seeing the impossibility of reaching Lapwai, he started back. When he came to the Cottonwood House (proprietor, B. B. Norton), he found Mrs. Norton, Hill Norton, Miss Bowers, Joseph Moore, and John Chamberlain with his wife and two children. Day informed these people of the threatening danger and caused them to make immediate preparations for flight to Mount Idaho, eighteen miles distant.

They set out in a wagon, with two on horseback, about ten o'clock that night and had traveled about ten miles when the Indians came up at the rear and began firing at them. Soon Norton and Moore, the horse riders, were badly wounded and compelled to abandon their horses and get into the wagon. Their team horses, however, were soon shot down, and the wagon came to a halt. Miss Bowers and little Hill Norton got out of the wagon and made their escape unharmed. Mr. Chamberlain, his wife and two children attempted to escape in the darkness, but had gone only a short distance when they were discovered by the Indians. Chamberlain and his little boy were killed. The boy was murdered, according to the mother's statement, by having his head placed beneath the knees of a powerful Indian, and so crushed to death. The other child was torn from its mother and dreadfully wounded, a piece of its tongue being cut and a knife run quite through its neck. Mrs. Chamberlain was repeatedly outraged by the Indians and received severe injuries. The remainder of the party sought shelter behind the dead horses. Here Norton was struck by a ball and killed. Moore was shot through the hips, Day through the shoulder and leg, and Mrs. Norton through both legs. The Indians kept up a desultory firing until about daylight, when they left. Miss Bowers in the meantime had reached Mount Idaho and the alarm was given. Several men started for the scene of the massacre, and the wounded were soon brought to town. Day died the following afternoon. Moore lingered for about six weeks and died. Mrs. Norton, Mrs. Chamberlain, and her child in time recovered.

After the first murders had been committed, the murderers rode into Joseph's camp, followed by White Bird and several of his men. One of them made a wild, characteristic speech as he galloped around among the tepees: "Look here; see this fine horse! Behold this rifle, this saddle, and all these good clothes! Why do you remain here talking and talking? The war has begun! I am mad! I have killed the enemies! Up! Get your horses and come on. There is plenty of everything if you only work for it!"

White Bird took fire, rode around the camp, and cried for war. "All must join now. The white men will never believe you if you ask for peace. There is blood. You'll be punished if you wait. Everybody get ready to fight."

A few hours later Joseph is said to have joined the malcontents. The peace men escaped, as we have before seen.

When the purpose of war had become general, Indians from all the bands of non-treaties except that of Looking Glass proceeded to commit the last terrible massacres, which we have related. Then, doubtless fearing the swift approach of the troops, Joseph's lodges at Rocky Canyon were taken down. He concentrated his whole force ten miles further away from Mount Idaho in the White Bird Valley, where stirring events were soon to transpire.

Chapter XVII

The distance from Fort Lapwai to Mount Idaho by the road usually travelled with wagons is sixty-two miles. The people near Fort Lapwai said it was twenty-four miles to the Old Mill, thence nineteen miles to Mr. Norton's ranch, thence nineteen miles to Mount Idaho. Grangeville is three or four miles nearer, so that there are fifty-eight miles from Fort Lapwai to Grangeville, and sixty-two to Mount Idaho. The road is quite direct, running southeasterly.

Let us look now for a few minutes at our little squadron of cavalry. They are toiling steadily along this road. The column appears long. That irregular moving mass behind is the mule train. The mules, with ammunition and supplies of every kind bound to their *aparejos*—a large, soft packing saddle—run in and out of the column, get now a little ahead and now behind, feeding by the roadside when it is light enough to see. They are a restless set of creatures, yet always obedient to the sound of the bell attached to the neck of the trained white mare, who never seems to forget her place or duty. Unaccustomed as these have been to long journeys, the horses soon fret themselves, and many of the staunchest and smartest of Perry's soon become weary. Add to the ordinary difficulties a hilly, mountainous road and plenty of wet, miry places that cannot be avoided, and the cavalry will even sooner show signs of flagging.

Packers always find the first day out a difficult one. So was it with our column. But it toiled bravely on all night, over Craig's Mountain and across Lawyer's Canyon and succeeded in reaching poor Norton's now deserted ranch by ten o'clock of the 16th of June. It was near night when the next fifteen miles had been accomplished.

Here the excited citizens gathered around the welcome soldiers. The Indian horrors which we have tried to describe had to be recited, and great excitement prevailed.

Frontier men are apt to undervalue the fighting ability of Indians. In times gone by, when we have been better mounted and better armed than the Indians and as well trained as they, we have beaten them in our conflicts, whether we have been grouped together as soldiers or citizens.

"Oh, Colonel, you can easily whip the scoundrels!" "They are cowardly wretches. We could destroy them if we only had the arms!" "You will have to hurry up, or you will not be able to overtake them!" "We will go and help you, as many as have arms and horses!"

Such were some of the expressions that saluted the colonel's ears as he halted at Grangeville and tried to take cognizance of the situation.

Grangeville is a small settlement consisting of a mill and two or three dwelling houses. After a talk with some citizens and volunteers, the commanding officer gave orders for a night march to White Bird Canyon, distant about sixteen miles.

A few citizens, perhaps ten, went with the soldiers as auxiliaries to show the way and to help shoot the foe, as yet much despised and much underrated.

They came to the top of the canyon about an hour before the dawn. Here Colonel Perry called a halt till dawn. Our men had been one day and two nights now without their accustomed rest, and yet they were on the very verge of a battle as we shall soon see.

I have before tried to give some idea of the Snake River and the Salmon, one of its tributaries. From the entrance of White Bird Creek to the mouth of the Salmon the distance is perhaps forty miles by the windings of its course. Colonel Perry, in the dim dawn, could not detect the valleys. His eye beheld nothing beyond the river but a succession of steeps with pointed or rounded tops. These were covered with flourishing greenness and behind them rose snowy peaks which were indistinctly mingled with the clouds.

The Salmon is a torrent with mountain shores. Its feeders, the creeks coming in on the right and left, are short and channel out the mountain masses transversely. White Bird is no exception. The top or head of the Canyon is where the scooping begins. A horse trail, broad for a trail

but narrow for a road, leads from this top down, down, by a
long descent to the rolling country that forms the bottom of
the canyon. When the light has come how plain it all looks!
A slight smoke from the Indian camp, not more than four
miles off, as it seems, down in the smooth-looking bottom.
The sides of the canyon are steep, but they have numerous
crosscutting ravines which you could ride up if you should
be repulsed!

When daylight came a few individuals were seen stirring at the Indian camp. As they came slowly out of their
lodges, each wrapped his blanket round his neck at one end
and allowed it to stretch to his feet, so as to get all the protection against the dew and chill of the morning. Some
moved to the war horses, which were picketed near at
hand, to change them to better grass. Some sought the herd
to relieve the night watchmen, and others, in order to scan
the horizon which everywhere appeared above them, went
quietly to the tall pile of rocks that flanked their encampment and lay down beside the sharp crags.

Among the latter observers were Joseph and his tall
brother. Suddenly, as the sunlight descended steadily from
the highest peaks and began to tinge with warmth and
beauty the broad edges and sloping surfaces of the west
side of the canyon, the brother's quick eye caught sight of a
stationary, motionless group of horsemen.

They looked as if they were painted on the sky, just
where the hills touched it. "Hu-hugh! Horses!" says Ollicut.
Joseph gazes steadily at the group.

"Get the white man's glass. Tell White Bird. They are
Indians up there, Jonah's men!"

Ollicut ran down the steep with long, springy strides,
sat down a moment by White Bird's blanket, wakened him
without disturbance and told him that the young war-chief
wanted him at the rocks. Then he went to his lodge and
returned quickly, fetching the field glass to his brother. The
purchase of this glass at some village or trading post just
before this outbreak perhaps indicated an intention to
begin the war, but perhaps not. These glasses enable
drovers and rangers to distinguish their herds miles away.
Old Blackfoot, one of White Bird's men, had extensive

herds of wild cattle, and he was quick to fall in with any improvements in their care and control. He doubtless imitated the Chapmans, the Crooks, and others who herded cattle on his ranges. They were never without the glass, and why should he be?

The three Indians now crouched, silent and motionless, among the rocks. Joseph used the glass, passed it to White Bird, and said, "Indians there!" pointing to a bluff to the west.

White Bird took the glass and quickly calls out, "Mox-Mox is coming."

Two horsemen were running their horses from a low height a mile distant. They constituted the outpost. Mox-Mox and another Indian had watched together. Now, as the glass was pointed toward the northwest, White Bird and Ollicut exclaimed at the same moment, "Bostons! Bostons!"

Colonel Perry had finished his brief rest and was leading his little squadron in close order over the crest of the first slope of the canyon, along the trail, while his friendly scouts of Jonah and Reuben were watching on the distant and commanding hill further toward the Salmon River, where the quick, piercing eye of Joseph had discovered them. Mox-Mox, having dismounted and ascended the crags, confirmed the tidings already revealed through the field glass.

Joseph then gave his instructions for the first battle. Ollicut was excited, though he had been fierce for war. The number of Perry's command now appeared to him great as they filed over the hill and down into the shadows of the ravine. "Cross over the Salmon," he urged. "It is big and swift; they cannot catch us!" White Bird gave a grunt of satisfaction at this safe proposal, but Joseph said, "No; their horses are new. They will scatter at the sound of firearms. Get the people ready—women, children, and stuff over there!" pointing down White Bird Creek. "White Bird, take your men and turn the Bostons when they get to this ridge. I will get over there behind the rocks and wait. Let every Indian be ready to mount. Mox-Mox and the women must take care of the herd and give us horses if ours are shot down. Ollicut must stay with me."

Soon there was busy preparation throughout the village. The lodges were mostly taken down; the pack animals loaded. The three main groupings were formed as Joseph had directed. At first there was heard in all directions the noise of hallooing and loud talking by women and men. Children screamed as they partook of the common excitement, but it was not long before everything of this kind was hushed. With arms and ammunition in readiness, with ponies standing patiently behind their lariats simply thrown on the ground, the Indians remained quietly waiting the attack of the soldiers.

Joseph had managed to conceal in the hollows and behind the buttes and rocks every sign of his force from anyone coming along the approaches to his front. Were it not for the telltale smoke rising from the late Indian village, his arrangement would have been a very complete ambush.

Let us return to our weary soldiers at the head of the canyon. With daylight, Perry's command began the descent. Before reaching the more level ground a white woman, Mrs. Benedict, made her appearance from the slight brushwood cover by the roadside, holding a baby in her arms and harboring a little girl about six years old by her side. Some of the Indians had released her from her horrid confinement, and she was hiding against recapture by the more brutal. She was burdened with her little ones and still more heavily with grief at her husband's death. Shivering with exposure, she was hastening as best she could to a settlement, the nearest being at least twelve miles distant.

Chapter XVIII

The little column continued its march till it neared two small knolls—the people here call them buttes. The Indian camp beyond these buttes was thought to be only a portion of the Indians who were on the warpath, for the talk of the citizens of Grangeville was, "They are getting away. They are crossing the Salmon several miles further on."

This was the order of the march as the cavalry approached the buttes, all with carbines loaded: A hundred yards before the main force with a little squad of eight brave men was Lieutenant Theller. Colonel Perry with the citizens was next, followed by his own company, then Trimble, with some forty or fifty yards' interval left between the companies. All were marching in column of fours. Suddenly the Indians appeared in skirmish order, stretched out in an irregular line. Their heads popped up from behind stones, from gulches, ravines and other cover. Those on foot took deliberate and deadly aim. Between the left butte and the creek an interval of at least two hundred yards appeared to be full of them—mounted and galloping to the left. It was White Bird, obeying Joseph's orders, with his flanking party. Indians always try to effect a flank movement.

While Theller began the work—to meet skirmish by skirmish—the citizens ran to the left butte, covered themselves by the inequalities of the ground, and prepared to shoot all Indians that they could see. The leading company of cavalry coming into line near them took position to their right. Trimble's company was ordered forward into line, and it was done quickly without closing the interval. Away the men went to the next butte. Trimble, looking after his exposed right flank (for there were, it seems, Indians enough to get beyond even this), went himself to the extreme point where at dawn Joseph was crouching and watching. The disposition appeared good under the circumstances. These cavalrymen will have to stay here now and fight it out as the Seventeenth Army Corps did when its line was enveloped in the same way at Atlanta, fighting on one side of the cover and then jumping over and fighting from the other side. With the cavalry under fire and spread out in a line, it was too late to plunge ahead through the Indians' line and camp towards the Salmon River.

Perry's men were firing, some of them over the horses' heads. The air was full of noise and smoke. Some of these horses proved wild and unmanageable at this time. Then Indians began to press up to a still higher point, to the right of our whole line. They were ascending the same kind of ledgy, rocky knoll as that now occupied. First a sergeant and six men went thither against them, firing rapidly. Those Indian flankers were driven back. All this moving, so thrilling and exciting, had not taken ten minutes. Perry and Trimble seemed to be together for the moment. Their left flank was now suddenly turned. Two of the citizens at the butte were wounded; then their companions gave way and began to fly. Some of the cavalrymen, too, had already taken the trail to the rear, at a run. Companies were badly broken. Colonel Perry endeavored to close all in together for mutual protection. The bugler, who sounds the calls and makes orders plain amid noise and confusion, was already dead, being the first man shot.

"Can't go on to Salmon River, Trimble."

"No, that's annihilation." Retreat was ordered and was commenced in pretty good shape. Whether Chapman, of the volunteers, or Trimble, or both, suggested it is not certain, but the word was, "Good position yonder. High ground among the rocks can be held."

The little column, now moving rearward, turned to the left and sought this position. But the Indians, too quick for them, were all around them and more to spare! The men were panic-stricken and began to cry out, "Can't stay here! Get back from here! Take ridge farther back!" Horses were galloping without riders. Lieutenant Theller's horse was gone; probably a panic had seized the soldier holder. Trimble and Parnell helped him to mount another, bareback. Probably the balking, plunging, kicking animal had been freeing himself from his saddle in a furious way, thus adding to the terror and confusion if anything could.

All soon became broken, and the rout was general—a kind of Bull Run on a small scale.

Perry and Parnell again found each other. Bearing over a little to the left, Trimble was soon separated and held by the bluffs. There was rallying and short resistance, from knoll to knoll, up the creek. Indians pressed along faster and faster, gaining the well-known trails up the flanks of the White Bird Canyon, while the American horses which our men rode were every now and then put to their speed to prevent a complete cutting off.

A tough struggle for life was made just as the soldiers came to the steep and narrow trail. Here, it appeared by the location of the bodies of the men who had been killed and by the place where Lieutenant Theller finally fell, the Indians had succeeded in heading them all on the trail. The most who were not already shot down, dead, or left to die, had deviated into the first available ravine to the left. Here, where they so thickly lay, must have been the last resolute stand made by our men in the valley of the White Bird. Defeated, losing their brave officer, Lieutenant Theller, the men who were still alive rushed to the top of the canyon ridge as fast as their horses could carry them. Here Perry and Parnell succeeded in getting better order of movement with the remnant. Perry, in an informal letter written the evening of the battle, said "It was only by the most strenuous efforts of Colonel Parnell and myself in organizing a party of twenty-two men that a single officer or man reached camp. The Indians fought us to within four miles of Mount Idaho, and only gave it up on seeing we would not be driven any farther except at our own gait."

The first account of our loss, brought to me at Fort Lapwai, showed over one-third of the one hundred souls that entered into this Indian battled killed and missing.

Only two or three of the missing ever came in. The closing words of Perry's note were, "Please break the news of her husband's death to Mrs. Theller." It is easier to go into a battle than to do this. I endeavored to control myself and break the tidings gently. But Mrs. Theller read them in my face before I could speak, and words had no place. "Oh, my husband!"

Joseph, Ollicut, and White Bird, each followed by squads of Indians, pushed their pursuit to within sight of Grangeville. Then they drew off and slowly rode back to White Bird Canyon. It was a wild and jubilant set of lodges that day! Clothing, arms and ammunition were now abundant.

The first thrill of victory is animating and sweet to those who conquer, but the humiliating, chastening defeat is ever hard for men to bear.

Chapter XIX

For a time we leave the victorious Indians at White Bird and our discomfited squadron at Grangeville—where Colonel Perry collected, reorganized, and put in as good condition as possible his scattered fragments—and return to Lapwai.

It is usually troublesome to turn back and begin a journey anew. It is doubly so at this juncture. How much more satisfactory if we could say that Perry and his comrades had finished their task and afterwards returned with victory perched upon their banners! And what joy to us if the brave Lieutenant Theller and thirty other gallant soldiers who set out on Friday full of hope and life could ever have come back! Still, such is the fortune of war. The hour of trial must precede the hour of triumph.

As the cavalry companies had departed in one direction, Captain Wilkinson had hastened in another with dispatches for Fort Walla Walla and for the telegraph.

Early on Saturday morning he entered that garrison, having accomplished the journey during the night, and startled everybody with his nervous messages. Then off sped a courier across the Blue Ridge to Whipple's camp at Indian Valley near the famous Wallowa. Thus the message was carried a hundred miles more before Sunday was over.

Colonel Whipple, ready at call, left a small squad to take charge of all luggage and set his column of two cavalry companies in motion. "Slow," say the excited citizens, and "Slow," say those furious scouts, who kill a horse every two days. Maybe it is slow, but when I said to the waiting people at Lapwai, "Colonel Whipple will be here by Thursday night," even an experienced officer thought not because the horses were fresh and not hardened to marching. My faith was pinned to the man in charge. Dark-browed, strongly built, apparently forty years of age, Colonel Whipple (called

colonel from volunteer remembrance, more properly the
Captain of Company L, First Cavalry) was a reliable man.
Neither reluctance nor delay was in the man, nor in the
three or four officers associated with him. Not hurry; a
kind of breathless double-quick for an hour, with a lagging
slowness the next hour—no, not that! But that steady,
care-taking, walking of men as well as horses, tramp,
tramp, from before the dawn till evening twilight, day after
day. The heart says, "Faster, faster, Colonel," but the judge-
ment remembers the proverb, "Too much haste makes
waste!" So that the steady pull is kept up. The few soldiers
that are at Fort Walla Walla, those near Wallula, where the
upriver boat touches, the available men from Forts
Vancouver, Stevens, and Canby, Townsend, Klamath, and
Harney are also in motion, some towards Boise and the
Weiser River northward, but the most towards me at
Lapwai. How quickly the mind fixes upon points that must
be occupied! Soon Lapwai and Lewiston draw like a load-
stone, not only these, but the artillerymen, on the wing
from Alaska, hurried on to the field without stopping to
breathe; and further help from California and Arizona. And
Boise draws its accessions from all the forts within the
range of three hundred miles, yes, even from the harbor of
San Francisco. So, afterwards, Lewiston calls loud enough
to be heard in Georgia, and the Companies of the Second
Infantry come flocking together and take the railway flight
thitherward. But during all this excitement and movement
a very few of us were only patiently waiting at Lapwai and
estimating the time before relief could come.

You can only get suggestive glimpses of the past; the
fullest memory only yields detached pictures, leaving the
blanks between them for the imagination or other memo-
ries to fill.

The diary for June 16th says, "A request from Colonel
Watkins for relief for Kamiah."

The immediate answer from me is a pictorial glimpse,
not flattering but truthful. "Dispatches just received and
noted. Captain Perry actually has with him less than man
for man. I depend on the superior skill and the experience
of the soldiers to overcome the odds. Wilkinson reached

Walla Walla at ten in the morning today (actually a couple of hours sooner). Steamer lies at Wallula and can return to Lewiston as well as not. I shall expect troops tomorrow morning and will send relief to Kamiah as soon as it will do to detach, but think the best possible relief is the vigorous push against the forces of Joseph at Cottonwood. We shall probably hear from Perry soon."

Second diary item for the 16th: "10 p.m. Jonah's wife (Jonah having gone with the cavalry to the front) came to the garrison with the woman who ran in from the hostiles; they believe Jonah killed, and all the troops."

This night was a peculiar and remarkable one, as it gave a view almost accurate of the general and particular features of the subsequent engagement and disaster at White Bird Canyon, an account given some sixty miles from the scene and at least six hours before the battle happened.

I was awakened by loud talking in front of the porch at Lapwai and went out. Jonah's wife, a large Indian woman, sat upon her horse. She was accompanied by another woman, the one I understood had just come from the hostiles. One of the half-breeds interpreted. Jonah's wife spoke so emphatically and so excitedly that she awakened everybody, and she declared, "The Indians had fixed a trap. All our troops had run straight into it. The hostiles had come up on every side and killed all the soldiers and all the scouts, including the friendly Indians."

The Indian scouts were for the most part unarmed and fortunately were not taken down into the dangerous part of White Bird Canyon. The next morning while Colonel Perry and our soldiers were actually fighting at the front as the Indian woman had predicted, I was writing a letter to Perry, of which I give a few extracts:

> Dear Colonel: We have been intensely anxious here, for we had not heard a word till the arrival of this messenger (the first one who had come, announcing their safe trip to Grangeville). Rumors have reached us that you were ambuscaded and all killed. Jonah's wife came at ten o'clock last night in great distress, with a story that a woman brought from the hostiles. The Kamiah people send a messenger in great

terror. Reports put hostiles, men, women, and children at or near the mouth of Cottonwood Creek—Looking Glass' camp. Take it for what it is worth. As the steamer can come up from Wallula as well as not, I expect reinforcements of two companies, perhaps three, today or early tomorrow. Will forward supplies just as soon as troops arrive. ...Be careful about those traps. Of course you will. They, the hostiles, have placed several for you, as this Indian woman explains them to Jonah's wife."

In these times of actualities, when it is difficult to make even Christians believe in special providences, we do not attribute prevision to the two Indian women. What is made plain, however, is that the Indians, or rather a part of them, had a clearly defined plan.

The Indians were to begin the war by a series of outrages, in the usual style. This would force the troops from Lapwai before they could be reinforced from distant points. It would also unite the malcontents themselves. The grouping of Indian lodges suited this view; to separate for warfare upon the scattered inhabitants, then to assemble near the mouth of White Bird in order to meet the soldiers of Lapwai.

The ambuscade, which the women described in detail, was made, as we have now seen, beyond the well-placed buttes, the rocky heights, and the favoring ravines of the White Bird Creek. The soldiers and citizens came; the Indians sprang their trap. The results were defeat and death on the one hand, victory and savage joy on the other.

Chapter XX

One has little idea of the fearful excitement which prevails at a military post like Lapwai, almost denuded of troops at the beginning of an Indian war. Citizens from all directions flocked thither for protection, including friendly Indians and their families who, without arms or ammunition, came from great distances to us. There, too, were very early gathered the Kamiah inhabitants, sub-agents, teachers, and other employees. They were escorted across the prairie by James Lawyer and his people. The excellent and successful lady teacher at Kamiah, Miss MacBeth, gave an interesting account of the journey: "The Indians treated us with great delicacy. They rode well ahead. They watched sharply to the rear. Some of them cantered off to round hills on our left, and they searched out all possible hiding places where an enemy could lurk or jump upon us suddenly, and they have brought us all without harm these sixty or seventy miles."

The Christian young men, Indians whom Miss MacBeth had so successfully taught, remained true to the friends of the government throughout the struggle.

Quite early in the morning on the eighteenth I wrote Colonel Perry: "Reports are not favorable, but my confidence in you, your officers, and men makes me distrust the stories of those who ran away from the field just as the battle began. I want a report, as soon as possible, from some reliable person." Then follows in the record other communications of the sad events now already familiar to the reader.

Lewiston was made the depot and base of operations. Every available man was set in motion. The able and experienced Colonel of the Twenty-first Infantry, General Alfred Sully, was called to Lewiston for counsel and to the field if his precarious health would permit. He was informed, "About thirty citizens reported murdered so far. ...Shall not

feed the enemy with driblets, but had to start the two companies to stop the murder of men and women and keep the
attention of Joseph and White Bird while I concentrated
my troops."

I had great experience with panics in the East. The
first was that of Bull Run, where the cry of "Black-horse
cavalry!" would in an instant clear the road and fill the
woods alongside with thousands of flying stragglers. The
next was that from Vienna to Chain Bridge, after
McClellan's return from the peninsula where in a dark
night a whole division of General Sumner was thrown into
complete disorder. But nothing there was so continuous
and feverish as the panics which took place at our small
fort while we were waiting for the troops. On one occasion
two friendly Indians, who had been chased and fired upon
by some unruly white men, rushed toward the fort with
the utmost speed of the ponies and cried out something
which the excited people of the garrison took to mean
"Indians are coming." Defenses were made; the little garrison was arranged for its best resistance. Some of the officers
were at the top of the hill in two minutes, looking out. Wild
with fear and with hair flying, laundresses and children
came running to the officers' line of houses. A resolute army
lady gathered and took charge of a large number of women
and children. Some incidents had a comic and ludicrous side
and in the retrospect afforded much merriment—as ladies
seizing rifles and pistols, barricading doors and cellar-ways,
stepping into water pails in dark passages. The alarm was
serious for a short time until the frightening cause was
made known through the interpreter, who had bravely met
the incoming Indians, friendly ones we knew, and learned
the truth.

It appeared that some wicked white man had pretended
that these friendly Indians belonged to the hostiles and so
ruthlessly fired upon them and sought to disarm them. Oh,
how angry the Indians were. Explanations and apologies
appeased them after a while.

On one of these interval days the ladies and the children who had come to the garrison for protection were sent
away to Lewiston by the seemingly harsh Department

Commander. It was a hard order and caused much gossip, and I fear the feelings of many friends were deeply touched but it was necessary, for we were getting ready for vigorous war.

Mule trains were hired, supplies of all kinds put in motion, couriers were coming and going. Indian messengers and escaping soldiers were arriving from a field seventy miles away with their mouths full of exciting rumors and bad tidings. By the 21st of June eight new companies of regular troops were on the green plat near the Lapwai post. A small organization of volunteers under Captain Paige joined themselves to Whipple, who was in command of the cavalry.

The friendly Nez Perces generously brought in their ponies for the infantry officers to ride. They were ready to drive in their herds in order to mount the soldiers of the infantry and artillery, but officers of experience in Indian warfare remonstrated. Colonel Pollock of the Twenty-first Infantry said, "No, the ponies are Indian trained and always go to their friends. A pony will buck and run away and always carries off a good soldier with him." To such speeches I replied, "It is good, indeed, to have your feet on the firm ground, but ponies' feet will speed faster than yours for the long marches. At last, using the ponies, we will wear them out."

The time from the first news of the terrible disaster at White Bird Canyon till the morning of the 22nd of June seemed long indeed. It appears long even in retrospect. Still it was only four days. Our effective men for the front, now at Lapwai, numbered but few more than two hundred.

Captains Whipple and Winters had arrived from their circuitous and tedious march from Wallowa. Captains Miller and Miles had reached Lewiston by steamboat and marched to Lapwai with several companies of the Fourth Artillery and the Twenty-first Infantry under their charge. The volunteers before mentioned, a little more than twenty strong, had also joined us. Lieutenant Bomus, the quartermaster of the post, had improvised a supply train. The numerous miners, employed in different directions about Lewiston, had been thrown out of employment by the

Indian outbreak. Their mule pack-trains and packers became available for our use.

The moment of starting is solemn. The air is full of rumors. The Indians who began the war, and who virtually have raised the black flag, are still more numerous than our column. The road winds over hills and mountains, through ravines, past the mouths of cross canyons which are full of pits and rocks; a wild range which is covered in places with forest trees and often with thick underbrush. The few daring messengers had skulked through by night from Colonel Perry to Lapwai. They had chosen the most roundabout and unlooked-for paths, and they naturally magnified the dangers in order to demonstrate their prowess. Our whole force numbered about one-fifth of a full regiment, such as those we took into the rebellion. Still this body of resolute men made a fine appearance. The cavalry-men sat on their horses waiting the word; the infantry, firmly grasping their rifles, were in line, ready to move; the artillery, who are really foot soldiers with a bright uniform, presented their perfect ranks slightly retired from the rest.

The mountain howitzer, heretofore used for the morning and evening gun, old and worn but fixed up for the occasion, and the two gatlings with their as yet restless animals flank the picture on one side. Bomus' train, now an irregular body of noisy mules going backward and forward, hither and thither, unstable as water, filled the space on the other. The few last loads of commissary supplies were being strung to their appointed *aparejos*, already upon backs, while the mules remained grouped around the storehouse door. As I moved out with my staff officers, received the salutes, and listened to the orders that put the small mass in motion, a little of the old thrill of war came back to me.

There was another notable spectacle when the column wound its way up the foothills of Craig Mountain. The cavalrymen led their horses two abreast. The infantrymen followed, arms at ease, talking, smoking, and apparently light-hearted as boys are when on a holiday tramp.

The mule column lumbered along, one and another of these indefatigable burden-bearers darting out and in, now ahead and now behind, to catch a bite of grass, while the bell mare kept up the unending ding-dong call, occasionally relieved by the packers' oaths. These oaths, I fear, are believed by the train-men to be essential in mule driving, and are adapted to the stubborn and eccentric natures under treatment! The column was stretched out and, including its intervals, covered more than a mile in extent. Doubtless Indian scouts from Joseph were watching it from the wooded crest of the contiguous mountain. Artillery, infantry, and cavalry were pressing toward them. When Ollicut had seen two companies of cavalry on the banks of the furious Grande Ronde River a month previously, he hurried to his brother, then at Fort Lapwai, and said excitedly, "There are a thousand armed men coming!" So probably at this time these sleepless scouts hurried off to the White Bird hostiles and reported, "More than a thousand armed men are coming." I soon found it the part of wisdom, for producing effect upon Indians, to elongate a column or stretch out a line to its utmost capacity. They never once attempted to break across a column or an organized line, but always tried to shower their skirmishers upon our flanks.

The memorandum of this day was very brief. It records the hour of starting, the length of the march, and the camp for the night. It does not mention the orders, reports and preparations for departure, the storings at Lapwai, the last messages to friends at home, nor the abundant news that went rearward to furnish the eager journals. It gives no idea of the camp in the woods at the crossroads where we might be attacked before the next morning, no idea of how the guns are put into artillery positions, of how the men encamped in line of battle, of the great carefulness in locating the outposts and pickets, of the manner of grazing the animals in the openings and then securing them at picket lines or fettering the mules and the bell-mare during the night, of how, when all this is done, the officers, hitherto so solemn in manner and authoritative in tone, sit around the small mess kits and unbend. Campfires must be small here and early extinguished, but this did not hinder the sounds of mirth as the story went around the mess table. Our wives and daughters at home sometimes declare that,

"While they are nearly dying of anxiety for us, we are having the best of times." Isn't it well for hearty work and clear-headed thinking that it is so?

Chapter XXI

Here is the record of the 22nd of June: "Left Lapwai at 12:00 m. Column under command of Captain Miller. Make camp at Junction Trail (Mount Idaho and Craig's Ferry Trail) at 5:30."

Who is Captain Miller? If I turn to the Army Register, I find, "Marcus P. Miller, a captain in the 4th Artillery with several brevets, the highest of which give him the appellation of Colonel. He was appointed from Massachusetts and graduated from the military academy of West Point in 1858. He served with distinction in the war of the rebellion and heightened his reputation by his brave work in the Modoc war." He was with me then: of middling height, well knit for toughness, with light beard and lightish hair, handsome forehead, blue eyes, and a pleasant face.

Next day the reveille was sounded at a little past four. We breakfasted at five and were on the march at six. Norton's ranch will be recalled by the reader. Mr. Norton, the late owner, was the man who was trying to get to Mount Idaho with his family when he and others were killed and his wife sadly wounded. We came to his house about half-past one o'clock, having marched nineteen miles. Mr. Norton had kept a sort of hotel. His house was now deserted. The Indians had rummaged everything; what the family had left here was found in complete disorder. Who can realize what it is to have savage warfare break upon a family with little or no warning, to kill and wound and scatter like this? It is worse than the desolation spoken of in the Scriptures, where one shall be taken and another left. None were left! There were the clothes, cut and torn and strewn about, the broken chairs, the open drawers, the mixings of flour, sugar, salt, and rubbish—the evidences indeed of riot run mad. Do we wonder that those who have passed through such experience have been slow to forget and forgive "mad Indians"?

The force was ordered to encamp here. The next day, the twenty-fourth, was Sunday. As I did not move my main body this day, the story was circulated and published that I halted because it was the Sabbath and spent precious time in giving religious exhortation to my command and in the distribution of some three hundred Bibles! Of course this would not hurt my reputation with a vast number of my Christian friends were it literally true and under ordinary circumstances would have been proper enough. But as it was not the case, I may speak of the occasion of the halt. First, I was not then quite sure of the position of the Indians. This I must ascertain beyond question in order to determine the direction of my movement. Perry came to us during the day from Grangeville and brought us the desired information. The Indians were still in or near the White Bird Canyon, not far from the scene of the disaster.

Next, I wished to send Captain Trimble and his cavalry company beyond the hostile Indians to Slate Creek. They were obliged to move by a difficult and circuitous route. I knew it to be wise for my main column to remain quiet, so as not to flush the game and press the Indians upon a small company of brave citizens who had been standing on the defensive in a little fort of their own construction and sending to Mount Idaho for help. Again I meant that there should be no question, when at last I should take the offensive against the savages, of my having a superiority of numbers. Therefore, for the additional reason that the troops at Lewiston might come up, I gladly delayed.

Mark well this place. Norton's ranch is to be historic, a central point. The broad and beautiful Camas Prairie opens out before you as you set your back to Craig's Mountain and look towards the southeast. The straight road in your front leads from you to Grangeville and Mount Idaho. What a beautiful stretch of rolling prairie land! Where is there richer soil or finer prospects? Towards the right is the Snake country. The Salmon, which flows northwesterly, empties into the Snake not more than twenty miles to the southwest. The Cottonwood, heading nearby, runs easterly into the curvilinear Clearwater, twenty miles off; and the Rocky Canyon Creek, close by, shoots out southwest to join the Salmon. White Bird, before described, makes its remarkable canyon and empties into the Salmon a few miles further up that river. This country is as well watered as Eden and as fertile as any garden which has been much longer under cultivation.

When the Pacific railroads shall be completed, the Camas Prairie will not be despised. These wicked Indians have loved these broad acres, which they have not been wise enough to cultivate. Joseph and White Bird understood the disabilities of their people and how they were letting everything valuable to them slip through their hands. But bright as they were, they had not sufficient ability to rise above the influences around them. Who indeed can do so?

If Colonel Perry could have anticipated the results which were to follow his haste to the White Bird Canyon and had halted here at Norton's and stood on the defensive till I came up, it would have been a good thing in a military point of view but that would not have had the effect, like his bold advance, of stopping the Indian murders.

The superior officer could not have known all the facts until he reached the scene of operations.

Defeats are always deplored. They naturally fill the hearts of the vanquished with great chagrin. They are usually interpreted against the commander. But every eminent commander has had his lessons of defeat. They are often the essential stepping stones to subsequent victories.

Perry, too, had hard work to make head against his accusers, till two courts of inquiry had by favorable findings put the matter at rest.

On Monday we made a brisk movement forward. The infantry, bearing off to the right, went to Johnson's ranch. It was the farm where Perry made his first considerable stand, where he was able to check his swift pursuers and enable his stragglers to catch up and close in. Deviating from the infantry's route, I took the cavalry to Perry's position at Grangeville, a little hamlet four miles short of Mount Idaho on the road leading to that town. The soldiers who were left alive of Perry's command here met us. How different they were in numbers and appearance from the brisk and hearty troopers that had left Fort Lapwai the

105

week previous! But our people rally quickly after defeat. They were glad enough to see us. The officers declared to Whipple and Winters, "You have made the long march and reached us sooner than we thought possible." The soldiers and the restless citizens, gathering in from the neighboring country or having come from Mount Idaho to meet us, were soon telling our men the story of the massacres and of the last battle. I delayed for an hour to examine the supplies that the principal citizen had in store and which he gladly put to our use, also to gather all the information known here concerning the enemy, his position, number of warriors, and intentions. Then leaving the cavalry to rest and feed till my return, I made a hurried visit to the already famous town of Mount Idaho.

A little rivalry, like that between New York and Boston, existed between Grangeville and Mount Idaho. Each village must have its own volunteer company. Each must have its guns for defense. If one has a fortification or a cannon, the other clamors for a like favor. The mounted citizens began to swarm around me as I proceeded. A prominent one—Mr. Croaesdale, an Englishman who had recently put a nice farm under cultivation in the neighborhood and brought hither a beautiful young wife of refinement and culture—rode ahead and guided us. On a knoll to the left of the town he had thrown up rough barricades and improvised a few quite creditable field-works. He manifested soldierly instincts and enthusiasm. I found that he had made a citadel on this knoll, which was already occupied by families whose fears had sent them in from the country.

Engaging, after a time, to dine with Mr. Croaesdale, I passed down the principal street to Brown's Hotel. Before entering this building, the crowd of curious, eager, solemn-looking men closed around me and expressed a desire that I would speak to them. So I said, in substance, what I had already written Mr. Brown: "We have now taken the field in good earnest. More troops are on the way to join us. I propose to take prompt measures for the pursuit and punishment of the hostile Indians and wish you to help me in the way of information and supplies as much as lies in your power. I sympathize deeply with you in the loss of life and in the outrages to which your families have been subjected, and you may rest assured that no stone will be left unturned to give you redress and protection in the future."

There is always risk, on such occasions, of promising more than one is able to perform. My brief speech, however, appeared to give satisfaction, and I passed into the hotel with Mr. Brown and others and went from room to room to see those who had suffered outrage at the hands of the Indians. Poor Mrs. Norton was there, very sadly wounded through her limbs. A lady lay in another room, pale as death, suffering from a gunshot wound and from other savage and repeated violence. Her little child was playing on the outside of the bed, to all appearance quite happy, but a part of its tongue had been cut off. There was an unusual number of people gathered in this place, shut up by a sense of danger and full of feverish excitement.

We dined at Mr. Rudolph's with Mr. and Mrs. Croaesdale and others. How patient and helpful were the ladies gathered here, yet how uncertain, how depressing were all the circumstances of this horrid Indian war! From the peaceful beauty of life in rural England to the appalling butchery in the wild canyons of Idaho, the transition was sufficiently abrupt.

Chapter XXII

The village realities passed before our officers as vivid pictures. Their sympathies were enlisted amid the terror and the suffering, but they could not delay over them. After a march of eight miles by southerly routes, we rejoined the main column at Johnson's. Here a messenger came with the news that our reinforcements were on the way. He also bore welcome words from home. How wonderfully news can spread. It is like the cloud no bigger than a man's hand when it leaves us. It is magnified several times before the journals at Lewiston and Walla Walla have put it into type, and by the time it has reached Portland and San Francisco, it has become a heavy cloud, overspreading the whole heaven. About this time the disaster at White Bird Canyon had shown this speedy and terrific increase. A friend stationed at Fort Colville two hundred and seventy miles from Joseph's field of battle told me he heard a story, with complete land graphic details, of the death of Colonel E. C. Watkins and myself, with other exaggerated horrors. All the people there believed the account, as it was so connected and so circumstantial. It was pleasant to us to find that our home people were not afflicted with these frightful stories. The stories existed, but the correction was ever at hand.

I remember that whenever I traveled after the war of the Rebellion, I used to continue to imagine peopling the hills, ridges, groves, forests, and ravines with soldiers and laying off everything for purposes of offense and defense into military positions for cavalry, artillery, and infantry. In just such groupings does that whole region around Johnson's Ranch lie in my memory today. Southeastward was a gradual slope, four or five miles in extent, to the head of the big White Bird Canyon, an open, rolling country; southward, rougher and rougher, filled with deep ravines, extending to Salmon River, which was boiling and rolling on in mad fury at the bottom of mountain banks. The largest transverse ravine in this direction was Rocky Canyon, at the head of which, three or four miles off, was one of the Indian camps at the time when the first murders were committed. The lodge poles and many of the lodges without their skin or canvas covering were still there, giving indications of the recent sojourn of six or seven hundred persons. To the north, twenty miles away in the direction we came, were the Cottonwood Creek and Canyon, Norton's Ranch with the tree-fringed Craig Mountain behind it as a fine background to a beautiful landscape; to the east, and sweeping around to the northeast, the rugged hills that border the Camas prairies and are opposite Craig Mountain and near Mount Idaho; and all the vast, charming expanse which people come hither to occupy and to cultivate, lying spread out between mountains and hills like an unrolled map for your inspection.

We left camp on reconnaissance at 6:30 a.m., and our column moved directly to the hill at the head of White Bird Canyon. This reconnaissance was for an important object. "Where are Joseph and White Bird?" "How many warriors have they with them?" Our march was occupying their attention and keeping them together. It was, further, the best method of gaining time for the companies now en route to overtake us, and for those moving northward from Boise City, some two hundred miles to the south, to get into such a position as would prevent an escape of the hostiles in that direction. This Boise movement, under Colonel Green, was intended to keep the disaffected Nez Perces and the Weiser Indians apart.

A reconnaissance which does not bring on an engagement, gives one the information he seeks, and does not drive off the foe has to be well conducted. Ours was thus successful.

We had another desire. It was to look up and bury our dead soldiers, who had been lying exposed for more than a week upon the hillsides or in the ravines where they had fallen. Miller commanded the footmen, increased by a company of cavalry under the diligent Captain Winters. These proceeded cautiously down the canyon trail, preceded by the watchful skirmishers and covered by vigilant flankers. Whipple stayed with our artillery and company of cavalry at the head of the canyon where the trail just begins to descend. Perry accompanied me to a good post of observation near the transverse ravine where the week before the greater number of his living men had, at their extreme peril, ascended from the canyon below to the broader space above.

Captain Paige, the brave volunteer of Walla Walla, with his little company of men and Arthur Chapman as guide, skirted the hills to the right of the canyon. The scene was so vast, the hills so high, and the ravines so deep, that our small numbers seemed even smaller by the contrast. As we peered down into the canyon, the bottom seemed level as a plain, though in reality there were many hills, knolls, and buttes between us and the battlefield. Little by little the troops uncovered the ground. The burial parties followed closely behind the moving columns, and as soon as they came near enough, sheltered with their blankets the poor boys who, stripped of clothing, were still lying there in death. It was quite late in the day before Lieutenant Theller's remains were found and identified. He was then carefully buried on the spot. Afterward his afflicted wife was gratified in her wish to have the body removed to the neighborhood of her home in San Francisco.

Paige and Chapman, pushing well forward to a promontory at the end of the ridge which they had followed almost to the Salmon River, at last discovered the Indians. Joseph, with all his warriors, his women, children and baggage, was now well across the swift river, and there, from some curious, sharp-pointed hills on the other side, was watching our movements.

A citizen, half starved and twice wounded, was brought to us. From him we gathered additional information. We learned the names of the poor settlers who had suffered most by the robberies and by the flames. We were told that Joseph's first intention was to have given me battle before going over the Salmon, but that he had changed his mind and wished to draw us into the vicinity of those snow-clad peaks called "Seven Devils" where our troops would be further from supplies and more easily handled.

The full purpose of this forward movement having been accomplished, the command slowly toiled up the muddy train in the midst of a heavy rain and returned to Johnson's for the night.

The leadership of Chief Joseph was indeed remarkable. No general could have chosen a safer position or one that would be more likely to puzzle and obstruct a pursuing foe. If we present a weak force, he can turn upon it. If we make direct pursuit, he can go southward toward Boise for at least thirty miles and then turn our left. He can go straight to his rear and cross the Snake at Pittsburg Landing. He can go on down the Salmon and cross at several places and then turn either to the left for his old haunts in the Wallowa Valley or to the right and pass our flank, threatening our line of supply. He has, at the same time, a wonderful natural barrier between him and us in the Salmon, a river that delights itself in its furious flow. We shall see next how we sought to solve the problem presented us by this shrewd savage.

Chapter XXIII

The troops were gathered near the mouth of White Bird Canyon. The main canyon forks a couple of miles back from the Salmon. One tine of the fork is White Bird Creek, running directly into the river; the other holds the main trail, which bears off to the left and leads to the river a couple of miles farther upstream. A very high bluff lies within the triangle thus formed. Standing upon this bluff you could see, hundreds of feet below, the restless Salmon, and beyond it, the irregular mountain valley held by the Indians. Their sentry-posts on pointed hills were scattered along between us and the mountain slopes.

They were shouting back and forth. We could hear the voices of Indians giving their orders. While we were preparing a ferry, by collecting boats and crossing a cable, the Indians suddenly started from the hilltops and from ravines and rushed towards our position. Paige and I were sitting near the right of our line, on the bluff overlooking the White Bird. It seemed for a moment that the little silvery thread far below that we call the Salmon River could really be no obstacle. I sent Wilkinson and others for long-range rifles and got ready with what artillery we had, to fire as soon as the Indians should be within range. Paige became more and more resolute, shouted loudly to the approaching foe, fired his rifle rapidly, while other rifles were coming. Some shots appeared to whistle among the Indians as they drew nigh the river. Away they turned and down the river they ran, like wild cattle just let loose from the corral, and in fifteen minutes they had disappeared. Surely all was ready for them had they re-swum the swift river. It was partly a ruse, intended to make me think that they designed to turn my flank at Rocky Canyon crossing, and partly the usual bravado of Indians who, by their wildness of movement and defiant yelling, hope to inspire surprise and terror. But our field glasses had shown us ponies grazing and figures sneaking behind the hills, and I was confident that the hostiles had returned under the cover of the rough ground and would go in another direction when they were ready.

Now that we were together, Miller had the artillery battalion, Perry having been sent to the rear for supplies. Whipple had the cavalry. Trimble was still at the Salmon River crossing near Slate Creek and prevented a turning of our left in that direction.

Chief Looking Glass, in the rear, was already beginning to give trouble. "Forty warriors have just left him to join Joseph. He is only waiting his favorable chance." Such was the information from our friendly Indians. As he was behind us and at the fork of the Clearwater, we must take care of him. "Captain Whipple, go with your cavalry and gatling guns, arrest the Indian Chief Looking Glass and all other Indians who may be encamped with or near him between the forks of the Clearwater. Turn all prisoners over for safekeeping to the volunteer organization at Mount Idaho."

It may add to the interest of the narrative to give Whipple's account of the execution of those instructions. He says, "On account of the distance, greater by ten miles than was supposed, and the difficult approach, the village was not reached at dawn, July 1st, as contemplated, but soon after sunrise such dispositions were made as seemed most practicable under the circumstances to carry out my instructions. An opportunity was given Looking Glass to surrender, which he at first promised to accept but afterwards defiantly refused. The result was that several Indians were killed, the camp, with a large amount of supplies, was destroyed, and seven hundred and twenty-five ponies were captured and driven to Mount Idaho. About twenty citizens, under lead of a volunteer officer, Captain Randall, (killed near Norton's on July 5th) accompanied me on this expedition."

Of course we thus stirred up a new hornet's nest and did not get Looking Glass and his treacherous companions into custody.

My men, those immediately at hand near the Salmon, were pulling some small boats over the torrent. Joined by the Slate Creek detachment and Hunter's and McConville's volunteers, they were winding their way up the almost interminable hog-back in a rain storm and following along the trail of the departing Joseph. The Indians had traveled down the Salmon toward the Snake country for twenty-five miles, to the raging crossing place at Craig's Ferry. Whipple, having completed his instructions, was waiting and watching at Norton's because, under our chase, Joseph might swim the river and turn again across the Camas.

These Indians excited our admiration by their dispatch in crossing rivers. James Reuben, an Indian who brought me a message at Craig's Ferry, told me how it was done: "Make skin rafts and load them, tie four horses abreast to the rafts with small ropes, put four Indians, naked, on the horses, and then boldly swim across." He gave us a practical demonstration by swimming his horse over to us and back across the fearful torrent. Brave Scout Parker attempted the same, but failed to get many yards from shore.

While this was going forward, Joseph did turn back upon the Camas Prairie towards Norton's ranch and threatened Whipple and the others.

I must try to afford a few glimpses of this detachment with their doings and surroundings.

Captain Babbitt, ordinance officer of my staff, had met Whipple at midnight near Mount Idaho with orders: "Proceed without delay to Cottonwood (Norton's) and form junction with Perry. The object being to gain the earliest information of the movements of the enemy should he (Joseph), as was thought probable, recross the Salmon." Such were the orders. Whipple tells how he fulfilled them.

"I marched," writes Whipple, "to Cottonwood, July 2nd and on the following morning sent out two citizen scouts, named Foster and Blewett, to examine the country in the direction of Craig's Ferry, the place where Joseph and his party swam the river, for indications of the presence of the Indians. Toward evening Foster returned rapidly to camp and reported that he had seen Indians about twelve miles distant, coming from the direction of Craig's Ferry, that they had fired a shot or two at him, and that he last saw his comrade about that time."

Whipple immediately prepared for action, delayed a little by unloading and distributing ammunition. Following his report again, "I directed Second Lieutenant S. M. Rains, of my company, with ten picked men and the scout Foster, to proceed at once toward the point where the Indians had been seen, for the purpose of ascertaining the strength of the enemy and to aid young Blewett. I particularly cautioned Rains not to precede the command too far, to keep on high ground, and to report the first sign of the Indians. The command was in motion very shortly after the detachment had started, and firing was soon heard on our front. A rapid gait was taken up, and after a couple of miles Indians were discovered about a half mile distant. On approaching nearer it was found that they were in large force, and that Lieutenant Rains and *every man* of his detachment had been killed." These were dreadful tidings!

Whipple continued a short distance, deployed, and dismounted for battle. The enemy, it seems, took the back track for a few miles on meeting the larger force, and at dark the Captain very properly retired with his men and guns to Cottonwood. During the night, couriers arrived from Perry, coming from Fort Lapwai with the pack train.

At dawn on July 4th, the command from Cottonwood set out bravely toward Lapwai to meet the escorting detachment, now in great danger, marched toward it eight miles, and returned in safety with Perry's escort and supplies. But this exciting morning ride was not enough for our Cottonwood celebration of the Fourth of July.

"About midday Indians began to gather, and but a short time elapsed before the camp was surrounded by them, and for hours they made the most frantic efforts to dislodge us. Every man of the command was kept on the lines this afternoon (rifle pits having been dug at a little distance from the Cottonwood House) until about sundown, when the enemy withdrew for the night."

This is very calmly described, but there were doubtless plenty of flags flying, plenty of firing from carbines and gatlings which made the old Craig Mountain ring. Add the Indian yellings and shoutings, and the day we celebrate was here thoroughly, if not formally, honored.

Cottonwood, July 5th. Perry, being the senior, was in command. Whipple was constructing some defenses east of Norton's when two mounted men were seen approaching at full speed. They came, pursued by Indians, from the direction of Johnson's ranch. These two were the messengers sent to me beyond the Salmon. Their mission having been performed, they had thus returned, but nothing befell them except the hot chase. Not so with the next party which immediately followed them! A short time after the couriers rushed in, Whipple was standing on the same hill where the defenses had been constructed. He says, "Noticing that there was some commotion at the brow of the hill where a few citizens had gathered, and that Captain Perry was walking towards me, I turned and met him, asking the cause of the excitement. He replied, 'Some citizens a couple of miles away on the Mount Idaho road are surrounded by Indians and are being all cut to pieces, and nothing can be done to help them!'"

"Why not?"

"It is too late!"

Still it is decided to try, and the entire force is ordered thitherward.

Here is another picture: "Arrived at the ground where the attacked party was. I found it to be Captain Randall's company of volunteers, numbering seventeen men. Randall had been mortally wounded, one man killed, and two slightly disabled. ...After I reached the point where the citizens were attacked and remained, Randall having been wounded at the first onset, I took position close at hand so as to relieve the volunteers from all duties but the care of their wounded comrades. A few shots were fired at us by the hostiles, small parties still hovering around, but no damage was done except that one horse was slightly wounded."

Lieutenant Shelton, First Cavalry, volunteered with his detachment of seventeen men and in a spirited manner drove the Indians from his front.

Then all returned to camp bearing the wounded. Much complaint arose because the officer in command at Cottonwood was not more prompt with his relief. A court of inquiry, after long sessions and much labor, exonerated the officer. After this return to camp, the Indians had the prairie to themselves and leisurely crossed the road between the Cottonwood forces and Grangeville and continued on eastward. Doubtless Joseph did so in order to pick up Looking Glass as, in this, we had not succeeded in anticipating him.

A little after sunset two companies of mounted volunteers reported from my main column, which was yet on the other side of the Salmon. On hearing of Lieutenant Rains' desperate struggle, I had sent these volunteers from us by the way of Rocky Canyon.

Let us return to our pursuing troops on the tableland beyond the Salmon. I pressed this column after the Indians to Craig's Ferry. Lost our raft in attempting to cross. Too much of a torrent to cross troops and supplies without it! James Reuben, the scout, had brought clear accounts that Joseph had not turned south toward his old haunts in the Wallowa, but northward and eastward, to gather up Looking Glass and reenforcements, catch small parties like Rains' detachment, and do what mischief he could. Therefore, by turning straight back, recrossing the Salmon at Rocky Canyon or White Bird, where there were boats, and going via Grangeville, where I could bring the Cottonwood force to me, I had a short line and hoped to get a decisive battle from our doughty chief. This difficult work was promptly attempted.

With some night marching and by getting alternate lifts to our infantry in country wagons, the 9th of July saw our advance, at evening, to Grangeville, and the remainder was not far behind. The enterprising volunteers, who had become a little disgusted with the slowness of regulars and angry at their own fearful discomfiture near Cottonwood, had suddenly left us and started on an independent movement. They had crept to a lofty height overlooking the fork and ravines where the Indians now were, near Looking Glass' old camp that Whipple had stirred up a few days before. The volunteers sent an officer whose message was, "Come straight to us." Shearer, a volunteer major with a few men from Mount Idaho, went thither for me and explained why I had borne off to the right, crossed Jackson's Bridge over a branch of the Clearwater, and worked my way down toward the fork, which was to be the battleground.

Joseph, in consequence of his success at White Bird, his eluding me at the Salmon, his massacre of Rains, and his escape from Whipple—as well as his skirmishes with the volunteers and his aiding Looking Glass in avoiding arrest, had come to boast of his prowess, so that he was rather inclined to try his hand with me. Probably he did not believe it possible that I could get my force concentrated so as to bring the whole of it to bear at once. But on our part, we were decidedly inclined to battle and so hastened with all our might thitherward. The chief advantage on the part of the savages lay in the toughness and swiftness in flight of the Indian ponies.

Chapter XXIV

Our infantry, artillery, and cavalry having passed without delay through Grangeville, the small army crossed the South Fork by Jackson's Bridge. It delayed at the crest of a height beyond the bridge until the ammunition train, the baggage, and infantry were closed up. Meanwhile, the volunteers were already at the round hill beyond the Cottonwood, looking down into valleys filled with men, women, children, and ponies.

The 11th of July was a day ever memorable to us and the people in North Idaho, even if such little affairs do not disturb places more remote. This midsummer day saw us creeping down carefully, hunting our way through the extensive forest, through the deep ravines, over the sightly hills, on toward the confluence of the two Clearwaters. About noon my aide, Lieutenant Fletcher, who had galloped away a few minutes before and was already a quarter of a mile to my left, discovered the enemy in a deep ravine near the mouth of Cottonwood Creek. He saw numbers of horses and a few Indians.

Let us try to sketch the picture which presents itself. We have just emerged from the forests into a country comparatively open. We are looking northward. One branch of the Clearwater is some half mile to our left, at the foot of high bluffs, and gives us only occasional glimpses of its current.

Trimble's troop, accompanied by an aide-de-camp, was sent forward to watch toward the front and right. I rode to the bluff at the left where Fletcher was and plainly saw the hostiles. Judging from their motions, they had just discovered our approach. By one o'clock a howitzer and two gatling guns were firing towards the masses of Indians below, manned by a detachment under Lieutenant Otis, Fourth Artillery. The Indians were running their horses up the South Fork of the Clearwater, on both banks near the river, and driving their stock as fast as possible beyond our range. In ten minutes more it was impossible to reach them with our artillery owing to the craggy mountain shores back of, and close by the river border. My guide, Mr. Chapman, assured me that they could escape only by a canyon on our left, which made a small angle with the river and led toward the rear.

The next bluff in that direction was beyond a deep and rocky transverse ravine, perpendicular to this canyon. Instantly the howitzer battery and gatling guns were ordered to go thither with all speed, supported by Winter's cavalry. Around the head of the ravine our distance was over a mile, the enemy having less than a third to go. So beyond the second bluff we found Joseph and his people, dismounted and already in position, while some thirty or forty mounted Indians had galloped just beyond range to encompass our left. Just in time Colonel Mason, the Department Inspector, appeared at hand with Burton's company of infantry. They deployed, stretching off to the right, and enabled Winters to take care of his left. They all now pressed forward in an open line. Firing became very brisk. I extended my line to the left by the cavalry and to the right by the infantry and artillery battalions, gradually refusing my flanks until the whole bluff was enveloped. Four hundred men, necessarily much spread out, held a line two and a half miles in extent. Our main pack train had passed by this position. Another small train with a few supplies was on the road near us. The Indian flankers, by their rapid movement, struck the rear of the small train, killed two of the packers and disabled a couple of mules loaded with howitzer ammunition. The prompt fire from Perry's and Whipple's cavalry saved the attendant ammunition from capture; luckily, the main supply train was saved by the quick work of a messenger guiding it within the lines.

Beyond this Clearwater stream is the high, rough hill, five miles distant in a straight line, where the volunteers were located; farther off is Craig Mountain, which recedes to the left and rises up as a background. From its nearest slopes the Cottonwood ravine makes its dark and crooked course toward us and disappears behind our shore of the Clearwater. The very steep and high banks of the river are roughly cut with numerous transverse ravines. The Indian camp from which the hostiles emerged, yet hidden from view, was beyond the river. Hundreds of Indian ponies were herded in ravines close to the camp. The warriors, the greater part of them mounted, had forded the river near our flank under cover of the bluffs and when discovered were racing up a transverse ravine whose shallow head we had some time since passed. Between these transverse ravines, some of which would be called canyons, there were large, level flats of open land. These were filled with rocks and gullies and their sides lined with small trees. We were obliged to work back toward the head of any one of them in order to cross it with howitzers or with horses. Our skirmishers were just sweeping over one of these plateaus, formed by the river and the canyon, when the quick, covert movement of Joseph which we referred to above was revealed to Fletcher's field glass.

For a few moments it was feared by lookers-on that the Indians would destroy all our food and our powder. The messenger had run his horse with all speed and to good purpose, for a loss here would have been a calamity indeed.

The fierce onset of the Indians requiring great haste, Wilkinson quietly gathered the trains and brought them under cover of Rodney's artillery and Trimble's cavalry companies.

The enemy manifested extraordinary quickness and boldness, planting sharpshooters at all available points, making charges on foot and on horseback, accompanying the charges with all manner of savage demonstrations. At one time an Indian paraded himself in plain view beyond our left flank and beyond the easy range of our rifles. He would dance around and leap up and down in a strange way with arms outstretched, swinging a red blanket. Doubtless this was done with a view to encourage others to follow him in the bold work of attacking the flank of the position.

These attempts were successfully resisted at every part of the line. At 3:30 p.m. a spirited counter charge was tried on our right, down into a ravine. Captain Miles, commanding the infantry battalion, led in this charge. Captain Bancroft, Fourth Artillery, and Lieutenant Williams, Twenty-first Infantry, were seriously wounded at this time. A number of Indians were killed and several wounded in the charge, and the ravine was thoroughly cleared.

A little later, Miller led a second charge near the center. He succeeded at first only in putting the Indians on their guard behind the barricades of stone which they had hastily thrown up. Wilkinson, with a view to a diversion, meanwhile led a demonstration on the right using artillery and infantry and every available man from the cavalry—including horse holders, orderlies, extra-duty men, and train. Fletcher also did effective service during the battle by lodging howitzer shells within the enemy's barricades.

Miller's charge at last gained the ridge in front and secured the disputed ravine near Winter's position. Further spasmodic charges on the left by the enemy were repelled by Perry's and Whipple's dismounted cavalry and by Morris' artillery. Yet a few Indian sharpshooters managed to so annoy every man who approached the spring, our water supply, that in spite of our successful charges the situation at dark was still uncomfortable.

During the night additional stone barricades and rifle pits were constructed by ourselves and by the enemy. Thus each party, still hopeful of a final victory, spent much of the night in the hard work of preparation.

In spite of the extreme danger from Indian bullets, a few officers went several times in the darkness to the spring and carried away full buckets of water which they distributed to their thirsty men. Promptness and courage had in the outset saved the ammunition and food. Gallant self-exposure during the night saved the water supply.

At daylight on the 12th, every available man was on the line. I directed that food should be cooked and coffee made at the center and carried to the front. This was not so easy to do. We had first to get complete possession of the spring, as sufficient water was not secured in the night. This feat was executed with great spirit by Miller and Perry, using Otis's battery and Rodney's company on foot. As soon as the battery had made a rapid firing, it ceased. Then a prompt charge at a run, with shouting, was undertaken by the men in support. The Indian sharpshooters were thus driven from their hiding places and the spring secured by our riflemen against recapture.

As soon as every man had been provided with food, I directed that the artillery battalion be withdrawn from the lines, thin though they were already, and that the whole stretch be held by the infantry and cavalry. This gave a reserve force to employ in any offensive movement. It should be remembered that the number of our men on the lines and the number of the Indian warriors that Joseph marshalled were about equal. Miller withdrew his battalion and at 2:30 p.m., the time I had selected, was preparing to execute a peculiar movement—to push out by the left flank and pierce the enemy's line just left of the center. He was then to cross a barricaded ravine, face suddenly to the right, and charge so as to strike the Indian position in reverse, assisting himself meanwhile by a howitzer.

Miller was fully ready and about to move when beyond the Indian position, toward the south, a dust appeared in the distance. Our glasses, quickly catching every new appearance, revealed it was an expected supply train escorted by Jackson's cavalry company. The artillery battalion, which was waiting for the other work, was immediately sent out to meet the newcomers. This occasioned considerable skirmishing and the delay of an hour, when the train was brought in in safety. To our joy Major Keeler, of General McDowell's staff, accompanied the escort and brought us cheering words from his general at San Francisco, as well as welcome reinforcements.

Upon my invitation, Major Keeler came forward to see the battle and took a place by my side.

Captain Miller, instead of returning with the train, was marching slowly in column by the right flank towards us when, as he crossed the enemy's line just at the right point, he faced to the left, moved quickly in line for nearly a mile across our front and repeatedly charged the enemy's positions. This manner of striking at an angle and following up the break is called "rolling up the enemy's line." This Miller accomplished most effectually. The usual attempt to double his left was made by the Indians. However, Rodney's company, held in reserve at Miller's rear, then deployed and flanked the flankers, driving them back.

For a few minutes there was a stubborn resistance at Joseph's barricades, then his whole line gave way. Immediately the pursuit was taken up by the whole force—infantry and artillery, Winter's troop dismounted, and the remaining cavalry as soon as they could saddle and mount. This movement was decisive. The Indians were completely routed and flying over the rugged banks, through the ravines, swimming and wading the river, with our forces in close pursuit.

Chapter XXV

Jackson's cavalry, just arrived, moved off quickly along the plateau. They followed the gatling gun in support at a trot as far as the bluff overlooking the river. The howitzers were brought to the same point, with Trimble's company, and shot and shell poured into the retreating masses of Indians and ponies. They were closely pursued through the ravines into the deep canyon, thence to the river—over rocks, down precipices, and along trails almost too steep and craggy to traverse. The footmen pressed them to that part of the river opposite the Indian camp. The river being too deep and rapid for the men to ford, they here waited for the cavalry under Perry. The cavalry worked its way as rapidly as it could from its position on the left, down the rugged mountain steeps to the deep ford, and crossed slowly into the Indian camp. But Perry, instead of pressing after Joseph up the bluffs on the other side, strongly posted his force near the Indian lodges. Meanwhile, the gatling guns and the howitzers, near which I was observing, were doing their best to reach the Indians, who were fleeing in every direction up the heights and disappearing to the left of Cottonwood Creek. At this time, about five p.m., I was following up the movement, descending a steep trail down the mountain side, when I discovered a number of the warriors apparently returning toward their camp from the Cottonwood ravine. They were at the time at least three miles from us. I warned Perry and directed him to immediately ferry over the footmen with his horses.

This action required time, and instead of returning to attack us as they appeared to have considered, the Indians crossed the Cottonwood Canyon and disappeared under cover of a ravine. It being evidently impossible to overtake the fugitives before dark, further pursuit was postponed until the next morning.

The Indian camp had been abandoned in haste, with the lodges still standing and filled with their effects—blankets, buffalo robes, cooking utensils, food cooking on the fires, flour, jerked beef, and plunder of all descriptions. The many wounded and dead horses in and near the encampment showed that our artillery had reached it.

We had, on our side, put into the engagement for these two days four hundred fighting men. The Indians, under Chief Joseph, over three hundred warriors, and a great number of women, who assisted in providing spare horses and ammunition—as did our packers and horse holders. They had twenty-three killed, about forty wounded, many of whom subsequently died, and some forty that fell into our hands as prisoners. Our loss was thirteen killed and twenty-two wounded.

The Nez Perces fought with skill and with the utmost obstinacy. Nobody could complain of our men on that field. "A small battle!" Yes, if we estimate by the numbers engaged. But the forces were quite equally matched, and it required just as much, perhaps more, nerve to do one's duty there, where the loss of a battle involves the direst consequences, and wounds and death were the same to those who suffered as in engagements where more lives are at stake.

The next morning we were early on the march. As soon as we reached the heights above Kamiah, we saw that the enemy's families, their stock and effects, were already mostly across the Clearwater a mile above the ferry. Our little force, now in hot pursuit, pressed down the trail as rapidly as possible and moved at a trot in two columns to the place of crossing. When the river was reached by our skirmishers, the last warrior was already over and well up the other bank. The gatling guns and musketry were quickly located and noisily used, but with little apparent effect except perhaps to increase the rapidity of Chief Joseph's retreat. As Perry's and Whipple's cavalry neared the enemy's crossing and were passing the flank of a high bluff which was situated just beyond the river, a brisk fire from Indian rifles was suddenly opened upon them. It created a great panic and disorder; our men jumped from their horses and ran to the cover of the fences. Little damage resulted, except the shame to us and a fierce delight to the foe.

We learned that the enemy had intended to make a halt and a firm stand before going over the river, but our rapid descent of the Kamiah hills and resolute approach, coupled with their defeat of the day before, they could not stand. Thus when our columns came in view on the heights they sprang upon their skin rafts and swam over, occasioning the loss of many of their supplies which their women had saved and brought off from their abandoned camp near the field of battle.

Joseph, with the same quickness of judgment which he had displayed at White Bird, the Salmon, the Cottonwood, and the Clearwater, took a position at the beginning of the Lolo Trail beyond the reach of our longest guns. Here his scouts, from every elevated point, watched the unfolding of our plans, so that the wary chief was always ready to conform his motions to ours. There was a junction of trails beyond him, fifteen or twenty miles off. Could I but get there! Perhaps I could, by going back a little and then downriver and across, quick, indeed, if at all, and secret!

The fourteenth was spent in reconnoitering. The fifteenth I started a column of cavalry with intention of ascending the heights to the rear, as if en route to Lapwai, but really to move in a westerly direction twenty miles down the Clearwater to Dunwell's Ferry and cross there to attempt to gain the trail to the rear of the Indians. They were still encamping in plain sight, not more than four miles from Kamiah. But their eyes were too sharp for the success of this maneuver, for I had not proceeded more than six miles before the Indians began to break camp and to retreat in good earnest along the Lolo Trail toward Montana and the east. Therefore, leaving Captain Jackson and his company and a few volunteers, who had just returned to me, to watch Dunwell's Ferry, I returned at once to Kamiah and prepared to move my entire command over the river as quickly as possible. My own return to Kamiah was hastened by a request, said to be sent in from Joseph, asking on what terms he could surrender. While I was talking to his messenger, not far from the river a shot was fired from the enemy upon our picket, which struck near the consulting parties. The messenger himself, his family, and some others subsequently surrendered, but not Joseph. It was doubtless a ruse, intended to delay our movements, but fortunately it did not affect them.

The seventeenth I sent Colonel Mason in command of the cavalry, Indian scouts, and McConville's volunteers, all of whom had been ferried to the other bank with great labor, to pursue the hostiles for two marches. The trail was exceedingly difficult and passed mostly over wooded mountains. The woods were filled with fallen timber. This condition of things enabled the Indians to form ambuscades with ease. Mason followed the enemy rapidly, as directed, for the two marches condensed into one, to within three miles of Oro Fino Creek. His scouts first ran into the enemy's rear guard. Three of the scouts were disarmed, one was wounded, and one killed. One of the enemy was killed and two pack animals captured. Having accomplished, as he believed, the object of his movement—to ascertain Joseph's intentions and to engage him if he could do so to advantage—and having found the trail unfit for action with the cavalry, where a small rear guard in the thick trees could easily throw our people into confusion, he concluded to return. At eight a.m. the eighteenth, the pursuing column was again at Kamiah. This really ended the campaign within the limits of my department.

The Indians had been well led and well fought. They had defeated two companies in a pitched battle. They had eluded pursuit and crossed the Salmon. They had turned back and crossed our communications, had kept our cavalry on the defensive, and defeated a company of volunteers. They had been finally forced to concentrate, it is true, and had been brought to battle. But in battle with regular troops, they had held out for nearly two days before they were beaten and after that were still able to keep together, cross a river too deep to be forded, and then check our pursuing cavalry and make off to other parts beyond Idaho. The result would necessitate a long and tedious chase.

Still, on our side, the Indians had been stopped in their murders, had been resolutely met everywhere, driven into position and beaten; and, by subsequent pursuit, the vast country was freed from their terrible presence. As it has since been proven, by means of these few months of hard work and some attendant abuse, the whole extensive region of eastern Oregon and northern Idaho was completely delivered from perpetual conflicts and just causes of alarm.

Chapter XXVI

I heard a quaint newspaper man once say, with regard to a congressional report, "I never read that kind of literature except under compulsion!" Military reports, with their technical terms, unembellished language, and their wearisome monotony of style, are equally forbidding to the common mind. If not so, I would venture to introduce here one or two military orders which were extracted from a campaign report, but I forbear, if the reader will but allow himself to be detained by a few dry statements of plans, in order to give him his bearings before he plunges into the wild forests which he must cross in passing from Kamiah, Idaho, to the Bitterroot River of Montana.

First plan: To leave a small garrison at Kamiah, go back to Lewiston, pick up supplies, press on to Missoula at once; consign Camas Prairie and thereabouts to Col. Green, who would be on hand from Fort Boise in about ten days; and entrust all else to General Wheaton, with Second Infantry, now fast coming from Georgia by railroad, steamship, and steamboat to Lewiston.

My first plan was abandoned because of some just reasons for alarm among whites and friendly Indians who feared that Joseph would come back before we were half way to Lewiston. Though I had halted my troops on change of plan, during a delay for supplies I still went in person to Lapwai. After sending dispatches and taking a brief rest, I turned back to my command. From a story that had reached me, I had hoped to have met my wife. The story proved false and the disappointment real. On the return, Lieutenant Pierce was my companion. Pierce was of the Twenty-first Infantry and had been detained at the fort as ordnance officer. His conversation was pleasant and refreshing during the long and tedious ride.

I then turned, with the main force, to Croaesdale's farm, situated on the famous Camas Prairie, and remained for some days looking towards Kamiah to support the little garrison which was left there if Indians should indeed turn back; looking towards Mount Idaho for Green's head of column, wishing it to annihilate space; waiting there eight days, while a fearful newspaper clamor came from the rear of "Slow! Slow! No ability; will never catch the Indians!"

Second plan evolved: Hostile Indians, with few exceptions (their rear guard back stealing ponies, causing the late alarm), had gone off by the Lolo Trail. My dispositions were to form two columns and a reserve, to accompany the right column myself, the left column to be in charge of Wheaton, and the reserve to stay on Camas Prairie under Green. The right column to take up the direct pursuit along Lolo Trail; the left column to go eastward by Mullan Road, look after old "Columbia River renegades" and malcontent Indians, keep the peace if possible, and then, like the right column, set out for Missoula, Montana. The reserve must watch out on all trails, keep intercommunication, be ready for hostile Indians should they double back, and give heart to all neighboring farmers, miners, prospectors, and friendly Indians by the show of protection at hand.

This new order of things being established and understood, we of the right column began the long march on Thursday, the 26th of July, 1877. The first stage, sixteen miles to Kamiah, was a rolling prairie with excellent grazing and wood and water in the canyons.

On July 27th the infantry, artillery, and Jackson's company of cavalry crossed the Clearwater.

The 28th, Saturday, I took what few there were of McConville's volunteers and made a reconnaissance to what is called the "Little Camas," marching a distance of ten or eleven miles through the rough, thicket trail, found no signs of Indian families, no stock of any consequence belonging to the hostiles, and then returned to Kamiah. It was pretty evident that the non-treaties had left the department. This day the head of Green's column reached us from Boise. Major Sanford was in command. He brought three companies of cavalry under Bendire, Carr, and

Wagner, and twenty Bannock Indian scouts. Two companies
of infantry, with Green himself, were reported still far back,
at Florence, but we could not properly wait any longer.

Next day, while the troops were finishing the slow
crossing of the Clearwater at Kamiah, closing up the supplies and getting everything ready for the long journey,
James Lawyer, the Nez Perce head chief of the friendly
people, called his Nez Perces together near the river and
invited the Bannock scouts and all of us who could come to
participate in a religious service. Archie Lawyer, who had
been so faithfully taught by the worthy Christian worker,
Miss MacBeth, stood forth and preached an earnest sermon to the Indians in the Nez Perce language. He frequently turned and spoke to us in English. He held a Bible
in his hands and translated its words readily into the
Indian tongue. Many officers and men were present and
manifested much interest in this meeting. The singing was
quite good. After service I made some remarks, which were
translated by Archie Lawyer for those who could not
understand the English.

Many Indians who cannot keep up with a connected dis-
course in English can follow a short conversation. I was
glad enough to have this service of prayer, singing, and
speaking before we left. I think many felt as I did. There is
a stern reality in going from all you love into the dread
uncertainty of Indian fighting, where the worst form of tor-
ture and death might await you. It is very wise and proper
to ask God's blessing when about to plunge into the dark
clouds of warfare.

On the 30th of July we were up before the dawn. The
headquarters were moved across the river at four a.m., and
the whole column was in motion by five. It rained heavily,
the mud increased, and the path was narrow, steep and
slippery as we ascended the heights beyond Kamiah.

We found an abrupt descent at the Lolo fork that none
but old frontiersmen and Indians could ride down, so we
slipped and slid, fell and scrambled up again. The pine
trees were abundant, and most of the way was filled in
with a thick underbrush. We had this day our first trouble
with the Bannock scouts. They had come from Boise, were

tired, and did not mean to go any farther. Buffalo Horn, a young Indian very handsomely decked off with skins and plumage, fortunately took the side of their white chief, Robbins, and induced all but three to keep on with us for the present.

At the Wee-ipe, the glade which we have before described, there was quite a lengthy opening in the forest and plenty of water and grass. The hostile Indians had pastured this plat pretty well and had dug over much of the land for the camas roots, which are often used by the Nez Perces for food. They are shaped something like onions, but more elongated, and have a sweetish, clammy taste which is quite palatable.

The weather cleared up before sundown, and we gladly put our weary soldiers into camp. They had marched sixteen miles up mountain heights by narrow, crooked horse trails where the mud was deep and there could be no firmness to the tread. It was slip, slip all the day. Sixteen miles here are equivalent to thirty on a good road in fair weather. We learned our trail ahead was much obstructed by fallen trees of all sizes and descriptions. They had fallen in every possible troublesome way so that even when small, it was very perplexing to get them out of the path. Nothing but axes would do it. We were, therefore, looking anxiously for our *pioneers*. Some forty or fifty of them with axes were coming from Lewiston. We named this glade-like opening in the almost endless forest "Camp Sanford" for our commander of the cavalry battalion. This was his first day with us. Miller continued in charge of the foot artillery, Otis of our howitzer battery, which is mounted on muleback, and Miles had command of the infantry battalion.

Every day's record of a march like this becomes monotonous. For the benefit of patient readers, after giving a brief picture of one camp and headquarters, we will only add here and there a scrap from the journal.

The camp was generally rectangular in form. One battalion covered the front, usually encamping in line and sending guard and pickets well out. A second covered the sides or flanks, and a third the rear. The battery took its place at will, selecting as good a position as the nature of the ground afforded. For headquarters a place was sought of easy communication and having a neat plat of ground with convenient wood and water. On coming to the place selected for the night's halt, Colonel Mason distributed the troops, guards, and outposts.

The "big tent" was a common square tent. Mason had a smaller one of special make, with joint and hangers in the uprights and in the ridge pole. This arrangement enabled him to fold all in compact bundles for packing on the mules. His was put on one side of the big one, and a tent fly was pitched with open front and back on the other. These now were made to house Dr. Alexander, the army surgeon, Lieutenant Fletcher, aide-de-camp, and the news correspondent, Mr. Sutherland, who had joined us at Salmon River. I took Lieutenants C.E.S. Wood and Guy Howard, aides, into my tent. The quartermaster, Lieutenant Ebstein, pitched still another tent-fly for himself and his clerks. A small pack train, under a Mexican named Louis, came up promptly after the night's halt was called.

The kitchen was placed some twenty paces off, to the left rear, near a clump of trees. The kitchen consisted of our mess-chest and one or two canvas bags—one or two mule loads, according to the state of the supplies. There was one man for cook and one for helper.

When the nights were damp or cold we always had a large fire made in front of the big tent. Our beds were common blankets or robes of skin, buffalo, fox, squirrel skins and the like, placed on the ground. Our table consisted of a square piece of canvas, spread near the kitchen in fair weather and within the big tent when it was rainy.

A more cheery, hearty and happy company than ours at headquarters is seldom found. Sometimes the officer is worn with anxiety, weary with long and tedious marches and loss of sleep, still he unbends at the mess table and tells lively stories to the circle around the campfire. There is no more intimate association among men during a lengthy campaign than that at a common mess. Generally we gave two hours in the morning, from the waking to the starting. Reveille at three or four, breakfast at four or five, and march at five or six.

On Thursday, the second day of August, the journal record was as follows: "The command left Camp Winters at seven a.m. Artillery at head of column. Day clear and pleasantly cool. Captain Spurgin came into camp at six a.m. bringing us news of his company of pioneers still several miles behind. He was left that morning at Camp Winters to bring them up. The trail led through woods of same general character as before, rather a slow trail, owing to mountainous country and fallen timber. The summit of the hills was covered with rough granite boulders, making the path quite difficult. There were plenty of excellent springs on trail. Our men travel it well and are in good order. We march sixteen miles and encamp on a slope of the mountain. Poor grazing here. The only feed consists of wild dwarf lupine and wire-grass. Several mules were exhausted, and some packs of bacon were abandoned by the way. Robbins, in charge of scouts, reports that 'loose Indian horses, always broken down, were seen along the trail.'"

We went into camp, named "Evan Miles," at about four p.m. Spurgin and the pioneers arrived at dark. Such was the record of a day. If one could stand on Mount Washington in New Hampshire and look off northward toward Canada, he could see on a clear day much such a country as this through which we were wending our way. It does not appear far to the next peak. It is not so in a *straight* course, but such a course is impossible. "Keep to the hog-back!" That means there is usually a crooked connecting ridge between two neighboring mountain heights, and you must keep on it. The necessity of doing so often made the distance three times greater than by straight lines, but the ground was too stony, too steep, the canyon too deep, to attempt the shorter course. Conceive this climbing ridge after ridge in the wildest kind of wilderness with the only possible pathway filled with timber, small and large, crossed and criss-crossed, and now, while the horses and mules are feeding on innutritious wiregrass, you will not wonder at "only sixteen miles a day."

"Didn't the hostile Indians go here?" the reader inquires. Yes, they jammed their ponies through, up the rocks, over and under and around the logs, and among the fallen trees without attempting to cut a limb, leaving blood to mark their path, and abandoned animals, with broken legs, or played out, or stretched dead by the wayside.

Our guide, Chapman, says in frontier parlance, "No man living can get so much out of a horse like an Indian can." Had we, for three days along the Lolo Trail, followed closely the hostiles' unmerciful example, we would not then have had ten mules left on their feet fit to carry our sugar, coffee, and hard-bread.

Chapter XXVII

Let us imagine now that we have toiled on over those mountains lying between Idaho and Montana, two-thirds of the way across, and that we have met Mr. Curley, the messenger who went from Mount Idaho to Missoula and was returning. Mr. Curley's face was cheery, but he brought us bad news. Joseph and Looking Glass, with their hordes, had come up to the hastily-constructed fort in the Lolo Valley and had promised good behavior in consideration for a safe conduct through to the "Buffalo Illahee." Captain Rawn was there at the time, in command of a few regulars and many volunteers. It was judged best by him and those with him to let Joseph's band go by, close on the right flank, and the whites promised not to fire. Who can think of the apprehension of a scattered population and blame these citizen volunteers for letting "General Howard's Indians" go on, provided they promised to do no damage?

Yet it was to us bad news that the Indians had gone, for the pass where the fort was situated was reported to be narrow, the cliffs on either side high and difficult, and therefore we hoped that these Indians would be stopped until we could come up and help the fort, by attacking from the west and rear. It might have saved us a long march, much public abuse, and perhaps have secured to us the enviable reputation of being good Indian fighters. We had passed the last tine of the Clearwater where, after twenty-one miles of the roughest country, with Spurgin's pioneers ahead cutting out the trail, we came into camp in the twilight. We heard loud echoes of firing by the advanced scouts and thought they had come upon Joseph's rear guard. Then we spurred the weary animals into a tired trot and along this narrow trail descended for miles through the almost impenetrable forest till we came to the narrowest of valleys. Here we found not a mouthful of food for horse or mule—but the nicest of salmon for the men, in water about knee-deep and clear as crystal, rushing and splashing over the rocks. The echoes which deceived us into thinking the enemy near were from the scouts' carbines shooting the bigger of the fish as they were swimming up the Clearwater. Glad were we to get beyond that valley where the poor mule was obliged to fast all night, and tremble and sway himself back and forth as he undertook to take his load up the steep exit at four o'clock the next morning.

How strong and firm his step became seven miles ahead when he came into a mountain glade where there were little swampy lakes and the greenest of grass in plenty. Here was the place where mule and man enjoyed a rest and a break-fast far more satisfying than in inhabited regions which are replete with abundance. Yes, we have passed this lovely oasis in the wild Lolo wilderness and have come to an open-ing in the mountains, which makes us feel almost as if the tug of war was over. But we must not be sanguine, for appearances are deceptive. My journal says: "Warm Springs, about four p.m. Nine miles from Summit Prairies (where the mule and man had the early breakfast), sixteen miles from our last camp. Fine camp here at Hot Springs—sulphur water, good grazing, and mountain brook."

It requires but a little imagination for the reader to fill out the picture: Several beautiful pools of steaming water, at the foot of a gently-sloping, thinly-wooded hill. Down the hill, sweeping swiftly over ledges and throwing up spray from fissures and crevices in the ledge, glides a broad, shal-low stream sparkling in the sunshine. It was a charming place. The wilderness was speedily changed into a beautiful village. Horses and mules were feeding on the green, as quiet and contented as if it had always been their home. The camps of the men were promptly arranged in order. Blankets and clothing were spread for airing, and already the underclothing was being wrung out by the half-naked owners in the hot water of the pools and was waving gently on the bushes as the sun and the breeze caused speedy dry-ing. This peaceful scene of rest and comfort, heightened by the statuesque forms of the bathers, was disturbed by the cry from the outer picket-post, "A horseman in sight from the East!" A tall frontiersman soon appeared, riding rapidly into our camp.

"My name is Pardee. I bring a dispatch from General Gibbon to General Howard." Pardee had brought us tidings of General Gibbon. He, Gibbon, had left his headquarters at Helena, hastened to Missoula, and arrived after the Indians had left Rawn's fort. He had with him less than two hundred men, but with these had pushed forward on Chief Joseph's trail. His command rolled on in wagons up the Bitterroot Valley as fast as horses could be made to go. He needed a hundred men more and hoped that I might send them by forced marches to overtake him.

Having left my infantry tamping along the crooked trail, I had already set out with my cavalry and was about a day ahead when this 6th of August message arrived. I had but two hundred souls, all told, and I had a fancy that I myself could push on more miles in a day that one less spurred by the sense of responsibility. Gibbon had then one hundred miles the start and was marching fast. We could not, of course, with tired animals, overtake him till he began a slower progress, which he must do to cross the Rocky Mountain divide, or until he stopped, as he would doubtless do if the Indians discovered the fewness of his numbers and decided to give him battle. In any case, he might delay somewhere for the needed accession of force.

A trusty sergeant by the name of Sutherland and an Indian scout were selected to go. They left at once with the answer, having been instructed to travel night and day until Gibbon should be overtaken.

"General Howard is coming on as fast as possible by forced marches with two hundred cavalrymen to give the needed reinforcement." Such was the substance of Sutherland's message.

Conceive of a brave man starting out at night in this wild country with only an Indian to guide him! The way was rugged, the night was dark, the distance was great, and he a stranger; but he was resolute and a soldier.

Chapter XXVIII

Sergeant Sutherland and his Indian guide found emerging from the rugged mountains between Idaho and Montana in the darkness no easy task. The Indian only knew the country generally and cared little about the character of his pathway provided his pony held out. Not so with the soldier. Sutherland liked, above all things, a strong, active horse. And he was not satisfied to follow faint trails and go merely by the stars. For a time the trail was pretty good, occasionally interrupted by fallen trees which were too long to get around. Then the path turned to the right and wound along a steep acclivity and over a knife-edge crest. By dismounting and slowly leading the animals, the sergeant and the guide managed to creep around to the other side without slipping off the shelving rock into a deep chasm below. When dawn appeared, the valley of the Lolo had opened out into broader proportions, the grass fields gave sign of cultivation, and an occasional hut showed that at some time not far back this region had been inhabited. Still, for miles there was not a domestic animal, not even an Indian dog to howl back defiance to the multitudinous cries of the coyotes.

When Lieutenant Fletcher, who will be remembered as the officer who discovered the whereabouts of Joseph's people just before the battle of the Clearwater, set out for Missoula the next morning at four o'clock with Gibbon's tall messenger, Sutherland had scarcely traversed twenty-five miles. The lieutenant's stock was rested, fed, and he had daylight, so that he gained rapidly on the sergeant and the latter was but a few miles ahead when Fletcher and his companion turned northward down the Bitterroot Valley toward Missoula.

The Indian guide deserted Sutherland at the most convenient point and time and also went off toward Missoula.

Sutherland's poor horse trembled in his joints, sweat at every pore. His sides, near the sergeant's boot-heel, were stained with blood from the often used spur when he dragged himself into the yard of the first settler encountered in ascending the Bitterroot River.

"Good morning, Mr. A."

"Good morning, stranger," says a jolly-looking man emerging from the farm house.

"'Pears you've had a tough ride, by the look of ye' horse."

"Yes, I'm bearing dispatches from General Howard to General Gibbon. I've authority to get a remount and am told you have some horses."

"Oh, yes, yes, stranger. You'll have to go right smart to catch Gibbon, for he streamed it with his men in wagons. He's got three days the start on ye!"

"Well, sir, I'm in a hurry. Will you let me have a horse? The quartermaster will settle. I must have one."

"I reckon I can. It's not tamed much, but you look like a spunky feller."

A colt is soon brought forward.

After a little food and coffee that Mr. A. kindly gave him, the sergeant mounted. There was first a stiff "I won't go!" then the leaping, jumping, shaking process. The girt-band gave way, and the rider, being hurled to the ground, strained his back. Still, after a time he managed to mount again and to break in his pony so as to proceed. Though in considerable pain and quite lame, he got over much ground before night.

Thus our messenger has gone ahead, followed by Lieutenant Fletcher, who had turned to Missoula for supplies. The latter was to meet us with the necessary food for men and animals before we reached the point where we were to turn off southward up the Bitterroot Valley in order to follow the trails of Joseph and Gibbon.

To return to my cavalry column: At half-past five a.m., Spurgin with his axemen was already out on the trail working hard to get well ahead of the command so that I might make today the utmost distance over this terribly rough and obstructed pathway. He cleared away the fallen trees, made bridges across chasms and, when there was time, he improved portions of the breakneck trail by side digging or walling with fragments of rock.

We set out at half-past six in the morning with some reluctance at leaving these hotsprings and this charming camp and made twenty-two miles. If this is considered a short distance for a forced march, it should be remembered that it was equal to forty miles on a fair roadway.

August 8th. Intent on reinforcing Gibbon, our two hundred cavalrymen were off just as the sun was peeping over the ridge ahead. We can truly say we enjoyed the march over this excellent road. Both men and horses were more cheerful. By nine a.m. we reached the mouth of the Lolo. The narrow pass where the temporary fort had been made by the men from Missoula and where the Indians had stopped to parley was inspected by our command. And as the excellent barricades of logs appeared in our front, the question arose, "How could the Indians get by?" All eyes were turned to the high hills on the right and on the left.

"Why did not Rawn and the volunteers stop them here?" "Joseph was too smart for them!" "Looking Glass is always a good Indian here in the Bitterroot country." Such were remarks that I heard from one and another as we worked our way crookedly past these obstructions in this famous Lolo Pass. While we were resting and grazing the animals for a couple of hours at the mouth of the Lolo, Fletcher came up with the needed supplies. Then on we went across the river with its broad and beautiful valley, passed the town of Stevensville, and kept on till seven o'clock in the evening. Between sun and sun, with horses which had hitherto been staggering and trembling on the stony and log-beridden paths of the mountains, we had accomplished thirty-four miles. So much for a good wagon road.

Soldiers who are pressing on toward an expected battlefield are very eager for news. Ears and eyes are wide open. Every sound is caught and accounted for. Every man met is stopped and questioned. Every unusual stir of cattle and horses in the distance is searched with eyes of the longest range and with glasses. Today, the 9th of August, on this level wagon road, we tramped along the Bitterroot Valley with few incidents to break the quiet of the column. It was a fine grazing country on our right and left—plenty of stock. The inhabitants appeared to thrive well between Stevensville and Corvallis, the next village above.

As the cavalry approached Corvallis we met a gentleman in a buggy. Yes, a covered buggy in the Rocky Mountains, far away from anywhere! It was the doctor of the region. Cautious, careful man! We did not learn from him that citizens had kindly remembered these Indians who had made through their country so many parallel paths—remembered them as very friendly and profitable traders as, year by year, they had come and gone while en route to the buffalo illahee. We do not draw from him that some very kind neighbors carried provisions in wagons into the Indians' camp and sold them for money, that their old and worn horses had been traded off for fresh ones, and that for these kindnesses, and this show of fraternal feeling, the entire valley had been spared by the placable Joseph. No, these facts crept out from other sources. The doctor told us where and when the Indians swept by—over yonder, across the Bitterroot, next to the mountain shore, beyond that fringe of cottonwood; also when General Gibbon rapidly followed. "He must be at Ross' Hole by this time." "Ross' Hole!" Strange name. It is some kind of crater in these highlands, we think, or short canyon too deep for the ordinary name. We shall see.

Soon we met citizens on horseback and some in wagons. They had started to catch the Indians, but traveling two days at ten or fifteen miles a day did not suit them. Their saloons, their stores, their farms were needing their constant care. "The Indians are already well out of the way, can run as fast or faster than we can follow, so we came back."

Why shouldn't they? These citizens were not employed as soldiers, and the danger to them and their families was past. No reliable news can be gained from these returning citizens.

A crowd watched for our cavalcade at Corvallis. It was composed of men and boys, roughly clad, with here and there a sprinkling of the brighter colors of female dress and a few hatless Indians standing listlessly with their red blankets wrapped around them. One such, a young Indian, sat quietly upon the flattish roof of an old shed near the outskirts of the town. He appeared like the rest. "Who are these Indians?" A most respectable-looking trader vouches for them. "They are all friendly Flatheads!"

As soon as the command was well out of the way beyond the town, this Indian who was on the roof slid easily to the eaves, sprang to the ground, mounted a Cayuse pony standing nearby, and made straight eastward. He reached the foothills of the eastern range of mountains which, in that direction, wall up the Bitterroot Valley, almost before he was suspected. Several young men gave chase but could not find him. He sped away to the mountains and then turned south toward Joseph's trail. He was a spy. As successful spies no men can excel these Indians, and none was swifter than this spy messenger, and none ever did greater service to his chief. His power of endurance was wonderful. The distance was probably one hundred and fifty miles by the route he took to enable him to overtake his people. Through the forests, over the mountains, across the stretches of prairie, the Cayuse never ceased to trot or canter till thoroughly exhausted; his legs bruised and bleeding, wet with foam, the trembling, staggering animal stumbled and fell. No coaxing, no whipping and kicking will restore his courage. So the spy, having slipped off the saddle and bridle and "cached" them close at hand, took careful observation of the place of concealment. Then he stalked away at a swift, steady walk till he had gained Gibbon's trail over the Rocky Mountain Range. It was a real range at this crossing, not so very high, but plain to be seen and felt as you ascended from the west.

I had become so anxious about Gibbon with his small force, that I resolved to pick thirty of our best horses with their well-seasoned riders, put them under Lieutenant Bacon, and add seventeen scouts under Chief Robbins; take also Lieutenant Wood and the quartermaster's active clerk, Mr. Bonny with me, and ride as fast and as far in search of Gibbon as the animals would carry us. Mason remained in charge of the remainder of the cavalry, to follow as rapidly as possible. In the cool, clear morning, just as the dawn appeared, we moved out of camp in a column

Chapter XXIX

Turning from the dismounted Indian spy to our command, we find them still wearily working their way through the mountains. It is wonderful how much distance can be made in a day by a steady pace, walking your horses as fast as you can, keeping them together. The men chat with one another and rest themselves occasionally by a puff or two from short clay pipes. At the end of fifty minutes, call the halt, dismount, and if there should happen to be short intervals, do not close them. Rest just ten minutes. Then mount and go on again for another fifty minutes. After just ten minutes' halt, proceed as before.

Where the mountains appeared to be shut in and it seemed no longer possible to move southward up the Bitterroot Valley without climbing, was a broad, level space covered with trees, not altogether the usual cottonwood, but mostly fair-sized oaks. Our camp of August 9 was chosen close by the one lately occupied by General Gibbon, so we named it "Camp John Gibbon." It was a fine camp. The swift water, with its lively mountain impulse still in it, shot over boulders in the shallow river bed, and a greensward strewn with the changing autumn leaves that had begun to fall invited weary men and horses to a pleasant night's refreshment.

I had become so anxious about Gibbon with his small force, that I resolved to pick twenty of our best horses with their well-seasoned riders, put them under Lieutenant Bacon, and add seventeen scouts under Chief Robbins; take also Lieutenant Wood, and the quartermaster's active clerk, Mr. Bonny, with me, and ride as fast and as far in search of Gibbon as the animals would carry us. Mason remained in charge of the remainder of the cavalry, to follow as rapidly as possible. In the cool, clear morning, just as the dawn appeared, we moved out of camp in a column of twos, took a steady, firm trot and, except in a few instances where the roughness of the trail prevented speed, kept at that gait all day. We rested at midday for one hour after passing the famous Ross' Hole. Our northern people would call it broad swampland hemmed in by hills. The Mexicans would name it a "cienaga." The frontiersmen say "hole." It is dry now, but doubtless when Ross and his party of emigrants went this way, their wagons and horses mired, and they indignantly named the cienaga, or swamp, a horrid hole, and in time, by the proper reduction of history, we have "Ross' Hole."

We could not trot up the mountain ridge; it was as much as we could do to walk. Horses and men toiled up the winding ascent. There were many paths. Every new climber tried to find an easier way. But if you took the left through the close trees and thick underbrush, you wished you had taken the right or another between the two. There was no dodging that abrupt six miles of mountain climbing. Only fifty-three miles as we came to this nice stream and broad, glade-like opening! We were already in the canyon that marks the eastern slope, and we wondered whether or not this Trail Creek sent its waters into the far-off Atlantic.

Soon after we halted at dark, Robbins and some scouts returned at a trot with seven citizens on foot. You do not often see this sight—citizens dismounted on a frontier road! In fact, you do not often see any human being in these mountains.

"Well, my men, what have you to tell us?" One of them replied, "General Gibbon had a fight with the Indians yesterday morning; has lost half his men. It was going hard with him when we left. We haven't had anything to eat for two days." So we invited them to our intended camp and fed them. General Gibbon and the Indians were not twenty miles from us. As these citizens talked much as men are apt to do who early in the conflict run from the field of battle, it is not fair to the gallant soldiers who remain and fight it out to give their story too much weight. Our horses were too exhausted to move another league that night, the 10th of August. We were so near the enemy—just how near we did not know—and there were so few of us that we barricaded a little with logs and built fires to make it appear that we had many troops. Mr. Bonny was started back to Mason at once with the news. How could he get his horse through thirty miles more, back beyond Ross' Hole?

A short time ago we saw the Indian spy in swift motion across the rocky range, first on horseback and then on foot. He had come into the wagon road just ahead of my brilliant camp, wherein we forty pretended to be five hundred. Our scouts found his plain moccasin tracks, and hence we felt sure that Joseph had already received timely warning. The spy doubtless took a good look at our campfires and then pressed on. We shall see what was the probable result of his message.

The seven countrymen who dropped in upon us the night before were a sorry-looking set. They gave us a graphic account of the fight, of their own part in it, their progress, their escape. One had had a brother desperately wounded. The troops had done nobly but were fearfully outnumbered. General Gibbon had shown wonderful gallantry and with many others was severely wounded.

They enumerated those who had been killed in the battle, but even after they had been comforted by a night's rest and a warm breakfast, they gave us but gloomy views of the final situation at the time they themselves, for dear life, were making their escape to the brush. Now, no offer of favor or money, not even the attraction of a brother wounded and needy, could induce one of those brave men to go back and guide us to the battlefield.

While we were making our forced march and taking the needed rest, others had not been idle.

Gibbon's messenger had passed near us in the early morning of the 10th. There was a part of the distance, just before that Ross' cienaga, where there were two roads. The messenger was galloping along the left while we were trotting over the right track. The high ground between prevented us from seeing this horseman, and him from seeing our cavalcade. It was too bad, for just the sight of him would have saved the brisk Mr. Bonny from the night ride of thirty miles, the poor horse under him being even more to be pitied than the man. The official dispatch which General

Gibbon's messenger was bearing made matters appear very serious. The message, written in pencil on a square piece of paper of the size of a visiting card, reads:

> General: We surprised the Nez Perce camp at day-light this morning, whipped them out of it, killing a considerable number; but they then turned on us, forced us out of it, and compelled us to take the defensive. We are here near the mouth of Big Hole pass with a number of wounded, and need medical attendance and assistance of all kinds, and hope you will hurry to our relief.
>
> Gibbon, Comm'd'g.
Aug. 9, '77

Though he passed me, the swift messenger met Mason, with the cavalry and the medical officers who were so much required. These tidings put them into swifter motion, and the news was sent flying to the infantry, then one day's march behind.

Strange as it may seem, another messenger passed my little troop without seeing us, and Mason, now pushing forward, first received him. This man brought a note from the sergeant who was deserted by the Indian guide and nearly killed by the bucking horse and yet, with his aching back, kept in the saddle. The note is so good, and it is so seldom that readers hear from an enlisted man, that I will insert a few extracts:

> On the Big Hole Trail, about 20 miles from Ross' Hole, 12 M., Aug. 9, '77
>
> General: I arrived here en route to General Gibbon's command ten minutes ago. I find the train of General Gibbon in camp, with a guard of about eighteen men, citizens and soldiers. General Gibbon left here last night, with a force of (say) one hundred and eighty men, and had been fighting all day, but his exact whereabouts not known to party here.
>
> In conformity with orders from General Gibbon, a party of three non-commissioned officers and seven

privates started from here at daybreak (with a 12-pounder mountain howitzer and ammunition) and were attacked about three and a half miles out; one corporal killed, two sergeants wounded, and two men missing. Howitzer lost, with fifteen rounds of ammunition; also two thousand rounds calibre .45; pack mule killed. As near as I can learn, the sergeant in charge scattered and destroyed the ammunition for howitzer; fired three rounds at Indians. It appears from the attack that Indians are between General Gibbon and this camp. I find the men here somewhat uneasy, but determined to stand off the Indians at all hazards. I take two men from here and start in five minutes to endeavor to reach General Gibbon.... .

Would respectfully state, in explanation of seeming delay on my part, that I was thrown from an unbroken horse at ____, and my back severely hurt, my progress from that point being attended with severe suffering. I am, General,

Very respectfully yours,

O. Sutherland,
Sergeant Company "B," 1st Cavalry

I am glad to preserve this brief record of a brave and deserving man.

On the margin of my notebook is written, "1877, August 11th. Saturday; clear and cool." Think of it, just over the highest ridge of the Rocky Mountains. "We sent our Indian scouts ahead at 4 a.m. and proceeded about eighteen miles by a trail through thick woods and underbrush—good ambuscades." It means excellent places for traps such as the Indians sometimes set. "We arrived at Gibbon's fortified camp at 10 a.m. and found the command all right and cheerful. The Indians had left at 11 o'clock, night before. Gibbon's final position was on a wooded ridge with heights above it and willow bottom, a creek, and tableland below it. He had no surgeon with him. The wounded were doing well, however. Gibbon's wound was a flesh wound above the knee. Sent courier to Deer Lodge with telegraphic dispatches to Terry and McDowell." The above is explicit enough and suggestive to those of us who were ever on the ground, but as this Indian engagement of General John Gibbon has gone into history from various sources, in the following chapter I will give the story substantially as I had it from his own lips.

Chapter XXX

Behold our cavalcade of forty riders with Indian scouts ahead as they descend the Rocky Mountain trail! Chief Robbins sees the smoke of a camp and animals grazing down there in the Big Hole bottom. The Indian scouts with Robbins had stopped on a bare knoll to the left of the road and from their manner and gestures appeared to be excited.

"What is it? Are they our men yonder?"

"They are soldiers, going from the smoke there under that hill, back and forth to the creek."

I knew at once that they were soldiers. It was a party bathing in the stream, some dressing, some sitting on the bank, and others wading in the shallow water. I had hardly said "They are soldiers!" before our horses were in brisk motion toward the smoke that was rolling up from the short pines, just to the left of the thick willows which completely covered the broad bottomland.

We passed rapidly along the trail, around another bluff, when the little camp came full in view. "There it is! It is Gibbon's camp!" A thrill of delight passed through our little party, and it found a voice.

It looked like a hospital at first, though there were lines of rifle pits and well soldiers enough to give one the impression of a heavy hospital guard. So many wounded, nearly half lying cheerful though not able to move, many white bandages about the head and face, some arms in slings. There were roughly constructed shelters from the heat of an unrelenting August sun. On the other side, in the northeast corner of the camp, reclined the wounded commander. His face was very bright, and his voice had a cheery ring as he called out, "Hallo, Howard! Glad to see you."

"Well, Gibbon, how do you do?"

"Oh, I'm not much hurt—a flesh wound in the thigh."

After a short time I asked, "Where are the Indians?"

"They drew off at eleven o'clock last night," Gibbon replied. "You'll dine with me?"

"How can I? You've no supplies."

"We have bread to spare."

"Where was the field?" I asked. Then he pointed out to me the ground.

We were standing on the north side of the valley. The willows, with grassy spaces between them, came next to us below the bluff. Perhaps three hundred yards across the level willow-land, rough and spongy in places, lay the main Big Hole Creek. It was twenty or thirty steps across. Then there was an open grassy bottom that now looked as if it had been mowed. A strip of this grassland stretched some fifty to seventy yards between the creek and the foot of the high ground that formed the other shore of the valley. It was on this grassy bottom that Joseph had pitched his lodges before the battle. Behind us the hilly hither shore rose rapidly into a mountain. Farther down on our side was a spur of the mountain, open and covered with grass, where Joseph's herd was feeding when Gibbon's men first approached, and a big herd it was. To our right, up the creek, the mountain was of easier ascent. Though covered with pines, it was only at intervals, so that the enemy had a plunging fire from two or three picket posts straight into Gibbon's camp. After the General and his generous staff had refreshed us with a dinner good enough for a soldier, he proposed to show us the battlefield proper and explain the situation.

"But you cannot ride, Gibbon."

"I think I can. I'll try, at any rate."

So, with some pain, he mounted. We rode to the place where many lodgepoles were lying. We found, just under the river bank, some of the Indians unburied and fresh marks of the hasty burial of others. He pointed to where women with their little ones in their arms had waded during the battle into the deep water to avoid the firing, and told me how it touched his heart when two or three extended their babies toward him and looked as pleasant and wistful as they could for his protection. This was while the balls were whistling through the willows nearby.

Now, my reader, if you should take up your skillful pencil, I think you could picture that touching scene and would sadly ask the question, "Is there no substitute for war?"

Let General Gibbon tell the story after his return to camp, for he is too lame and sore to dismount on the field or to stay long enough to satisfy my curiosity. The excellent Doctor Fitzgerald and his assistant had arrived. The wounded were already attended to. The messages had been sent to the outer world, and the plans for further pursuit were agreed upon. The General reclined under his bush cover, favoring the sore leg as much as he could. I took a camp chair, while our respective staff officials, grouping themselves at hand, sat, half knelt, or squatted upon the ground.

"You know, Howard, when the Nez Perces had avoided Rawn with his small force there in the Lolo, they ascended the Bitterroot. At first they travelled slowly enough, delaying to trade with the inhabitants. Wasn't it a shame of those Bitterroot people to traffic with the horrid murderers, giving them fresh horses and all sorts of provisions, as readily as if they had been the best friends in the world? I am glad to say that one man had courage enough to shut his store in their faces. I set out with a little short of one hundred and fifty rifles on the fourth of August from Missoula, using wagons to make all the distance possible. I don't think we could have got through to this place if I hadn't been most lucky in running across Mr. Blodget, a frontiersman who had piloted wagons over this country before. The packs were on hand if we had failed with the wagon train. Wasn't it a rough road though? It took us a long time to get over the divides, but in the bottoms we made grand time.

"We ran across a number of the Indians' camps, and they made some twelve or fifteen miles a day, so that, by doubling on them, I knew I should in time catch up. But we were delayed beyond measure at the Rocky Mountains. Our men had to draw the wagons up with ropes. It took us hours to get to the top. Well, we accomplished it and worked our way down this slope into Big Hole, rested a while, then leaving a small detachment three or four miles back with the howitzer, where you saw the camp, I came on with the remainder slowly and silently under cover of the night. We heard the sound of Indian ponies on the next spur, over there to my left. Pushing along quietly between them and the bottom, we at last discovered the Indian lodges.

"Here I halted my command, for it was altogether too dark to move to the attack. We could catch sounds from the tepees. Occasionally a dog would bark, or a child cry, but evidently our presence was not discovered.

"On the edge of the bottom I deployed my companies into line, putting the citizens on the left, for quite a number of them had volunteered to come on and help us. You notice the big sloughs there beside the creek. The willows are thicker in spots. The command now moved forward rapidly. But the Indians discovered the attack as soon as we had started, and several of them put themselves across this creek, into that bend and, using the bank as a cover, opened fire. Some of our men swept past these and through the tepees, driving the Indians before them.

"At first we had passed the low ground and had taken the camp and appeared to have carried everything, but I soon found that the Indians had not given up. Some were in the willows working as skirmishers. Some rallied up yonder on that hill and started across the bottom to retake their herd. Others got behind trees and rocks and were picking off our men, one by one, and you know we couldn't spare any. Some of my officers were wounded already and myself among the number.

"At last I ordered the move back to this side, and we took this wooded point. Here we were a good deal exposed to the sharpshooters, and several officers were wounded, but we drove them back, defeated every attempt to assault our camp and inflicted great loss upon the Indians. Of course they yelled, crept up close at times, fired, and set the grass on fire, but all that time we were digging those trenches, and barricading, and giving to the hostiles as good as they sent.

"Next day, until night, parties of them were lurking about between me and my train. The attempt to fetch up the howitzer brought up a severe skirmish, and the howitzer was lost, but that night (evening of the 10th) the last of them gave us a sharp volley about eleven o'clock and cleared out. And here you find us, some killed, many wounded, but in no way discouraged. It was a gallant struggle. Who could have believed that those Indians would have rallied after such a surprise and made such a fight?"

Chapter XXXI

The engagement was a bloody one indeed, whether viewed from our own or the Indian side. "Captain William Logan, killed!" It is a short notice. Strangers are not much interested. "War is his business, general." He takes his chances. A brief biography, a two days' notice, the regular army record. But I am not satisfied with this. Heroic devotion to duty in Indian warfare saves lives by interposing one's own. Let the reader write the name of William Logan on the tablets of his memory and think again of those that loved him and have ever since suffered on account of his loss.

Lieutenant James H. Bradley fell in action to rise no more. You do not know his face? Never mind. In order to punish guilt, to secure peace, and serve faithfully his country, he gave the full measure—his life.

Lieutenant William H. English was wounded severely. All hoped that he might recover, but he did not. He lingered for several days, but before the campaign was over the news of his death came to us. Several other officers were wounded, some being hit two or three times. I do not name them in this narration lest I extend too much, though I feel toward them a strong desire to honor their service in some practicable way.

There were twenty-six others, soldiers and citizens, who laid their bodies away in this place of sepulcher. Their names are not before us, but, thank a kind Providence, comrades talk of them, and somebody keeps a place of love fresh and warm in remembrance of them.

Look on the other side. See these women's bodies disinterred by our own ferocious Bannock scouts! See how they pierce and dishonor their poor, harmless forms and carry off their scalps! Our officers sadly look upon the scene and then, as by a common impulse, deepened their beds and covered them with earth. Poor Jack Carleton hardly dared own his motive for his hard work in the burying of so many people with poor instruments and too little help. "Oh, General," he says, "let us bury them. The settlers on the Big Hole below will desert their ranches if we leave 'em here."

"But," says one, "aren't you disgusted with war when you walk thoughtfully over the bloody field after the battle?" Yes, yes, deeply disgusted, horror-stricken; but it is the same with railway accidents and with fire and pestilence. Indian warfare is horrid, but Indian massacres, outrages, and brutality are a thousand times worse.

Some such thoughts passed through my mind while we waited for the troops. It was on Sunday the 12th of August that the different groups of bodies were counted and buried or reburied. We had two Nez Perce scouts, or herders, drawn from the loyal Indians of the same name. These loyal ones, it should be remembered, though they constitute seven-eighths of the tribe, though industrious and true, though far in advance of the renegades, still are too often forgotten. Two of them, Captain John, and Old George, will be remembered by all who went across the continent in this long and persistent pursuit. They were capital herders of broken-down horses, could recruit the horses' strength and fetch them on when such seemed impossible. Old George had an Indian look but kept his hair short and always was good-natured. On all occasions when you spoke to him, his under lip, like that of some attentive and aged listener to a sermon, would drop. Old George was caught by the enemy some days after Gibbon's battle and held a prisoner for a few hours. When he had made his escape and returned, he told me that Joseph's men said, "Your men kill our women and children; your men are worse than the Indians." "Werte! Werte! Werte!" cries George; that is, "No, no, no! My chief is kind. I saw him and his staff officers tenderly bury the women and children with their own hands. They don't want to hurt the women and children." George said his captors were pleased to hear his account, and when he told them he carried no gun, they simply robbed him of his horse and let him escape.

We were ready to push on the 13th, turning southward, yet still keeping to the left of the main hostile trail. Our scouts had followed Joseph over a level stretch of country till they struck a spur of the Rocky Mountain ridge which divided the Bannock City valley from the Horse Prairie Valley. Across this ridge the hostiles had gone by an ugly gap, or pass, probably hoping to surprise our small advance detachment had it ventured on the direct pursuit. But we were too wary for them this time, and I had a firm belief that this southward turning of Joseph was only a feint to get me hopelessly in the rear. The Indians were as industrious as was General Lee after Gettysburg in attempts to deceive us as to their intentions. "We are going back by Salmon City," they gave out; or, "We are going back by a more southern trail." Always, going back! Old Captain John shook his head. "Werte, werte," he said. "Buffalo illahee. Joseph, Looking Glass, White Bird!" I agreed with Captain John, so I moved forward, keeping far to the left of the Indians' trail and did not forget that the said buffalo country was still eastward.

Captain Browning, with Lieutenants Wright and Van Orsdale and fifty men of General Gibbon's command, volunteered to accompany us a few marches. Gibbon's wagons lumbered off, going northward—hard, shaky things they were at best. They were carrying some thirty wounded men whom Doctors Alexander and Fitzgerald had made as comfortable as possible. Cheerful sufferers these. They were sure their friends would appreciate their gallant work and their sacrifice.

The first night towards Bannock City we named our clean and pleasant camp "Camp James H. Bradley." Our men hoped that the Bannock City people would retain for the spot the honored name we gave it.

At this camp we had word from two excited messengers that eight men, all citizens, had been murdered by Joseph's Indians in Horse Prairie.

The women and children had all been previously carried to the mining town just mentioned for safety. The Indians had also gotten two hundred and fifty of the finest American horses. This made us look despondingly at our poor cavalry, which had begun to mope so much as to excite the contempt of our frontiersmen. "Why don't you ride? Why not put your cavalry ahead every day? You never can catch Joseph if you don't!" How truthful, yet how sad, these very apparent facts. Still I never felt these taunts so deeply as I did those eastern witticisms which I read afterwards: "One day ahead!" "Beautiful panorama! Joseph and his Indians, Howard and his soldiers, running a race for the amusement of mankind!"

The 14th of August we had almost a review; women and children came out and watched the column for a mile, to the road junction, where we turned away from Bannock City toward the Horse Prairie country. These people were so happy to see us, so pleasant in their manner and speech, that I could not resist the temptation of stopping for a few minutes' conversation. Old people took me by the hand and pointed me out to their children as a soldier who had seen service. That little girl at Gettysburg town in July, 1863, who waved her white kerchief to the passing troops inspired them anew with heartiness; so did the Bannock City ladies cheer our little band by their happy faces and welcome words, such as before and afterwards during this campaign we did not often have the privilege of enjoying. The Bitterroot people, on the other hand, had stoutly blamed us for chasing the Indians to their neighborhood.

We were, the 15th, in that famous Horse Prairie Valley. We entered the valley at the lower end. The Indians had crossed it higher up. This was that wonderful country that Washington Irving described in his *Bonneville's Adventures*, containing the first historic account of the Nez Perces.

I do not know why it is that this valley appears to be such an exception to the lands of the interior in point of fertility. We encamped upon a grand farm, well fenced and well kept. Other farms stretched off in the broad valley, above and westward, as far as we could see. Good horses, good cattle, abundant grain and grass.

Our second camp was named for Captain Logan; this one for Lieutenant English. "Camp English" is to me memorable, for here I had two annoyances. First, from some volunteers who thronged my tent and severely called me to account for the way I did things in the military line. Second, from citizens who came from the next valley, situated to our right and across another spur of the mountains where old Fort Lemhi is located. They declared, "The Indians are upon us; they are surely turning back, they will destroy Salmon City. Colonel Shoup with sixty volunteers and Tendoy's Indians have retired to Fort Lemhi. We are forted up at the crossroads. Push straight for the fort and you'll have them. Indians went west, passed us at the crossroad, and are camped between that and the old fort."

I finally decided to yield a little to the pressure. I feared to move off much to the right for reasons before given, but I would take a trail to Lemhi Valley ten miles east of the hostiles and reluctantly began my preparations. To my great relief, a swift messenger reported after midnight, "The Indians have broken camp and rushed past the crossroad and its forting-up, doing us no harm, and have gone eastward as fast as they could." The annoyance was over, then, so that, as first intended, we made a drive for the Corinne and Deer Lodge stage road, hoping almost against hope to catch the Indians as they emerged from the mountains and attempted to cross this road.

Browning and his men kept on with us, while Captain Norwood, one of those gentlemen who seem born to command, was reported as not far behind with his company of the Second Cavalry. A few of the volunteers also continued with us. With a renewal of strength and energy, we pressed down the Corinne road. Joseph was yet west of this line, and was running, as Indians only can, to get past Dry Creek Station before we could possibly reach there.

The evening of the 17th of August brought us as far as Junction Station. Firewood three miles off; poor grazing, owing to the superabundance of alkali. Here fifty-five Montana volunteers, under Captain Callaway, came up—good, sturdy-looking men, well mounted and well armed. This camp was sort of a new place of departure, so we will defer an account till next chapter.

The morning was fine, with seldom a cloud in that sky. The dust was lying a little closer to the earth in the morning, and the air was clearer, O that we had the ability to get more rapid motion from the tired animals! A horse will look reproachfully at its rider, settle down into a solemn, hopeless gait, which neither scolding, kicking with boot-heels, nor use of whip will quick for more than five paces at a time.

Chapter XXXII

Take a map of the United States and look along the Union Pacific Railway till you find Corinne. Then follow a north line past Fort Hall, up almost to Virginia City, to a junction of stage roads, where we arrived on the night of the 17th of August. The road from Corinne to Virginia City is very direct. It supports a daily stage.

Junction Station, where we were encamped for a night and forenoon, was a lively place indeed. The stages and stage lines are institutions, *sui generis*. Passing through a wild, uninhabited region, a station is planted about every fifteen miles.

The hostler and his assistant live sometimes at their stable, where horses enough for the daily changes are kept, rested and fed. In places where hay is convenient or where there is a promise of crops in the near future as a reward of labor, the population increases to a hamlet. A fertile valley always stretches out with farm houses and often, as at Pleasant Valley some fifteen miles south, has its village, stores, saloons, and shops. Thus gradually a newly established stage line, here in the interior of the continent, is peopled by fully as many souls as such a dry region will support. We must not forget that much of this country is rough and mountainous, and that many valuable mines of gold and silver have been discovered and are worked not far from the road.

The morning was fine, with seldom a cloud in that sky. The dust was lying a little closer to the earth in the morning, and the air was clearer. O that we had the ability to get more rapid motion from the tired animals! A horse will look reproachfully at its rider, settle down into a solemn, hopeless gait, which neither scolding, kicking with boot-heels, nor use of whip will quick for more than five paces at a time.

This clear, fresh morning I had arranged for part of the animals to have a few hours' rest. This was the plan. A line of mountains leads off to the left, meeting another line at an angle at the head of Madison River. At this point is a charming lake, where an enterprising citizen, Mr. Sawtelle, had a fishery. East of this lake is the gap or pass in the ridge that forms the western gateway to the national park. It is called Tacher's Pass. It becomes evident to my mind that Joseph would attempt this pass. I hesitated at first, owing to the stage men. They thronged me. They declared that it was the nearest way to go by Dry Creek, plain road there; no trail in the straight line. I deliberated whether to take my main force by the straight line north of the mountain ridge to that key point or send thither a smaller body. I yielded, finally, to the positive reiterated information, chose Lieutenant Bacon, with forty picked men and Robbins with his Indians scouts and sent them direct to Henry Lake and Tacher's Pass, while I moved by the more circuitous road recommended. They had already been six hours on the march when I sent for Callaway, who had been a volunteer colonel during the war of the rebellion.

"Colonel, my horses are so jaded that I wish to rest them a few hours. My white scouts are beyond Pleasant Valley, and I wish to be nearer them. Will you escort me?"

"Oh, yes, General, I'll go and get the boys together. You know we have a little town meeting. We can't do as you do, just give orders and have done with it."

I said, "All right, Colonel. I wish to leave very soon."

In about ten minutes, the volunteers came in a body to see me, and I told them my wishes, as I had already done to their commander. They delayed a little to talk it over, and then said, "Come, boys, let us go and get our horses."

My team—for we were to ride to Pleasant Valley in a wagon—was ready. Lieutenant Fletcher, with his carbine in his hand, sat by me. Just as we were leaving, a fine-looking young citizen, fully armed and equipped and riding a handsome fresh horse, rode on beside the wagon. This gentleman, Fletcher, and the driver constituted the actual escort.

Joseph had reached the stage road beyond Pleasant Valley. Shortly we met a half-breed scout who had become frightened, lost his gun, and deserted. Next we met a citizen scout.

"What's the matter, my man?"

"My hoss is played," he replied.

"Well, come with us and try to keep up."

In a few moments more another scout came with a note from the front.

"Indians are on us! We are skirmishing with them beyond Dry Creek."

I looked back to see if I could catch sight of the dust of the volunteers. The road was dangerous, and Pleasant Valley itself would soon be threatened and might be taken. No volunteers! At last I sent back for the entire command. Lieutenant Wood's record reads: "General Howard leaves word for volunteers under Captain Callaway to come on as escort. They held a council of war and declined to do so until all their comrades had caught up and rested their horses."

The result was that the dangerous journey of eighteen miles was made without escort. The cavalry, increased by Norwood's company, overtook me at Pleasant Valley, and on we went to Dry Creek station. There we found that the Indians had already crossed the stage road several miles below and had gone on to Camas Meadows.

One of Robbins' scouts, the famous Buffalo Horn, who has since fought against us and was killed, crept with two others to the top of the mountain ridge and succeeded in getting upon a prominent point whence he could see Joseph's camp in the Camas Meadows below. They were fifteen or eighteen miles from the Dry Creek Station. Buffalo Horn sent one of the Indians with a message, "Joseph and all his Indians are here." How confident I then felt!

Bacon and Robbins ahead of Joseph, and my cavalry only eighteen miles behind and on the direct trail! If it were possible, I would reinforce Bacon, but he is seventy miles off.

"He can annoy and stop them, if he cannot do more!" I exclaim.

It was after dark when at the end of some twenty-eight miles we came to Dry Creek. A fine-appearing man, apparently over sixty years of age, saluted me. He used so good English in conversation that I was surprised. He did not curse and swear or piece out every sentence with some crude provincialism. He had been a sea captain, was a native of Maine, evidently well educated and well bred. "Uncle Mac" knew every path in that country. The quartermaster arranged with him for forage, wood, and for guiding me in the morning. He told us that the Indians had done great mischief along the stage road. They had destroyed Shoup's train of wagons, killed several men, broken up a station and run off the stock.

The cavalry horses were indeed slow in their progress, and the command had been much reduced by Bacon's detachment. The volunteers were behind at Pleasant Valley, and the footmen at least a day's march farther in the rear, so that the general aspect of things affected our best officers quite unpleasantly. That night my bright hopes were greatly dampened in consequence of a formal remonstrance against further progress till the Infantry should join. But I decided that we must not let this opportunity slip, so with the aged guide to lead us, at dawn the next day we broke from the stage road to the left and marched rapidly to Camas Prairie to the very camp the Indians had occupied when Buffalo Horn had looked down upon them. These are the famous Camas Meadows, where we gave most occasion for sport to our good friends in the east who make and love caricatures. It is where "Howard was surprised by Joseph and lost his mules!" How the enterprising young chieftain made a fair march, established his encampment for women, children, and surplus animals beyond our reach, and then, with his freshly stolen horses and picked men, returned in the night and surprised and circumvented our pickets and sentinels, presents in the following pages a subject of special interest.

Chapter XXXIII

Almost the only English writers who have succeeded in giving to my mind a clear conception of the location of troops and of their actual movements during military engagements are Carlyle and Thackeray. The former gives a careful description of the ground, the streams, the thickets, the villages, and the hills. He arranged the troops in a graphic way, so that if you had your pencil and sketch book you could map out the field of conflict. Thackeray is less formal and precise, but seizes upon prominent points and gives enough of minutia to help the imagination fill out the picture and does not, as do most writers, leave you with a confused impression. Perhaps, however, a confused impression is the true one to give concerning a surprise and the terrible din of arms like that of Sunday night, the 19th and 20th of August, 1877.

But as there was no confusion in the arrangements and operations after the dawn began, we will proceed to lay out our field and for observation drive down a few prominent stakes.

Conceive a broad, grassy meadow. You enter it midway from its western edge. To your left is a chain of hills, or mountain spurs. On the nearest height, Buffalo Horn and his comrade scout had sat and watched the meadow the day before. Straight ahead of you, and a half mile forward, were a few large stacks of meadow hay, from fifty to a hundred yards asunder. Just beyond the mown flats, from which the hay came, were two streams of water, running quite swiftly. Each stream was fringed with bushes higher than the men's heads. The two streams ran across our path and were nearly parallel with each other. Beyond, some two hundred yards, we touched the higher ground. The meadow sweeping off to the left, northward, becomes narrow near the mountain spur and extends eastward. Here on the higher ground, acres upon acres, for ten miles or more, are thrown into curious lava-knolls, each knoll so much like another that you cannot fix your whereabouts by the distinct and diverse features around you. Should you drive to pasture five horses over these wave-like knolls for a mile and then leave them for an hour to graze, it would be next to impossible to find them.

We took for the center of our night camp one of these knolls which was near to the meadow bottom. From my tent I looked back to the parallel streams. Across the first one, the Callaway volunteers encamped. Norwood's Cavalry and the forty infantry occupied the west side. The other companies of cavalry covered all approaches to my central position. This position was strengthened by knolls and lava-rocks on three sides, north, east, and south. We took plenty of room, and Mason, as was his custom, located the outposts and pickets well in advance of each front. The Indians had gone up the north sweep of the meadow, as we knew by their full trail, and when we arrived at the Camas, were in their camp fifteen miles in advance. Ahead of them, forty miles or more, was Henry Lake and the Tacher's Pass, which leads into the National Park; and as I had hoped, there likewise was Lieutenant Bacon and his command.

"Well," says Lieutenant Wood, as we were preparing for rest, "I'll take off my pants tonight, it is so safe a place."

Lieutenant Howard laughed and said, "I've loaned my pistol to a scout for tonight, so think likely the Indians will come back."

We all ventured, in spite of the latter's humorous prediction, to get between the blankets without the pantaloons. How quiet was the night; starlight, but no moon. It is wonderful, that stillness of a sleeping camp, so like death. I remember to have slept beside some soldiers at Antietam. They, with their heads covered, appeared sleeping soundly. In the morning I was shocked to find that they were the dead whom their comrades had laid there prepared for burial.

After midnight, nothing could be heard but the tread of a sentinel, the occasional neigh of a horse, bray of a mule, or bark of a startled dog. But suddenly, while the darkness was yet intense, there came a terrific noise, the rattling of musketry, a sharp, quick, multitudinous roaring, followed by the shrill Indian yell.

"Here they are!" we exclaim, as we all sit up in our blankets.

"Lie close or a stray bullet will hit you."

"Oh, no, I must be up for this. Nothing can be better, if they only will stay and give us a battle."

Our clothes and equipments were resumed quickly enough. Horses and men were ready by the time we were beyond our tent fly.

Callaway and his volunteers, not so used to sudden alarms, find it hard to get in order. One takes another's gun, some get the wrong belts, others drop their percussion caps. Their horses get into a regular stampede and rush in the darkness toward the herd of mules, and all the animals scamper off together, while the citizens plunge into the water above their knees and cross to the regular troops at a double-quick.

The Indians, under Joseph's lead, had crept in slyly between the pickets. They cut the hobbles of the bell-mares and took off the bells and were ready at the signal to give the herd a direction the instant the firing began. The yell was so terrible that mules tied to wagons tried to break loose, and the horses at the picket ropes did all they could to manifest their fear by pulling, pushing, and springing.

Joseph had so organized a few of his Indians and marched them toward camp as to make the picket think it was Bacon's party coming back. They, the Indians, came on by fours, steadily and very like our troopers, till challenged. Not being able to reply correctly, the picket fired upon them. This was doubtless the first sound. Then came the big firing and yelling, and then, quickly enough, the reply from our camp.

When I had advanced to Norwood's wagons, I could just get glimpses of the herd of animals making off beyond the first stream, but whether westward or northward could not be determined till the sun should get nearer to the rising.

The cavalry was put in readiness. Norwood's, Carr's, and Jackson's three companies under Major Sanford. With orders to pursue and recover the mules and horses that had been stampeded, away they went at a gallop, company after company, while we organized the camp for a possible attack from the knoll to the east of us. I had remaining Wagner's and Bendire's Cavalry and the fifty infantry under Captain Wells with a couple of pieces of artillery.

As we had to wait for results, our breakfast at the headquarters was prepared as usual, and we sat cross-legged upon the ground around our canvas table. I confess it was a little exciting to be aroused from sleep in this way, and so the bread and coffee had to be forced somewhat. The first messenger, a soldier, came galloping in and quickly dismounted.

"The compliments, sir, of Major Sanford. The mules have been overtaken, and some fifty to seventy-five of them have been brought back."

"Tell the major, all right. I do hope that he may get them all."

Another messenger galloped up in hot haste before we had finished breakfast.

"The major says, sir, the Indians have come back to attack in large force and are turning his left."

The remainder of the cavalry was soon brought out, with the infantry and the artillery, and moved on toward the threatened point. Through the irregular ravines, over the rough lava knolls, we crept along. A few volunteers who still had their horses followed the artillery from point to point till we came in sight of the line—our line retiring.

"What is the matter, Major?"

"We were rushing ahead, Carr in front, when we ran into a sort of ambush. The Indians began to get first around Norwood's left and then around Jackson over on the right. I thought as there were so many of them that I would draw back a little."

"But where is Norwood?"

"That is what I am trying to find out."

"Why, you haven't left him?"

"No, I sent to him the order at the same time as to Carr, but it seems that he has stopped."

"Well, let us return to him at once."

So, stretching out our line, making it as long and formidable as possible, we keep on.

"Come here, Carleton" (the citizen scout). "Where are Norwood and his company?"

"I left him over yonder, fighting hard, over there by the bushes."

I asked two or three others. One pointed in one direction, and another two or more pointed to the right or left, so confusing were those lava beds. But we continued marching northerly and easterly, ready to make a good fight if the enemy should turn back.

At last a little clump of thick cottonwood appeared and to its left a pile of rocks, more sharp-edged and craggy than the rest. Here, to our joy, was Norwood's company, dismounted. He had fought quite a battle, and the Indians had been beaten back. Some of our crazy mules, which we had recovered, were stampeded again and in the most senseless manner ran off in the wrong direction—to the Indian herd.

Here among the trees, we found Norwood's wounded, including Lieutenant Benson who, gallant fellow, had volunteered but two days before, his own company not being with us. It was now afternoon. The Indians were ahead eight or ten miles. They had stopped now and then to fight, but had made off again toward Henry Lake.

Not being prepared to advance farther that day, much to Buffalo Horn's disgust, I ordered the troops to camp.

We returned slowly with our six wounded men and one dead. "One dead!" It seemed strange to us there at the edge of the meadow in the middle of the continent, that but one should be taken, and that one the favorite orderly and bugler of Captain Jackson. He was tenderly prepared for burial. The grave was dug by his comrades. Mason read the touching Episcopal service beside it, while officers and men stood around with solemn and often tear-moistened faces. The farewell volleys were given, and the remains of young Brooks were left to rest there in loneliness till the resurrection.

Chapter XXXIV

When Miller heard that the cavalry had struck the Indians, his command instantly quickened with a surprising energy and seemed to move with the swiftness of fresh horses. He came up some forty-eight miles in less than twenty-four hours. Cushing, who had under General McDowell's instructions started with his company for San Francisco, now joined us. Captain Bonneville's interview with wild Indians on Horse Prairie and its picturesque ceremonial have been referred to. We had at Camp Benson, the second day after the battle of Camas Meadows, a repetition of the effects, if not of the ceremonies of that occasion. First a gay cavalcade, riding with the speed and easy grace of Indians, appeared in the distance. It proved to be the advance guard of a company of scouts from Fort Hall about one hundred miles to the southwest. Their feathers and fur strips were flying in the breeze, and the bright colors and tasteful decorations of each man and horse added to the brilliant effect. They carried a white flag in the front rank and rode grandly into our camp.

They brought messages from Captain Bainbridge, who himself joined us before midnight with the remainder of the scouts and his small guard of soldiers. Bainbridge brought the good wishes of General Crook, as well as an increase of our scouting force. Everybody knows that there are times when a little help, or even a word of cheer, goes straight to the heart. A thrill of joy ran through our weary and almost discouraged company at this accession.

The leader of these scouts, or the "chief scout," as he was called, deserves a special notice. He was a tall, pale man of fair proportions, being slightly deaf. A stranger would see little that was remarkable in him. Yet of all the scouts in our Indian campaign, none equalled this chief, Fisher. Night and day, with guides and without, with force and without, Fisher fearlessly hung upon the skirts of the enemy. The accuracy, carefulness, and fullness of his reports were a delight to one attempting to chase Indians across a vast wilderness.

For the remainder of the march our record will be swift and graphic. On the narrowest trails we were obliged to ride or march in single file, but habitually Mason or one of my aides rode by my side, and the command came on by twos. What did we not talk of? Science, art, literature, poetry, homes; yes, *homes*—theirs and mine. Every soldier will understand me when I say that in these conversations, whenever the word "home" is spoken, moistened eyes, gentle tones, and tender hearts are the rule and not the exception.

August 23rd. We had just crossed one of the branches of the Snake. We were nearing its headwaters. A mile or two beyond was a charming glade in the forest. This glade occupied the angle between the Snake and a small tributary. The animals must have all the grass, so we put our rough shelter and wedge-tents around the glade in the edge of the wood. The Bannocks, our scouts, had for their tepees a slight knoll near the water, not far from the general's bivouac. Buffalo Horn came and asked if the Indians might have a dance.

"Oh, yes, let them dance."

The echo of the wild singing, the weird shapes passing the fire during the dance, and the actual sense of danger after Joseph's late night attack appeared to impress the whole command with a feeling of apprehension, almost a panic. Added to this, the general was intending to wake the command at two o'clock, so by a forced march we could come upon Joseph's heels before he passed through the Tacher's Gap into the Yellowstone Park, and therefore an unusual stir of preparation was kept up. It was a night to be remembered. The neighing of the horses and the braying of the mules, one occasionally giving a high and prolonged screech, sounded during this still night ten times louder than usual.

About midnight, after the war dance and its council had subsided, Buffalo Horn and a thick-set, semi-savage half-breed called Raine came to headquarters and asked for authority to kill our Nez Perce herders, Captain John and Old George, and one other Indian of the tribe. Raine said George and the other Indians were traitors, that they had rejoiced openly at Joseph's success in surprising our mule herd, and that old John was a Nez Perce and ought to die.

We had George brought forward to face his accusers. He was so frank and evidently so honest that the story against him was not for a moment believed, and Buffalo Horn was denied the small favor of killing the three. He was very angry in consequence and never quite forgave me for this refusal. The third Indian may have been guilty. At any rate, he so much feared these suspicious and exacting Bannocks that he escaped into the forest that night and went back to Kamiah. But the jolly Captain John and the demure George, herding and bringing up the played-out horses from day to day in a wonderful manner, remained with the command to the close of the campaign.

How vast appeared this opening, this immense prairie, into which the column emerged from the forest at peep of day! Miles of tall grass; yonder, straight ahead, the mountain ridge, rough and irregular; a beautiful lake off to the left and north.

"That must be the gap, Tacher's Pass," says Wood.

"Oh, yes, and sure enough there is an Indian camp where the smoke rises," Mason quickly replies.

Our scouts and advance guard are close on them. "Let us ride." So we did, as fast as the poor horses could get on. Finally, the command had mastered the stream, ditches, and unexpected gulches that turned us off wearily to the right and left, and we came to the mouth of the famous pass.

"Well, General," says Chief Robbins, "we found 'em gone. Fisher and his Indians have followed on through the gap." Being thus eluded again, the greatest discouragement seized upon officers and men as they were put into camp that day. They appeared to themselves much like a poor dog watching the hole from which the badger had just escaped.

Bacon and his party, not seeing any Indians at or near Henry Lake on his arrival there, had turned back and were obliged to complete a junction with us by a stern chase. What a disappointment! Bacon had come into full view of

181

the beautiful lake and the pass just beyond, two days before the Indians rushed through. If Bacon only could have known! If the cowardly messengers only had gone to him, instead of returning to me with a statement that they could not find him our tedious work might have terminated at this point.

Fisher, with the Indian scouts, was still pursuing. "They are not far ahead," I said to myself and issued orders to move. "We cannot, we cannot, General! Come, look at your soldiers, look at their clothing, ragged already and tied with strings, look at their feet, some barefooted, and the most with shoes so badly worn that in one or two days they will be gone. The ice froze an inch in our basins last night, and we have no overcoats, nothing but thin blankets now falling to pieces. There are no spare blankets for nights like these." "You can go no farther," says Doctor Alexander. The inspector, the aides, the quartermaster, and the other officers echo the sad response, "You can go no farther."

The general decided to telegraph for instructions, sending fifty miles to the nearest station, then suspended his orders and changed his plans; for, in view of these terrible facts, what else could be done? It will be remembered that this was almost the only halt for upwards of two months.

Virginia City was seventy miles away. "Take the best team you can find, Guy, and I will go and get clothing and supplies. Let Cushing and Norwood, with their companies, proceed to Fort Ellis and take a resupply by way of Crow Agency and join us again two hundred miles on, while the main body rests here for four days, keeping its scouts close to the Indians and well informed of their movements." The needs of the command were written out, and with such memoranda Captain Adams, as quartermaster, Lieut. Howard, and I set out. We had a pretty good team and a good driver. The stout wagon wasn't made for comfortable riding, but it could rumble over small and large boulders and across acres literally sowed with stones. We were so exhausted that it was a comfort to change, as Mason says, from the "clothes-pin method," to ride even in a springless lumber wagon. Thus we were pulled on, all day and all night.

Before noon, the 24th, we crept out from under the seat, from fitful dreams and a sort of make-believe sleep, to catch a glimpse of a few houses. Soon we reached the town, a mining village planted here in the midst of a wilderness of hills and mountains.

"Plenty of stores, such as they are," says Guy.

Imagine the delight of traders at this visitation, for shoes, clothes, and blankets we must have. We nearly bought them out. Our jaded cavalry horses were remembered, and a goodly supply of fresh animals were ordered from the most accommodating of ranchers, and I fear also from the shrewdest of jockeys.

"Horses, is it?" asked a bystander. "Why, yes, I have an abundance on my ranch, all in good order, and well broken to the bridle and saddle."

You should have seen these same horses when Indians, frontiersmen, and packers tried to put on the bridle and the saddle. Such a pitching and plunging, hooting and yelling, running and falling, made one think of danger ahead from something beside Indians!

After a few hours' work at Virginia City, we set out on the return. The Madison and the Jefferson are two mountain peaks near the grand dividing ridge, not far from Henry Lake. They are also the names of two mountain streams, tributaries of the Yellowstone. Our wagon had to ascend to the mountain divide along the bank of another stream, the Galatin, crossing it several times. Its water is very clear, tumbling and rustling over its strong bed, hereabouts always wide, but shallow enough to ford.

After crossing the divide, as we descended the clear woodland slope, we soon caught a glimpse of Henry Lake and then of our camp, which during our absence had been moved around to the side of our approach. What a grand view was before us! Nothing more picturesque! The mountain ridges, the broad meadows between, and the lake at the foot of our glacis, with a small city of tents and temporary shelters in the foreground. These were flanked on either side by the numerous horses and mules that were grazing peacefully along the shores.

After our one hundred and twenty miles ride, we find at camp telegrams like the following:

"Where Indians can subsist, the army can live.... The country and the government expect you to do your duty. No troops near enough to take your place. Continue the pursuit. If you are tired, General, put in a younger man and return to Oregon, but the troops must go on."

How hard to bear some things are! The general wasn't tired, of course, nor did he mean to be tired. His business was to die in his tracks if need be. But the chafing, stern order to the general worked like a charm upon the command. Officers and soldiers, now resupplied, were ready to a man. "We will go with you to the death." It was worthwhile to bear a little chagrin in order to awaken such a loyal spirit.

Beyond us, then, setting forth bright and early the Monday morning of the 27th of August. That beautiful camp by the lake, where in weariness, poverty, and heartsickness we had been halted for four days, where we renewed our supplies and were finally inspirited by a gentle reprimand, we named for our quartermaster "Camp Ebstein." Lieutenant Ebstein's equanimity had never failed him. He came speedily out of difficulties. This name headed the numerous letters and reports which left this neighborhood and which, like water coursing from banks of snow in springtime, always flow from a halted camp.

Our column looked well. Even the horses had picked up a little, and the movement was passably brisk as we wound like a silvery serpent around the lake and passed through the mountain gorge to new fields and to dangers still unknown.

Chapter XXXV

Officers and men were naturally enough on the *qui vive* as our little pursuing column made its way through the western gateway and rough avenue into the grand National Park.

The smallness and sparseness of the trees were the first things noticeable. The level, lengthy openings, the beautiful mountain streams, the dryish, grassy bottoms and occasional bubbles of land named "buttes"—these, for the first three days, afforded a pleasant change. Then the extraordinary geyser landscape, with its vast seas of almost barren sulphur-crust, burst upon our view.

Here we met that unfortunate geyser party which caused at the time so much public interest on account of having fallen, during a pleasure trip, into the hands of the hostile Indians. The first man we encountered—breathless, hatless, almost starved, with his feet wrapped in rags—was so wild that he could give no intelligible account of himself. "Three Indians fired on me, and I got away. They are all killed. The rest all killed!" The next one was Mr. Oldham, a tall, stout young man with very straight, black hair. He was shot through both cheeks and of course could hardly speak. The very next day we encountered the third, a lawyer, Mr. Cowan, who was twice wounded and left on the ground for dead. Cowan revived enough to be able to explain the situation and give important information: "The Indians surprised us. Our camp was not far from here—over there where the broken wagon is. At first they treated us kindly. Two of our number got away into the bushes when the Indians fired at us for sport. Then they took our horses. Abandoning me while unconscious, they carried off my wife and a young lady, her sister, and their brother."

It was not long before we found the body of the missing one of this party. The women and their brother were spared by Joseph and were afterward rescued.

We named this camp of the 30th of August for the wounded lawyer, "Camp Cowan." Lieut. Wood in his notes called it the sulphurous camp.

A woody height, or butte, just to the south of us furnished a picket post with a good outlook. North of this butte were several hot springs. These springs were only a few feet across the mouth and appeared like wells of water. They betrayed their presence by constantly sending up clouds of steam.

As I sat on the crest of the picket's butte, a barren sulphur plain stretched off southward, presenting here and there very regular mounds of slight elevation. Here, for the first time, my eye was delighted by the curious spectacle of those water spouts which we now call geysers. I do not wonder that they are named as if they had life, as Giant, Giantess. Some of them, for fifteen minutes at a time, would throw jets of water straight up into the air. The action was like that of a steam fire engine with its hose, the nozzle being held erect; the important difference was that the geyser really propelled a column larger than a hogshead. It was of course the distance that gave these geysers the appearance of smaller spoutings. During the short time before sunset, officers and soldiers, except the pickets, guard, and herders, were allowed to investigate these strange phenomena. The most curious results of this intense chemical action, so near the crust as to be constantly breaking through and overflowing, were found also in occasional deep chasms, at the bottom of which was a muddy fermentation like that in the plasterer's lime bin in active operation. The mud was of various colors, from the clayey white, through varying shades of red, purple, and brown, to the blackest muck.

In one corner, with a crater-like opening, the dark, hot mud was in perpetual motion. It was thrown up and then fell back from ten to twenty feet, producing an effect of a pit of sulphurous smoke and darkness and noise not easily described.

There is no end of surprises in this wonderful park. Following the Indians' crooked trail after the march was resumed, our scouts led us of a sudden against a mountain which bristled with extensive forests of small trees. The trees had been killed and hardened by the forest fires which had swept hither and thither through them. By a zigzag course everything in the command, except the wagons, managed to get to the mountaintop. But how were the wagons ever to be hauled up the height? If you conceive of a man so constituted, broad-shouldered and deep-chested, sufficiently tall, as to have a weight of two hundred and twenty-five pounds without corpulency, with a bearing such as to make the roughest frontiersman obey his slightest command and so plucky as to regard obstacles as only made to be overcome, you have imaged Major Spurgin of the Twenty-first Infantry, our chief of the pioneer battalion.

While we camped for the night just beyond the beautiful Mary Lake in the top of the mountain, a practical wagon road was made by Spurgin's pioneers, and the wagons which had joined us in Montana were brought on so as not to detain the march of the next day.

We were next in camp on the Yellowstone, near one of those noisy, dirty, heated smoke holes such as I have mentioned, bearing the descriptive name of "Muddy Springs." The Yellowstone bottom broadens out in this neighborhood, giving to us plenty of grass and a good encampment, notwithstanding the immense herds of Chief Joseph which had here just preceded us.

We received news at this point from Fisher, in the shape of a discharged soldier whom the Indians had captured, and whom Fisher's scouts had recaptured and brought in. He pointed out the direction the Indians had taken. They crossed the Yellowstone and went up the river toward Yellowstone Lake quite a distance and then struck off along a tributary creek in the direction of that wonderful river with an odorous name—Stinking Water, and then, turning square to the left, endeavored with much detention and loss of animals to make their way through a dense, tangled forest.

They left the Stinking Water trail doubtless because Joseph heard that the prairie ahead of him had been set on fire and that some of General Crook's troops were coming up from that direction. By this information my command was saved nearly a hundred miles of the circuitous following, the toughest journey which this pursuit occasioned, for we traced the chord of the arc which the astute young chieftain was forced to describe.

Next there came to us here evidences of a Bannock treachery which culminated a year later in the murders and outrages of the Bannock campaign.

At the foot of the mountain, near Mary Lake where Spurgin made his zigzag road, forty horses belonging to citizen teams which were doing the transporting work for us were turned out to graze. During the night these horses all mysteriously disappeared. The quartermaster's clerk, encountering some Bannock scouts who had suspiciously lingered in the rear, was treated to very rough language by them. I sent at once a small detachment of mounted soldiers, who soon returned to camp with ten of the Indian scouts as prisoners.

Their leader, a half-breed and brother to the Raine who had desired to murder old George and Captain John, was cross and mutinous in his manner and language. I had them all disarmed and their handsome horses and rifles taken from them. I found also on inquiry that all the Bannock scouts, except one or two, had deserted the brave Fisher, had come back to the troops, and were planning to return to Fort Hall.

An old chief of the tribe soon begged of me to let the prisoners go free, assuring me of their innocence. I said, "What you say may be true, but Indians are good to hunt horses. They follow blind trails better than white men. Send out some of your young men and look up my lost horses. I will never set the prisoners free till the horses are brought back." The old man replied, "Yes, Indians good to hunt horses. I will send them." In a few hours twenty of the horses came galloping into camp, chased by his young Indians. Then, with the old man, they came to me and declared that these twenty were all they could possibly find. I said, "All right; I shall never let the prisoners go till I see the other twenty horses." The old Indian gave a grunt and shrug of the shoulders and left me. Soon I saw him mounted and then leaving camp with his party. That night the remaining twenty horses overtook us, and the prisoners were released except the leader, Raine, who was dispatched as a prisoner to Fort Ellis.

Under our new guide Irwin, the discharged soldier brought in from Fisher, we took our course across a mountain range; we pursued a route that our guide believed would be a fair wagon road. But, though the trail did lead in the right direction, it took us over such fearful steeps and across such deep and rough ravines with precipitous banks that it seemed utterly hopeless for our train of supplies ever to get through.

One canyon, "Devil's Canyon" near the remarkable Yellowstone passes, proved so much worse than all the others that my heart almost failed me as my poor horse worried his way into the water channel and up the crest to the opposite heights. I said to myself, "Impossible for wagons!"

These difficulties being in view, the troops gave up the wagon train, took what provisions they could carry with the pack train, and went on to cross the Yellowstone at Baronet's Bridge. The indomitable Spurgin was to get to that point if he could and then, bearing to the left, go on to Fort Ellis. If that was impracticable, he was to turn back and go to Ellis by another and much longer way. It was not till after the campaign was over that I found, to my gratification, that Spurgin had actually made a wagon road and brought his teams over the seemingly impassable chasms as far as Baronet's Bridge, and proceeded thence directly to Fort Ellis. So much for will, energy, and work!

At the river crossing the hostile Indians were already abreast of us, on the other side of the Yellowstone, and our scouts found too abundant evidence of their usual murder and rapine for twenty miles down the river to the Mammoth Falls, where a raiding party from Chief Joseph had met and robbed some wagons and burned a store.

The Baronet's Bridge, a slight structure stretched across the roaring torrent of the Yellowstone, had its further end so much burned by the raiders that it had fallen out of place and was not passable, so that we were allowed to rest three hours, long enough to repair the broken bridge.

Chapter XXXVI

In order to show where we were on the morning of September 6th, and where is Baronet's Bridge, we will again invite the reader's attention to the map. Find the southeastern point of the Grand National Park, then run the eye up the Yellowstone about twenty miles, and you have the location. Our bridge has just been finished. The beams, shortened by the fire, were tied to some heavy timber that was fortunately on hand. Mr. Baronet's house, the only one we had seen since Henry Lake, stood a few hundred yards away on Joseph's side of the river. It was appraised at three hundred dollars, and much of its lumber was brought to the river for replanking. The bridge, which was probably fifty feet above the water, extended from bank to bank, had but one intermediary support, and that fearfully near to demolition. As the first animals were started across the patched-up structure it trembled and swung laterally very perceptibly, but by a little setting of teeth and what a Chicago orator called "clear grit" on the part of our improvised bridgemen, in the short space of half an hour the work was done. Led horses, loaded pack-mules, and marching men had crossed the flood. I think we must have realized something of the feeling of the Israelites when they had reached the other shore of the Red Sea and looked back. This joy at a great obstacle overcome is, indeed, a living force in leading men on to success.

At the Mammoth Falls, twenty miles below, where the store was burned, there were signs that Gilbert's Cavalry had been there and suddenly departed. Lieutenant-Colonel Gilbert, with two companies, came so near as that to forming junction with us, but the proximity of the Indian raiding party and want of knowledge of our whereabouts swung him off by a remarkable detour a hundred miles to our rear. He then pursued us for days, till his horses were exhausted and his command worn out with the chase. He finally turned back to Fort Ellis.

Cushing, whom I had sent with foot and horse to Fort Ellis, had been shorn of his cavalry to reinforce Gilbert, yet he bravely took up his supplies and pressed his remnant, now but two foot companies, down by the Crow Agency in order to head off Joseph when that Indian should emerge from the mountain gaps into the valley of Clark's Fork. Cushing did not succeed in anticipating the Indians, but he brought up the supplies in time to prevent any delay of the pursuit by our main body. Clark's Fork cuts the Yellowstone after its big bend and forms almost the only practicable crossing in that quarter.

As we wound along the sharply-marked tributary valleys which here run at right angles to the yawning river, we found a bevy of mounted frontiersmen watching us from knolls and heights which were in plain view to our left. Cautiously the horsemen approached and at first showed a singular reluctance to join us or communicate. The partisan leader is apt to dislike the regulars, is probably jealous of his independence. At last I learned that the greater portion of the hostiles were thirty miles from us, trying to make their way among the mountains and forests to Clark's Fork. They were avoiding the Soda Butte Canyon, which is a shorter cut across a mountain range that rises more and more grandly to the left of our pathway. This Soda Butte Canyon in itself afforded a magnificent picture. The little land bubble, which has some symptoms of soda about it, lifted itself at the entrance to the canyon.

Select grass, a variety of small trees, a clear mountain stream, and then a gradual rising by slopes, steppes, and precipitous evergreen acclivities to the right and left, and finally, old castellated formations, towering above you from two to three thousand feet in height—select these features and arrange them with an artist's skill; thus you may give a faint picture of this wonderful region.

Judge of our joy to find at the famous Soda Butte Silver Mine, near the back entrance to this canyon, some twenty miners still hovering about their new crushing mill, resolute and well-armed, ready to defend their treasure with their lives. George Houston, one of the miners, was a favorite and already celebrated guide. Houston and all his companions were employed to scout the country and, if possible, bring us upon Joseph before he could get past the point where we should debouche into the before-mentioned Clark's Fork Valley.

Indeed, we made a run for this point, but fortune or Providence was against us. The Indians' big trail, now in plain view, swept down the valley, and not a soul was in sight for ten miles and more.

George Houston knew a curious and shorter path just beyond the Indians' course, which had the significant name of "Lodgepole Trail." Away we went then to follow where the Crows fled from the victorious Sioux and strewed their narrow forest road with lodgepoles which, nicely peeled and pierced, indicated their previous wealth. The scouts, many of them who had fresh horses, followed the hostiles directly for thirty miles around, while we accomplished the twenty-five across.

The terrible work of our enemy was developed by the scouts. Four miners were encamped in the valley. They had with them horses, guns, mining implements, in brief, their all. Three, begging for their lives, were killed outright, while one, a young German and a recent immigrant, dreadfully wounded and losing everything he had in the world, escaped. How my heart ached for him as he tried in broken English to make me understand his deplorable situation. A part of our white scouts, having with them, I think, one or two Indians, coming suddenly upon Joseph's last bivouac at the foot of a broad mountain ascent, surprised and killed and scalped an old, ailing warrior who had been left behind by Joseph that morning. Twice before had our scouts committed a similar savagery. It is hard to make them understand any other war principle than "a scalp for a scalp."

Perhaps, as the Quakers allege, the inconsistencies are all with us who profess to be a Christian people. If we do not believe in the savage operations of war, in taking life for life, property for property, in giving deceit for deceit, and in the inflictions of extreme injuries and penalties, why do we set the example?

However we, who are the nation's soldiers, may stumble over troublesome queries such as these, still we certainly do like to keep pace with civilized nations in mitigating the horrors and evils of war as much as lies in our power. The taking of life may be necessary, but the savage triumph and the savage tokens of triumph, such as fingers cut off and scalps severed from the heads of the dead and the dying, are certainly not. They fill our breasts with horror!

Chapter XXXVII

It was during this march from the Soda Butte mines to the foot of Clark's Mountain that we were watched by three unique, distinctive persons—a jolly half-breed, more French than Indian, an Indian of the Crow Nation, and a veritable, though timorous, American. They were couriers from General Sturgis who had ensconced themselves near the summit of different sightly hills till they had obtained unmistakable signs that our moving men were not Indians.

We were delighted to find that Sturgis, with six or seven companies of the Seventh Cavalry, was within fifty miles of us, and that the hostile Indians were surely between us and Sturgis. The latter, when the couriers left him, was just about to move to Hart's Mountain, with a view to block the only practicable pathway which led from us to the mouth of Clark's Fork.

It would be gratifying, indeed, if Sturgis only could know that our force was so near. His messengers had come out, not to meet our column, but to warn the miners, for none of my later couriers had succeeded in reaching his camp.

It was the 10th of September at dawn. Our small force, scattering out and leading up their horses a short distance at a time near the fresh Indian trail, began in earnest the ascent of the mountain.

"This is hard work," says Mason. "I don't know which is the worse, for me to walk or for my poor trembling horse to carry me."

Fletcher, pretty well blown, sits down with bridle in hand and, noticing the dead or half-alive ponies and an occasional deceased mule which the hostiles had killed and abandoned in their haste, exclaims: "What a pity General Sturgis could not have known of this trail and moved to yonder crest! The worn out rascals would have fallen an easy prey to his force and ours."

"True, but one must be behind the scenes to know everything."

This conversation indicates the situation. At the crest of the toilsome ridge an immense expanse of mountains, hills, valleys, and rivers broke upon our vision. An aide declared, "We're out of the woods at last!"

Hart Mountain, ten or twelve miles straight before us, is a single elevated peak. There we supposed Sturgis was waiting with his cavalry, or that he had already broken out upon the hostile flank as Joseph, with his people and herds, was attempting to pass.

Fletcher, with Chapman and Roque, the little Frenchman who came from Sturgis, set out at once for Hart Mountain, while our expert signalmen began to wave their flags furiously toward the mountain and watched with strained eyes, with telescope and field glass, for some return signal. But it was all in vain. General Sturgis, we afterwards found, getting information that the Indians were going toward the "Stinking Water" and probably misled by some treacherous Crows, had made a forced march off to our right in that direction just at the opportune moment, that is, opportune for Joseph and his followers. With consummate generalship the latter made a regular feint towards the odorous water, while he plunged into a forest which, to us, was apparently thick and impassable, and under its cover kept around the base of an immense ledge. He then passed into a narrow and slippery canyon without exposing a man to the view of General Sturgis. My command, discovering Joseph's ruse, kept the trail which Sturgis had been so near but had not seen. We finally slid down the canyon, many a horse in his weakness falling and blocking the way. The mouth of this canyon, which debouches into Clark's Valley, was not more than twenty feet across from high wall to high wall. And one may imagine the scene of cavalry, infantry, and pack mules crowding through it and admire the quick wit of an Indian who had the hardihood to try the experiment and break the almost impassable roadway.

Near our second encampment from this point, Sturgis, who had at last turned back, soon overtook us. Though

Sturgis and I were disappointed, we formed at once a close combination. I was delighted to observe the elastic tread of his horses, which could in a very few minutes walk away from ours. Noticing the general's feeling of disappointment at Joseph's adroit escape and also believing that this feeling would be a spur to extraordinary exertion, he was given a slight addition to his force—some scouts, artillery, and cavalry, picking the horses—and placed in command of the swift advance. With considerable reluctance and much protest by Wood and Guy against it, I myself remained behind to form junction with Cushing, who was coming from our left, and to bring up the reserve and supplies. But my personal chagrin at Joseph's success was soon relieved. After Sturgis had crossed the Yellowstone by the South Fork road and reached the heights beyond, the Indians were before him in full view. The sight of the game we know is inspiriting. I need not say that he charged the foe, fought a gallant battle, and had a running squabble with them through the canyons and rocky barrens, even to the Musselshell. He captured hundreds of ponies and delighted not a few of his Crow allies with the opportunity afforded them to steal. It seemed to matter little to them whether they took from Indians or white men. They were made happy just to steal!

It was in this Clark's Valley where was drawn up and sent to General Miles, who was then located far below our front at Tongue River, the letter which was to apprise him of the situation. Colonel Merrill, of Sturgis' command, seeing me about to send a messenger, said: "Why not use a boat down the Yellowstone?"

"Sure enough," I replied, "if we can find one."

The boat was found, and the dispatches were sent, in duplicate, by boat and by a horseman. Some twelve or fifteen miles from the ford—I had just come into camp the evening of the 13th of September—I received a brief note from Fletcher, who had gone with Sturgis: "We have struck the enemy and are fighting."

I rested from six to nine at night and then set out with fifty cavalrymen. It was a bitter-cold night. In the darkness and swamps our guide soon lost his head, and we were obliged to pick our own difficult way without his help. Chilled through and shivering, at last the tired escort wore out the night. At sunrise we crossed the Yellowstone and reached the battlefield by half-past ten in the morning.

It was the most horrible of places—sage brush and dirt and only alkaline water, and very little of that! Dead horses were strewn about and other relics of the battlefield! A few wounded men and the dead were there. To all this admixture of disagreeable things was added a cold, raw wind that swept over the country. Surely if anything was needed to make us hate war, such after-battle scenes come well in play.

Sturgis and Sanford, already twenty miles further on, were declared to be in hot pursuit. But as the Indians, who were running night and day and still had remounts, had managed to outstrip Sturgis and get away beyond hope from his movement, my only remaining chance of ultimate success lay in my confidence that General Miles, now notified, would strike diagonally across our front and reach the Missouri before the hostiles. Should they succeed in crossing that river, the British line [at the Canadian border] was too near to afford much prospect of thereafter dealing a successful blow. So Sturgis was requested to rest for a while at the Musselshell till I had gathered the remainder of my somewhat scattered troops upon the left bank of the Yellowstone. Then we would move forward together.

Chapter XXXVIII

It was a charming place, on the bank of the Yellowstone some ten miles below the Clark's Fork crossing, where the escort, Mason, Cushing, Sanford, and Lieutenant Otis came together. We were to push down the Yellowstone to the old Baker's Battlefield—a ground already known as the place of a fierce engagement with the Sioux several years before. We were to meet some of our supplies of clothing and goods coming thither from Colonel Buell's post, which was forty miles to the south, and rejoin Sturgis at the Musselshell and follow to the Missouri. We trusted to General Miles to deliver one more blow to the swift-footed hostiles.

Our Yellowstone camp, at which a part of us remained a whole day, the 16th of September, became a lively one. Here I received a note from Colonel Gilbert explaining his futile chase of us. Here, as we sat on the ground around our square canvas, each contributed something to the news.

Fletcher described Sturgis' battle and pursuit. I asked, "Why didn't the artillery do something?"

"Oh, General, horses so played out that one piece never got up, and the other only succeeded in putting in one shot!"

"Why didn't the General head them off in the canyon?"

"Why, the rocks were too precipitous, but the trial was made. The Indians were off before we could get in there and hinder them."

"What has Mason to say?"

"Not much. I found Cushing all right. He was vexed enough because Norwood (commanding the cavalry company) was taken away from him at Fort Ellis, and all sorts of hindrances were thrown in his way."

"Did any couriers come up?"

"Yes, sir, that fellow whom you sent to Sturgis did not go to him at all, but went to the Crow Agency, and he is now back. He doubtless saw those messengers and scouts who were lying dead along the Indian trail near Hart's Mountain, became frightened, and so made off."

"What have Wood and Howard to say about the people who ran from us so rapidly this morning?"

"I think, General," says Wood, "the scouts have overtaken them, and they have come back. At first they took us for Indians. Another party was hidden in the brush, one of them being a woman. Some of them are ranchmen, and some were passengers on the coach that Joseph captured. The Indians were at this very place when Sturgis' scouts first discovered them. The sight of him made them leave."

My son said, "I went as far as the second house below. The buildings were burned to the ground. The remnants of the old stage coach were lying around. I learned that the Indians, in wild sport, took an active drive in the coach before they dismantled it and destroyed the mails."

Such are specimens of the table chat. Of course there was fun as well as serious talk, but habitually the songs, the stories, and the jokes had their place after the dinner.

This was a prairie-like country, much of it very dry and dusty but vast in appearance. Low mountain ranges afforded here and there landmarks in the distance. In order to show what energy can do, I may tell how Major Earnest left the Yellowstone camp the 16th, rode fifty-seven miles, obtained teams with supplies, and drove them back thirty-seven miles to a junction with us before ten p.m. of the next day; and how Fletcher and Otis, by remarkable forced marches, brought up further necessaries to the moving column.

The 20th found us in camp a few miles below General Sturgis on the Musselshell. It was a beautiful camp on a fine plateau, like an oasis in the vast treeless desert, adorned with handsome shrubbery, abundant grass, clear running water, with fish plentiful enough for every soldier's mess.

Here it was that we received the return messenger from General Miles, who was stationed at Tongue River. Merrill, one of Sturgis' battalion commanders, was looking over the maps of this country before Miles' messenger arrived. He said, "Miles is ambitious. He will start at once and head

Joseph off before he gets to the Missouri. I know the country." Then, pointing out a diagonal course which extended from Tongue River to near Carroll on the Missouri, he said, "He will go across there! He will never allow such an opportunity for a brigadiership to escape him." I said, "Yes, if he gets his message in time." A few hours later, glad, hearty tidings from Miles did come. He promised to move at once and indicated how long it would take him to accomplish the march.

I know of no period of my life when I needed sympathy and encouragement more. These dispatches from a brave officer and a tried friend were full of cheer, and I shall never forget the lift they gave me nor grudge to him a grateful acknowledgment for them.

Our movement was much enlivened, not only by this news but by the presence of the Seventh Cavalry under the command of Sturgis. It spurred up our way-worn command, and helped it to keep in sight of our new friends, but as Sturgis declared in one of his notes to me, "We must not move too fast, lest we flush the game." So I recognized the necessity and for a time moderated the rate of marching.

We knew from a long experience that the Indians watched well to the rear and moved very much as we did, keeping one and two and sometimes three marches ahead. When we stopped to rest they did so; when we moved short distances they shortened their journeys. Therefore we planned for the same operation to continue. Meanwhile I endeavored, through our numerous scouts, to keep informed where the Indians actually were.

On the twenty-seventh Sanford's weary cavalry, now being replaced by Sturgis', bade us goodbye just as we were entering the famous Judith Basin.

Robbins and nearly all of our old scouts went back. George Houston, the National Park guide, and his companions continued with us and followed the Indians very closely. Then, in this broad and open country, trails began to diverge, multiply, and grow dim. Between Houston and the mouth of Judith River, where it flows into the Missouri, thousands of acres of the prairie were on fire. The new trails were annihilated. Great uncertainty began to press upon me, but I had resolved to go at least as far as the Missouri and to carry out my orders "to chase the Indians to the British lines."

One day Colonel Mason and Doctor Alexander were riding near me. I had in my heart earnestly petitioned for God's help, expressing a sentiment that I hope was sincere: "If thou wilt grant my request, do so, I beseech Thee, even at the expense of another's receiving the credit of the expedition."

I said to Mason, as my spirits grew lighter, "Colonel, I believe that we shall capture these Indians yet."

Alexander asked, with a hearty laugh, "What is more hopeless? There isn't one chance in a million for Miles. I cannot see, General, where you found your hope."

"All right," I answered, "mark my words and see if I am not right!"

Mason hoped, with a slight despondency of tone, that my prediction might prove true. It was not long after this conversation before some message-bearers hove in sight. We had not met horse or man for several days. A manifest excitement quickened the motion of the entire command as two horsemen were discerned coming on at a steady gallop and every moment approaching nearer.

"Well! What news?"

"A dispatch from Fort Benton for General Howard or Colonel Gibbon." The courier dismounted and handed me a note. It informed me that the Indians had crossed the Missouri at Cow Island, had a fight with some of Gibbon's men, burnt a freight-train of wagons, but had all moved over and gone. Miles reached the mouth of the Musselshell, twenty miles or more below, crossed the Missouri there, and was still in pursuit. Such in substance was the startling information brought.

It did not take us long to pass the next fifty or sixty miles to Carroll. Leaving headquarters and part of my command with Sturgis and Mason, I took passage on the little steam "Benton," which, doubtless by General Miles' kind provision, was tied to the shore and made subject to my orders.

The Artillery battalion under Miller sprang on board, along with my two aides and a few scouts.

We steamed up the river as rapidly as possible. The Missouri is shallow at the season when we were there, and our vessel often ran aground. I was curious to see how the river could be navigated with so little water. Soon I noticed that when the steamer struck a sand bar, as she often did, she put out her immense wooden arms, which are vitalized by a steam windlass, and lifted herself little by little over into deep water.

Cow Island was reached early the next day. With a small escort of seventeen mounted men, I made a push along the large Indian train with the hope of reaching Miles or communicating with him. Dispatches which I had received at Carroll on the Missouri were confirmed at Cow Island by a messenger from him. The tidings were to the effect that his movement had not yet been discovered by the hostiles and that he hoped still to be able to strike them in flank. The messenger had left him near a line of abrupt hills, which were called "the Little Rockies," and he was moving then northwesterly towards the upper extremity of the Bear Paw Mountain Range. With this man for a guide and the Nez Perce herders Captain John and George for interpreters and keen-scented scouts, we followed the Indian trail for a time, but finally deviated from it, hoping to intersect Miles' course. The weather was fearfully cold and the ground covered with a fresh coating of snow. Fortunately for me, Sutherland, the correspondent, had wrapped me at starting in his own enormous great-coat. It had a warm hood secured to the collar; this attachment, occasionally thrown over the head, kept me very comfortable.

We found plenty of wood the first night, but the water was alkaline and made every man who drank it sick, so that the second day was attended with great delay and discomfort.

Just as we passed the bluff at the north end of the Bear Paw and had been some time following Miles' plain trail, and while Lieut. Wood was amusing himself in taking the skin and nice cuts from a young buffalo which he had killed, two very handsome, well-mounted scouts were met. They had descended from a neighboring height where they had been watching a party of Indians who were hunting antelope between Miles' position and theirs, so they told us. They declared that these Indians were hostiles. They said also, "We have carried the news of a battle going on when we left, from Gen. Miles to your troops with Sturgis and Mason, and have got back this far." Lieut. Howard declared to them that he didn't believe that the hunters were hostile and laughed at their fears. One of the scouts became angry at this and said, "We are going back to your troops. We know as much about Indians as you do."

This colloquy had proceeded thus far, before I had come close enough to hear. The excitement was soon quieted, and the scouts invited to join us and ascertain whether the Indians were hostile or not.

This they did, though their horses, doubtless partaking of their riders' feelings, appeared very nervously inclined during the next ten miles. It was difficult to keep them in the column. The distance from the head of Bear Paw to Miles' camp was not more than twelve or fourteen miles. Still it became quite dark before we had approached near enough to catch a glimpse of it.

Chapter XXXIX

October 4, 1877, we not only encountered the messengers who knew of Miles' engagement, but also another curious and solitary courier by the name of "Slippery Dick." He was approaching us to rejoin General Miles, with his tall, black horse at a rapid gait, having returned from Sitting Bull's camp by the way of Tongue River. He described the position of the famous Sitting Bull. He believed that this chieftain had about twelve hundred warriors and stated that he was in British territory not more than forty or fifty miles from us toward the northeast. It appeared evident that when he encountered our troops, Joseph was attempting to cross the line and form a junction with Sitting Bull. Our several parties were now consolidated, and we rode rapidly toward the point where the messengers had last seen Miles.

Suddenly, as we neared the brow of a hill, numerous small fires made their appearance, scattered over the breadth of a mile. Continuous musketry firing was heard. At first we feared that in the darkness the outposts had mistaken our party for hostile Indians and were therefore firing at us, but soon we found that it was not so. It was the Indians in the ravine who, from their holes and trenches, were firing at Miles' investing forces.

When Miles heard that I had come forward and was approaching his camp, he came out to meet me. We were guided to his tent, where he explained to me the situation.

The journal of my aide-de-camp for the next day says: "October 5th. Firing is continued by our troops, with an occasional reply from the enemy. They are evidently saving their ammunition for a siege.

"About eleven o'clock, Captain John and George were sent into Joseph's camp with a flag of truce. General Howard and Colonel Miles were awaiting their return, near the advance rifle pits. After much communication, Joseph, at 2 p.m., agreed to surrender on condition of good treatment, and White Bird said, 'What Joseph agrees to is all right.' ...Joseph, first offering it to General Howard, delivered his rifle to Colonel Miles. The coming-in was prolonged till long after dark. The lame, maimed, halt and blind came crawling up the hill. Meanwhile, White Bird and two wounded squaws, with a party of fourteen, escaped between the pickets under cover of the darkness."

October 6th. Miles received information at 2 p.m. from the Red River half-breeds, of thirty Indians, twenty of them wounded in Miles' fight, who had escaped across the boundary. Also from scouts, of six killed by the Assiniboin, of two or three killed by the Gros Ventres, and a squaw and two children captives in the Assiniboin camp. We sent for these prisoners.

These notes sufficiently indicate the situation, which may be briefly described as follows:

When Miles had passed Bear Paw Mountain, he had struck the flank of Joseph's march, surprising him while resting in camp. Joseph was well posted in a ravine. His immense herd of ponies and captured mules were permitted to feed along the slopes. Miles' force was immediately deployed and hurled upon the Indians and upon the herd in such a way as to defeat the former, driving all but the killed and wounded and the few that escaped into the narrow, crooked ravines and capturing most of the herd. The work was bravely done, though the gallant charge cost the lives of several officers and many men and disabled many more. The Indians, quickly putting themselves under the cover of the uneven ground, dug holes and rifle pits and were thus able to stand on the defensive.

Finally, after a series of interesting and exciting negotiations, the surrender of Joseph and his Indians took place.

My force proper was stopped twenty-five miles back, at a point which was more nearly opposite Sitting Bull's position than the battlefield. After the surrender had been completed, all our forces slowly returned to the Missouri. With my staff and escort, I separated from Miles at the battleground on the 7th of October, and we came together again the 13th, on the Missouri. The force was now divided into three parties. Sturgis' command remained to watch the Sioux. Miles, taking the Indians with him, crossed the Missouri and returned to Tongue River by the same route that he had come. With my infantry, artillery, and staff, I again embarked on the Steamer Benton and set out for home. A part of us made our way via Chicago, and the remainder via Omaha, the Pacific Railroad, and the Pacific steamers, to our several stations in the Department of the Columbia.

After Miles' march and engagement, there arose all sorts of heart-burnings, reports filled with claims and counter-claims for credit. There were necessarily diversities of statement, rivalries, crimination, and controversies, such as we read of in Europe after an important battle or campaign.

Such jealous disputations, like the smoke on the field, often obscure for a time the results of the conflict, but have a way of correcting themselves by the lapse of time. Accomplished results are the things that, in the main, concern a general, an army, a historian, a man.

I was sent to conduct a war without regard to department and division lines. This was done with all the energy, ability, and help at my command, and the campaign was brought to a successful issue. As soon as the Indians reached General Terry's department, Gibbon was dispatched to strike his blow, then Sturgis, in close alliance, and finally, Miles in the last terrible battle. These troops participated in the struggle with exposure, battle, and loss, as we have seen. They enjoyed the appreciation and thanks of their seniors in command and of their countrymen. But when, with the fullness of an honest and generous recognition of the work, gallantry, losses, and success of all cooperating forces, I turn my attention to the troops that fought the first battles and then pursued the swift-footed fugitives with unparalleled vigor and perseverance amid the severest privations for more than a thousand miles, would it be wonderful if I magnified their doings and gave them, were it possible, even an overplus of praise for the part they bore in this campaign?

Personally, according to the covenant which I have recorded, I shall be satisfied to let another bear the crown of triumph, while my heart is deeply moved with thankfulness that the work itself was brought to a successful conclusion.

It is a difficult matter to ascertain the doings and sayings of Indians after they have gone on the war path. As soon as Joseph's Indians had passed Kamiah to traverse the Lolo Trail, I had but a few opportunities to gain knowledge from the inside of their lodges.

At the obstructing barricades in Montana, which were dangerous to pass, Looking Glass appeared as the diplomat. He succeeded by his ability in deceiving the commander of the defenses and brought past the hindering works Joseph's whole people in complete safety.

After Gibbon's battle, Joseph showed his influence over the Indians by rallying them on a height just beyond the reach of the long-range rifles. He gathered the warriors, recovered lost ground, and recaptured his numerous herd of ponies, which had already been cut off by Gibbon's men, buried most of his dead, and made good his retreat before the force with me was near enough to harm him. Few military commanders could better have recovered after so fearful a surprise.

At the Camas Meadows, not far from Henry Lake, Joseph's night march, his surprise of my camp and capture of over a hundred animals showed an ability to plan and execute equal to that of many a partisan leader whose deeds have entered into classic story.

Again, his quick penetration into my plan of delaying my march between the Musselshell and the Missouri, so as to make all speed, cross the broad river at Cow Island, defeat the guard, and then destroy an immense freight-wagon train, replenish his supplies, and make off beyond danger from the direct pursuit, is not often equalled in warfare.

And even at the last, the natural resources of his mind did not fail him. Broken in pieces by Miles' furious and unexpected assault, burdened with his women, children, and plunder, suffering from the loss of his still numerous, though badly crippled herd of ponies, he was yet able to entrench and hold out for several days against twice his numbers, and succeeded in pushing out beyond the white man's pickets a part of his remnant to join his allies in Canada.

The cheery brother Ollicut and old Too-hul-hul-sote were among the slain on Miles' field.

From the beginning of the Indian pursuit across the Lolo Trail, until the embarkation on the Missouri River for the homeward journey, including all halts and stoppages, from July 27th to October 10th, my command marched one thousand three-hundred and twenty-one miles in seventy-five days. Joseph, taking with him his men, women, and children, traversed even greater distances, for he had to make many a loop in his skein, many a deviation into a tangled thicket to avoid or deceive his enemy.

Whichever side of the picture we examine, we find there evidence of wonderful energy and prolonged endurance. It will be indeed fortunate for mankind if these same qualities, which we cannot help commending, can hereafter be turned into a common channel and used for the promotion of the arts of peace. What glorious results would have been effected could these non-treaties have received the same direction that the worthy missionaries were, in early days, able to give to the remainder of their tribe, and have shown the same ability and persistence in peace that they did during this fearful Indian war. Certainly it would be gratifying to me, at any time, to see the remnant turn from savagery to civilization. They are a people, even in their wildness, picturesque and replete with interest. May not these, in the far-off Indian Territory where they have been sent, have a portion in the labor and the comforts of the world's progress?

Part II

Through Nez Perce Eyes
A Trust Betrayed

by

Duncan McDonald

Introduction

On April 26, 1878, *The New North-West* of Deer Lodge, Montana, began publishing a series of articles about the Nez Perce War written by Duncan McDonald, then the Agency Trader for the Flathead tribe at Jocko, Montana. The series was entitled *The Nez Perces: The History of Their Troubles and The Campaign of 1877*. The first article was preceded by this introduction:

> The writer, a relative of Looking Glass and White Bird, has entered into arrangements with *The New North-West* to prepare a series of papers giving the Nez Perce version of their troubles and their remarkable campaign. It is a condition of the publication that the views shall be related from their standpoint, and as full particulars as possible will be given of the tribe and their great expedition. The author has been for some time collecting data from the prominent actors in the great drama, and the time yet required to elicit incidents of the campaign will be occupied in preliminary narrative.

In other introductory remarks *The New North-West's* editor advised his readers, "Last summer, at the instance of *The New North-West*, he [McDonald] made a six weeks' trip to British America, for the purpose of obtaining correct particulars of the campaign from White Bird. The data thus obtained is being presented in these articles and can be relied upon as authentic from the Nez Perces' standpoint."

Thus unfolded a different account of the Nez Perce war in Idaho and Montana and the history that led up to it—a story of friendship forgotten and trust betrayed. Seventy-two years had passed since the Nez Perces had first welcomed members of the sick and starving Lewis and Clark expedition into their lodges; only twenty-two summers since the Great White Father had promised them in perpetuity the exclusive ownership to five thousand square miles of their traditional homeland. The non-treaty Nez Perces could not understand how only eight years later the size of their reservation could be reduced by ninety percent and they could subsequently be forced "by bullet or bayonet" to abandon the graves of their ancestors. They could not understand how the white man's justice applied only to the killing of white men. Finally, they did not understand that they were, in 1877, at war not only with General Howard and the people of Idaho, but with the entire United States government and its forty million citizens.

Through Nez Perce Eyes

It will be remembered that in the year 1847, Dr. Whitman and wife were murdered by a Cayuse Indian named Ta-ma-has, who was supposed to have been influenced to commit this by a Mexican named Jo. This murder resulted in a conflict between the U.S. Government and the above named tribe. After the Indians were defeated, the Government demanded the murderers, and Ta-ma-has and several others were hanged in Willamette Valley, Oregon. At the time the Cayuses were engaged in this war, a young man of the Nez Perce nation named Yellow Bull abandoned his parents and tribe. Ta-ma-has had a young and beautiful daughter, loved and respected by all who knew her. Yellow Bull, by his coolness and personal bravery, had won her affections and the confidence of her father, and it was soon agreed upon that the two should wed each other.

After Ta-ma-has was hanged, the young couple came back to the Nez Perce country, and shortly after the girl gave birth to a son. Little worthy of note transpired regarding this couple until the boy reached the age of manhood. One day, whilst conversing with his mother, he asked her if he ever had a grandfather, and if so, he would like very much to pay him a visit. Hesitating for a few moments, the woman told him that he had a grandfather, and that his grandfather was dead, having been hanged by the Americans a long time ago. This same young man was one of the three who committed the depredations in Idaho last summer.

Later on, in the year 1854, the Nez Perces, then under Chiefs Lawyer and We-we-tzin-mae, concluded a treaty with the United States Government. Shortly after this treaty was formed, several Indians and their women were murdered by the whites, probably without just cause, as we shall endeavor to show. We refer to one instance in particular when three

Indians started out to the mountains in search of game. Arriving where game was plentiful, they had little or no difficulty in procuring a reasonable supply. After caching it, they returned to their homes, making an agreement to return at a certain time and take the game home. This being agreed upon the three separated, and upon their return, two met at the cache about the same time. Feeling somewhat fatigued by their trip, they dismounted to take a short rest, when two white men approached them in a rude manner, disarmed them, and asked one of the Indians whether or not he was the man who interpreted for Chief Joseph. The man answered him to the contrary. Thompson, the white man, called him a liar, at the same time knocking the Indian down and abusing him in a brutal manner. The Indian's companion made no resistance or attempt to save him, but the third one of the party referred to, named Willatiah, arrived while the scuffle was going on and made inquiries as to the cause of it. On being informed that the Indian had been thus treated without any cause or provocation whatever, Willatiah at once interfered in hopes to stop the white man from offering any further abuse, when suddenly the white man sprang upon him. But Willatiah, being a man of considerable nerve and strength, soon had the white man upon the ground, when the latter called to his companion to shoot the _____. The companion obeyed this command—Willatiah fell a corpse. The white man who committed this rash act was one of the squatters of Wallowa Valley, and it was supposed a little difficulty he had had with Chief Joseph a short time before was what prompted him to do the deed. It seems Chief Joseph had ordered him to quit Wallowa, as he himself claimed that section of country, and requested him to ask Lawyer to give him land, as that he, Lawyer, had sold his country for molasses sugar to the Government. As soon as Willatiah expired the remaining two Nez Perces started off quite panic stricken. A short time afterward another Indian reached the scene of the late conflict and found his dead friend and companion, and immediately set out to ascertain the cause. Satisfying himself, he informed Chief Joseph, who at once summoned his warriors and started to interview Agent Monteith, demanding at the same time the murderers. This request the Agent refused to comply with, only trying to satisfy them by telling them that they ought to kill the white men.

Walitze was the man who fired the first shot in the late Nez Perce war. He was the son of a well-to-do farmer named Tip-piala-natzit-kan, who is a brother of the once favorite Eagle-of-the-Light, and who was murdered by a white man four years ago. Tip-piala-natzit-kan was well known throughout the tribe, and his duty it was to call the councils together. As was mentioned before, the father of Walitze was a farmer, and in good circumstances, peaceably inclined toward all, accommodating, and he undoubtedly desired the settlement of the country in which he lived. About a year prior to the murder of Tip-piala-natzit-kan, a white man came to his house and stated that he would like to take up a piece of land. The man requested Tip-piala-natzit-kan to show him a piece of land unclaimed by anyone, promising him (the Indian) to be a good neighbor. Tip-piala-natzit-kan, liking the appearance of the man, at once granted his request and proceeded to show him the unclaimed land. No difficulty arose between the white man and the Indian until about a year afterward when the white man wanted to fence a piece of land that the Indian claimed. It seems that early one morning the man was engaged in hauling some rails a short distance from the Indian's house, when the wife of the Indian roused him up and told him that his white friend was putting some rails upon their land. Tip-piala-natzit-kan at once aroused the other Indians who were living in his house and asked them to accompany him, as he wished to talk with the white man and find out what were his intentions, and said that he was afraid to visit him alone. But it seems that no one wanted to accompany him, and accordingly he went alone. Upon reaching the designated place, he asked the white man if he had forgotten the promise he made to him during their first interview and asked him in a friendly manner not to put any rails on his land, but put them on the land that he was owner of. The white man at once became wrathy, took his rifle from the pile of rails and shot the Indian, wounding him mortally. The Indian at once started for home, suffering great pain, and much exhausted from the loss of blood. His son Walitze was then in the Cayuse country. The wounded man addressed his people in the following words: "I know that my days are short upon this earth, and it is my desire that you do not get excited at this event. Send this message to my son Walitze: Tell him for my sake, and for the sake of his brothers and sisters, and in fact for the whole of the Nez Perce Nation, to hold his temper and let not his heart get the best of him. We are as a nation poor in circumstances, in fact we have nothing. The white man has plenty of things that we have not. We can manufacture neither arms nor ammunition. We love our country and above all our families. Do not go to war. You will lose your country by it, and above all the loss of life will be great. Tell my son I should like to see and shake hands with him before I die, but I am afraid I cannot. When I am dead tell him all I have said, and lastly of all not to wage war upon the whites." Saying this, he expired a few moments afterward. A few days later his son came home, and naturally enough his relatives delivered to him the message left by his dying parent. Walitze hung his head as the message was related to him, and with tears running down his cheeks said that he was very sorry to hear of his father being killed in that way and that he felt proud of his last remarks warning himself and people to keep at peace and hold in abhorrence war. Chief Joseph and others demanded the murderer of Tip-piala-natzit-kan, but the authorities refused to take any steps to either arrest or punish him. Joseph then warned the whites that if they did not punish the murderer, there would be trouble. Walitze, Tap-sis-ill-pilp, and a young boy whose name is not known, are the three who commenced the depredations in Idaho last summer. Both Walitze and Tap-sis-ill-pilp were killed in the battle of Big Hole.

As further evidence in proof that the attack of the Nez Perces on the white race was not the result of inborn deviltry on the part of the red man, but rather a continuous abuse and violence exercised by the former on their so-called savage neighbors, I will now give you the history of the murder of a native in the vicinity of Slate Creek, Idaho. Ta-wai-a-wai-we, or Bear Thinker, one of the chiefs of that region, with the accustomed friendliness shown by his people ten years ago toward the whites, received into his family as son-in-law and endowed with a portion of his worldly goods an American whose love of ease o'er leapt his ambition. Unfortunately also for Bear Thinker, the mind of his son-in-law was as stagnant as his body and seemed to have belonged to the Dark Ages when the superstitions of his race were more remarkable than those of the Indians today. Among other beliefs indulged in by him was one that his father-in-law, being a chief and a medicine man, or wizard, was proof against death otherwise than by old age. This conviction being conveyed to a white acquaintance and backed by a bet, the pair tested the matter by administering to the chief a dose of strychnine, which, it is hardly necessary to add, quickly conveyed him to the happy hunting grounds. Granting that this act originated in an almost incredible ignorance, it appears that a devilish recklessness went hand in hand therewith, as the Indians state that the poisoners enjoyed a hearty laugh while the old man was "kicking his last" and remained wholly unpunished for their crime.

About nine years ago a Nez Perce woman was murdered near Kamiah, but I have not been able to gather any particulars. I have also been informed of the killing of Ta-akill-see-waits, son of a chief of the same name. Of his death nothing is known except that he started on a short trip with a white friend from which he did not return. Sometime after, however, some Indians engaged in hunting discovered traces of blood which, being followed, led them to the bank of a small creek, where they found the remains of their friend covered with earth and brush. Their applications for the arrest of those involved and other of their assailants and murderers were of no avail, meeting always with the response that the punishment of a white man would instigate a war, and as yet they were not sufficiently desperate to accept such an issue.

On their annual trip to the plains, about the year '64, the Nez Perces, having dug what camas they required at Big Hole, proceeded down the Missouri and camped at the junction of a stream which heads in the Rocky Mountains southeast of Deer Lodge. While at that place it seems that a party of Flatheads under Stalassna, which had been on an unsuccessful horse-stealing expedition to the Snake country, arrived within a short distance of the camp. Upon discovering it, however, instead of making themselves known, they cached themselves till night, when they stole four fine horses and also stole themselves away. On the following day, while the Nez Perces were moving camp, they were overtaken by four well-armed white men who accused them of stealing horses from the vicinity of Virginia City. Their denial was, of course, received with utter disbelief because the whites had tracked their horses almost into the camp—in fact to the stopping place of the Flatheads who were the true thieves. Although the Nez Perces declared that there must be some mistake and they themselves had had horses stolen, their assertions still met with no credence. The white men accordingly followed the camp until it reached the neighborhood of Bozeman when, emboldened by the proximity of the settlements, they shot two Indians, named respectively Ta-wis-wy and Hym-py-ya-se-ni, who had gone there to trade. The former was killed at once, but the latter escaped and recovered, although a bullet entered at the base of the nose and made its exit at the back of his neck.

At the same period also the whites, determined on a supposed revenge, caught and killed another Indian who was hunting about eight miles from Bozeman. These acts were more than Indian nature could be expected to submit to, and accordingly the Indians determined on an assault on the settlements. Such an unfortunate occurrence was, however, at that time avoided by the intervention of a Delaware named John Hill who, acting as interpreter between the races, procured the holding of a common council in which the Nez Perces were promised that the murderers should be arrested, taken to Virginia City, and made to undergo a lawful punishment for their acts. Of course the promises were a dead letter. Equally of course, no one who has followed the published accounts of the Nez Perce War will argue that the then peaceful result of the conference was due to cowardice on the part of the Indians.

Reckless as the actions of the above-mentioned whites really were, there are yet many men in the west who would sympathize therewith and with some show of reason, as the former certainly had strong cause for belief that the Nez Perces had stolen their horses; but who can excuse the killing of U-mas-na-cow and Key-la-tzie-augh (Hand-Otter), two of the tribe murdered in the vicinity of Lewiston in '68 or '69, simply because they attempted to prevent two white men who had brought whiskey into their lodge from debauching their women. The next murder of my list seems to have been committed merely on account of the belief (shared and stated, according to a late report, by Gen. Sheridan) that only a dead Indian can be a good one. The circumstances connected therewith being as follows: In 1871, my informant had his lodge pitched on the present site of the Missoula post when two Nez Perces arrived there on the way from the main camp, then on the Galatin, to their homes in Idaho. During the night of their stay with him, another Nez Perce en route from Idaho also made his appearance, and in giving the home news told one of the others that his wife was anxiously awaiting his return. This much pleased the Indian addressed, for in some manner he had been led to believe that during his winter's hunt on the plains, the woman had allowed proximity to have the stronger charms and replaced him with another husband. Such a story having been circulated in the camp, the forsaken husband, being a man of mark, had been offered as second wife, a young girl, one of the most eligible of the tribe. Being, however, of a constant disposition, before stating his acceptance he determined to more accurately inquire as to his wife's faithlessness. For this reason he had started for home ahead of the camp, leaving therewith his baggage and extra animals. Upon hearing the news as above stated, he concluded to return to the camp for his belongings so as not to arrive at home empty handed. He therefore left the Bitterroot and was on the road within twenty or twenty-five miles of Bozeman when a man stepped out of a roadside house and, without speech of any description, shot him through the body. By catching the saddle he managed to remain on his horse until he was carried some distance from the scene of the attack. He then fell to the ground and crawled sufficiently to be out of sight of white passers. Thus he remained for two days and nights without food or water, when at last some Indians came along and they bore him to their camp a few miles on the other side of Bozeman. Soon after his arrival there, some soldiers appeared with an order for the camp to move, the order having originated on account of some depredations committed in the vicinity by other Indians—Sioux or Crows. All the Nez Perces then—with the exception of Eagle-of-the-Light, who had a dying brother in his lodge and preferred to take the responsibility of staying to either leaving his brother or killing him by travel—left for the Yellowstone, and on their way the wounded man died.

An Indian more or less is truly no great matter, but surely a great country which can afford to free her Negroes and boasts of her Bergh may also exhibit a slight feeling of humanity for the family ties of a poor red man.

Many more cases of outrage committed against the Nez Perces as individuals could be added to the foregoing, but a surfeit, perhaps, having already been given, it is now appropriate to call attention to the great cause of dissatisfaction on the part of that tribe. The Stevens' Treaty of 1855, under which the Government claims the control of those Indians, was obtained by a ruse which, if understood, could hardly receive the commendation of a great nation. Not being able to gain to his aim the consent of any of the real chiefs, Governor Stevens, a man of much ability and few scruples, cut the Gordian knot for the Government by providing a chief freshly manufactured for the occasion. Lawyer, recognized by the Indians as a tobacco cutter (a sort of undersecretary) for the chiefs Looking Glass, Eagle-of-the-Light, Joseph and Red Owl, was the chosen man. In other words, for certain considerations he was prevailed upon to sign away the rights of his brethren—rights over which he had not the slightest authority—and, although he was a man of no influence with his tribe, the Government, as if duty bound on account of his great services, conferred upon him the title and granted him the emoluments of Head Chief of the Nez Perces. The feelings of the Indians were at that time aroused to such a pitch of indignation that they at first determined to hang their new superior, but as so often has been the case with them, milder counsels prevailed and indifference and contempt took the place of revenge. However the Government chose to look upon the result, the true chiefs and body of the people regarded the treaty as void. Thus the case stood—gradual encroachments being made on one side and protests being made by the other—until last year when the old story of a love affair produced the grand *denouement*.

Before, however, proceeding with a description of attendant circumstances thereof, I will, to prevent misconception, give a short resume regarding the chiefs connected with the council held during the formation of the aforesaid treaty. As previously hinted, there were at that time four noted chiefs and these were: 1st. Eagle-of-the-Light, Chief of the Took-peh-mas and Lum-ta-mas, first among his peers as to eloquence, and chosen by them as main spokesman at the council. Partly on account of old age, and partly due to a conviction arrived at through an intelligent intercourse with white men that his people had no chance of redressing their wrongs by fighting, he declined to take part in the later war, and has since its commencement chiefly resided in Montana.

2d. Flint Color, or as better known by Americans, Looking Glass, a chief of the Took-peh-mas and perhaps the most influential man of the nation. He was father of the late Looking Glass, known to the Flatheads as Big Hawk, who was killed in the battle with General Miles north of Fort Benton.

3d. Joseph, Chief of the Ca-moo-ey-nahs, father of the present well-known leader. Before death he cautioned his son against giving white men any opportunity to claim his land. "The Wallowa Valley," said he, "is yours. It is a fine country and belonged to your fathers, who are buried here. It will yield a subsistence for you and yours. Let the white man travel through it, and while doing so, eat your fish and partake of your meat, but receive from him no goods or other presents or he will assert that he has purchased your country."

And 4th. Red Owl, another chief of the Took-peh-mas, an eloquent, sagacious Indian, noted as an Apollo among belles of the tribe. He was wounded during the attack made by Miles, but whether fatally or not I have been unable to learn.

It may be here added that at the period now spoken of, White Bird, latterly of so much notoriety, was young and of no particular prominence. Since then, however, he gradually rose in the estimation of his associates, and on the resignation of Eagle-of-the-Light, became first chief of the Lum-ta-mas.

It seems the Nez Perces and the Crows were greatest of friends once. They used to camp together and kill buffalo every winter for many years. The "Women Nation," the Crows, is what the Nez Perces have called them since the Nez Perce campaign against the United States government in 1877. The Crows are named women and sometimes traitors. It will be explained how they were named. It seems the Nez Perces were influenced by the Crows and urged in a good many respects. The main blame lies on the shoulders of the Crow nation. It is true a man has no right to murder when he is told to do so by another party, but ignorance commits the crime sometimes. Ignorance makes the Indian think all white men are thieves and nothing else, and sometimes they think they can whip the United States government and they really think that there are no good, honest white men. We know that many an Indian has been made chief not for his shrewdness but for his bravery. Any brave Indian can be made a chief. If he were really an idiot, as long as he is brave, his valor covers a multitude of sins. But it is not often the case with wise Indians. It is a hard matter for a wise Indian to become a chief, but any stupid brave can be one with but very little opposition.

No doubt the well known Crow chief, named The-Eagle-that-Shakes-Himself, was a brave man, but he was not a man of knowledge. Many a day and night the Crow chiefs and Nez Perces spent their time counciling in their lodges about the pale-faced white men. We remember about it. For three years before the war broke out in 1877, between the U. S. Government and the Nez Perces, it was told around our camp fires what the Crow tribe were trying to do to make an agreement between the two mentioned tribes. We will state an incident that took place about two years ago between the Nez Perce and Crow nations.

We know it to be a fact that The-Eagle-that-Shakes-Himself once spoke and told Looking Glass and White Bird about the time when the two Nez Perces were murdered by white men, one of them near Bozeman and the other near the Missouri River. Exclaimed this chief, "I understand. You are chiefs. Listen to me. I want to let you know how my heart feels towards the white man. Do you see my eyes are open? As long as I live these eyes are open. Never will I allow a white man to take or kill any of my people. You are cowards. You have not the heart that I have. You are a lot of cowards and like to eat the white man's sugar and molasses. You allow them to take your people's lives. You allow them to spill your own blood on your own soil because they don't tell the truth to the red man. I say, fight them. Take their murderers and kill them. What are they good for, only to murder the Indians and take our country away? You will get all the help from me. Let us go to war against the white man. You go back to your country and start in, and as soon as I get the news I shall do the same thing. At the same time move this way and I will go to Sitting Bull and make peace with him, and we will all give the white man a game." Unfortunately, this chief was made a game of by Sitting Bull's warriors. He was killed by the Sioux Indians in a fight between the Sioux tribe and the Crows.

This kind of advice from the Crows had quite an effect on the Nez Perce tribe, especially among the young braves. It was repeated over and over. But Looking Glass never was made a fool of, never was fool enough to take such advice from any of his Indian friends. Looking Glass, after the Crow chief had made his speech, raised his head and, resting his eyes on The-Eagle-that-Shakes-Himself as though they would pierce him, said to the Crow chief, "You say you have eyes. You say you can see. You can flatter a fool, but not me. Those eyes of yours and your heart do not see far. You are like a child; you can see, but cannot see far ahead. You are the men who are fond of sugar and molasses. You are the men who suckle the white man. You are the men that can be bought and sold for a plug of tobacco. I, Looking Glass, Eagle-of-Light and Joseph's father were the ones who wanted to hang Lawyer for signing treaties with Governor Stevens. What right had he, or authority, to sign treaties? He does not belong to the blood. He is the offspring of a foreigner. We blame him in signing the treaty. But he was not half as bad as Stevens. What right has Stevens to put Lawyer at the head of a nation that really does not belong to him? Is it right for any Indian to go to whoever the head man of the United States may be and put him out of his office and have anyone he pleases succeed him? Will the people of the United States like it? No. The Indian that would put the President out of his office would be killed at once. This is what Governor Stevens did with our Indians. We don't want any treaties. Whoever made this world never told the red man to sell his country. For this reason we want to live in peace. If we sign treaties and then turn and fight the Government, it would be breaking up treaties. We do not want to fight as long as we have justice. That is all we want. If the white man punishes his murderers, we shall do the same. But he does not. He does not even ask us to help him. The first thing he calls on is his weapons to kill the Indians. I want peace with the white man. My hand is open to the white man. I do not know what they mean. Whenever one of my Indians gets killed, they do not even arrest the perpetrators. By the looks of things, we will be compelled to go to war."

These Indians, on reaching Idaho from the buffalo stamping ground, learned that Willatiah was innocently murdered in the mountains by two white men. This Indian's life was really a cause of many a poor innocent settler losing his life in Idaho. Willatiah was the last man murdered before the war broke out in 1877.

I give below a list of Nez Perce Indians killed by whites before the war of 1877.

Chief Bear Thinker was poisoned; Juliah was killed near Bozeman without cause; Taivisyact was shot while passing a house on horseback near the Missouri River on the road to Bozeman; Took-kay-lay-yoot, Lapwai, by a soldier on account of liquor; Yalmay-whotzoot, Lapwai, was killed while looking for horses; Him-p-augh, was killed on account of buying a pistol; Tip-iala-huana-chino-mouch at Elk City, cause unknown; Koyotes was killed on a spree with supposed friends at Slate Creek; Maltze-qui was killed because he was falsely accused of stealing a bottle of whiskey; Eya-makoot, a woman, was killed with a pick on account of her dog whipping a white man's dog; Cass-say-u was accidentally killed by the son of their own minister, Spalding, who shot at another Indian while gambling and killed the wrong man; Took-ooghp-ya-mool on Salmon River; Usay-kay-act was taken away by a white friend and never seen again; T-nan-na-say, a councilman, was shot by a soldier in a council south of Yakima; Tipia-la-natzi-kan because his field was taken from him; Willatiah in the mountains near Wallowa.

As I have stated before, none of the murderers of these people were ever arrested or punished. At the time of this last occurrence, Joseph and his band were so excited at seeing the murderer of Willatiah go at large that they threatened the settlers of Idaho. The settlers, frightened by these threats, sent a dispatch to the soldiers at Walla Walla. When the soldiers arrived the officer in command asked Joseph if he wished to fight the whites. Joseph answered, "If I am compelled, I will have to fight. The man we wanted to fight for is dead and gone. It is better to be at peace once more. But I warn the whites to not kill any more of my Indians. I would not mind if you were killing Indians who are trying to do something wrong, but it seems you want to kill my best men, and for this cause I will not stand any more murder. I did not ask you to come and settle in my country. If you do not like us, keep away."

It was then the Nez Perces first heard there was a Big Chief of the soldiers coming to see the Nez Perce nation.

They were told this by the soldiers, and the Big Chief coming was Howard. This was in 1876. It should be remembered that there are two brothers, each named Joseph. Joseph, Senior, [Chief Joseph] is the one now a prisoner at Leavenworth [Kansas]. On hearing of this appointed council, Wa-lame-moot-key, a Cayuse chief and a relative of the Josephs, sent for all the Nez Perce chiefs saying he wished to have a council with them near Walla Walla. But the chiefs were not disposed to have a council and remained at home.

But Joseph, Junior, [Ollicut] who had heard from other sources that Howard was at Walla Walla, took four or five other Indians and went there to see him.

Howard met him and said, "Joseph, I am glad to see you. But you have come alone; I would like to see the other chiefs also, and tomorrow I will see you." Howard told them to find lodgings in some of the houses of the town and ordered that they should have something to eat. Joseph declined to be quartered off on the town or to accept government board and did not remain in town.

Next morning they were called to the military post by Howard and entered the room where he was. Before taking their seats, General Howard said to Joseph, "The Sioux chief Spotted Tail has concluded to move to a new reservation."

Joseph merely replied, "And so Spotted Tail finally concluded to remove."

While Joseph was being seated, Howard drew some papers from his pocket and said to him, "These papers are my instructions from the Great Father to move all Indians to the reservation. I want to move the Indians to three different reserves. These Indians must go either across the Columbia, to Lapwai or Kamiah reserves." Joseph made no reply. Howard drew out more papers and said, "Joseph, do you understand? All Nez Perce Indians must move to their reserve. Have you anything to say?"

Joseph replied, "Yes, I have. Howard, you are a chief and I am a chief. You know what is good for your white friends and I know what is good for my people. I think it is better to leave all the Indians alone and to leave all the whites alone. I always feel happy in seeing both living in peace. Both peoples are getting civilized and making progress in this part of the country. Both are growing wealthy. When the whites first came here, they were poor and we helped them by trading. We gave them everything they wanted. All these things I tell you come from the root of my heart. It is impossible to order all white men to leave; I think it is impossible for all Indians to leave. As I said before, the white man helps the Indian to become civilized and the Indian helps the white man to get rich."

Howard answered, "Yes, Joseph, but you must move."

Joseph again said, "Howard, you had better leave the Indians alone. You are well paid to move Indians from their homes. These Indians are rich and well fixed. I like to see both nations progress. Let the white man raise his children and harvests. The Indian will do the same. We are non-treaty Indians. Therefore we wish to live among the white men and live in peace. It makes me happy when I travel through this fertile country and see that it will support both the Indian and the white man. I have good reason for not wishing to remove to the reserve. It is too small to sustain half my stock. How could we keep our stock on a reserve that is only half large enough to feed it?"

Howard replied, "You must go to the reserve."

Joseph said, "Well, you will have to talk with the other chiefs. You are made a chief by your people. You have now a good part of the country. It is better to leave the Indians alone on their own farms. You are working for the white man and I am doing the same for the red man. We are self-supporting Indians. We ask nothing from the government but protection in our rights."

Howard answered, "Your argument is very good, but I am sorry to say you must go to the reserve." At the same time he told Joseph that he would telegraph to Washington.

Joseph rose and said, "I am telling you how the Indians feel about this country. You say these Indians must go to three different reserves—Lapwai, Kamiah and across the Columbia River. If I must go to a reserve, I want to go to the Cayuse reserve, and if the Cayuse Indians want to go to Lapwai, they can. My Indians can do as they please, but I know they will not go. I do not want a white man to select a place for them. Let the Indians select a place for themselves as white men do. I do not wish the Nez Perces to go to three different reserves. If the Cayuses go to Lapwai, I want the whites to leave that part of the country because it is too small for the Indians alone. We are rich and have many horses and cattle."

Howard replied, "There are too many settlers in the country to be removed on account of the Indians' wishes."

Joseph said, "There is the trouble. You say your people are too well settled to be disturbed, and I say the Indians are too well settled to be disturbed. So it is better to leave the Indians alone. Why are you so determined to remove them? This is where we were born and raised. It is our native country. It is impossible for us to leave. We have never sold our country. Here we have all we possess, and here we wish to remain."

Howard merely said, "It is impossible. I wish to have a big talk with all the Indians at Lapwai in ten days' notice."

Joseph then drew out a paper on which were written the words of his father a few moments before he expired. It was as follows:

"My sons, this country is ours. My sons, do not give up this part of the country to the white man."

The paper was handed to Howard who, after reading it, said, "Joseph, you and all the other chiefs come to Lapwai in ten days." It was so agreed.

In fulfillment of the wish expressed by Howard to Joseph, Jr., the Nez Perce chiefs congregated at the Lapwai Agency at the time specified. Joseph, Jr., on reaching home, had related to the Nez Perces what Howard had said about removal, and they were much alarmed. Joseph said to his people that he had done his best to prevent their being removed, and asked them to keep quiet, and so they went to Lapwai. After arriving there, Monteith, the U. S. Indian agent, told a member of the tribe named Reuben, "You go and see Joseph and tell him to come to the reservation at once. Why are they humbugging and holding councils?" Reuben reported to the Indians what Monteith had said, and it seems had said still more that the Indians "must move." Much anger was created among the Indians at this message.

On seeing Howard afterward, Reuben told him, "If you are determined to move these peaceful Indians to a place where they cannot graze half their stock, you will have to do it with soldiers. We will always tell you the place is too small."

Howard did get soldiers, and when the Indians saw them reach Lapwai, they became more angry than ever. The next question was who the Indians would have for a speaker at the council. They held a council among themselves to select an Indian who was a good talker. The Nez Perce chiefs were all present except Looking Glass and Red Owl, who were in the mountains hunting, and neither they nor their people had any intimation of what Howard proposed to do with them. The result of the council was the election for speaker of an Indian named T-whil-who-tzoot, who was supposed to be a smart, intelligent Indian. Joseph, Jr., was barred out, the council deciding that he was not smart nor bold enough to represent them in a council with Howard.

When the day for the great council arrived, all the Indians were present except the two chiefs mentioned and their people. Joseph, Jr., feeling aggrieved at the action of his people in electing another instead of himself as speaker, withdrew from active participation and the reader will not often see his name mentioned during the campaign. When the council assembled, General Howard and the Indians took their seats. The General then arose and said, "I want all these Indians to go to their reserve at once. If you do not go voluntarily, I will compel you to do so with my soldiers. I have instructions from Washington to move all Indians to their reserves, and according to my instruction I must make you move. If you will not move for my words, you shall go to the reserve by the points of my soldiers' bayonets."

The elected chief, or speaker, T-whil-who-tzoot, rose and said, "Howard, I understand you to say you have instructions from *Washington* to move all the Nez Perce Nation to the reserve. You are always talking about Washington. I would like to know who Washington is. Is he a Chief, or a common man, or a house, or a place? Every time you have a council you speak of Washington. Leave Mr. Washington, that is if he is a man, alone. He has no sense. He does not know anything about our country. He never was here. And you are always talking about your soldiers. What do we care about your fighting qualities? You are chief, Howard, and I am elected by the Nez Perces to speak for them and do the best I can for my people. Let us settle the matter between you and me."

Howard replied, "I have instructions from Washington to move all Indians to the reserves and put them under charge of Agent Monteith."

T-whil-who-tzoot said, "Howard, are you trying to scare me? Are you going to tell me the day on which I shall die? I know I must die some day."

Howard then turned to White Bird and said, "Have you anything to say?"

White Bird answered, "We have elected T-whil-who-tzoot to speak for all the Nez Perces. Whatever he says or does is law with us."

T-whil-who-tzoot was at once arrested and put in the guard house, where he remained about a week. If I have been rightly informed, Howard in the council came near being a victim at the hands of the Nez Perce warriors.

When Howard saw the Indians abandoning him on account of their elected speaker going to jail, he sent for White Bird. When the chief arrived, Howard said to him, "I want you and Joseph and all the rest of the Nez Perces to go to the reservation."

Little Bald Head (also known as The Preacher), said to Howard, "I would like to select a place for my people. The place where I want to live is opposite Lapwai."

"I don't want any Indian to select a place outside of the reserve," said Howard. "I want Joseph, White Bird and all Nez Perces to go where I want them to go. If not, as I said before, I shall move the Indians with bullets or bayonets. I only give you ten days to move to the reserve. If you do not do what I have said, I shall send my soldiers and drive all your stock to the reserve, and also the Indians, and disarm them."

White Bird replied, "We like our country; we are wealthy Indians and self-supporting; we do not wish the government to spend a dollar toward the Nez Perces. My white neighbors are my friends."

Then and there Joseph, Sr., said to Howard, "You give us ten days to move our livestock and property. You must be joking. I notice when you want to move, it takes a long time to do it, especially when there are rivers to cross. I notice whenever you go after Indians in time of war, it takes you months to cross a river. I want you to understand that we have more horses than the soldiers ever had in the Indian wars. We want time. Ten days is not time for us. When the generals have a handful of soldiers and a few animals to cross a river, it takes them weeks and months to cross. We have plenty of children, women, horses and cattle, and the rivers are high." This is the only speech Joseph, Sr., ever made during the year of 1877.

Howard said again, "I don't want any humbugging. Do as I tell you to do—move immediately to the reserve."

Joseph said, "We like hunting; why should we stop on the reserve all the time for the balance of our days?"

Howard said, "If you want to hunt, you have to get a permit from the United States Indian Agent. Whenever you want to hunt, do not take many horses; take as few as possible, then you will not bother the settlers. Those settlers are the ones who sent a petition to Washington to get all Indians removed."

All this time Walitze, Tap-sis-ill-pilp and U-em-till-lilp-cown were listening to what Howard and their chiefs had said. Howard told the chiefs, "You can have any houses on the reserve belonging to the whites, and white men will leave their homes and go to some other places. Those houses are on the reserve. If you wish to occupy those houses, all right, and those white men can take your places outside of the reserve—a kind of an exchange."

On these conditions, Joseph, Sr., White Bird and Little Baldhead, or The Preacher, started out with the General to select homes for themselves. While riding around the country Howard had a few soldiers and an interpreter along with him. Howard said to White Bird, "What made you a chief? I am a chief because I lost my arm while fighting in big battles and fought bravely." Joseph and White Bird were surprised at these remarks, and said amongst themselves "Howard is anxious for war."

All this time there was news amongst the Indians that the soldiers were increasing at Lapwai or some place near.

The Indians were advised by their white friends they would be compelled to move, that Howard was determined to move all Indians. Young Joseph, on hearing that there were plenty of soldiers arriving near them, exclaimed, "I see that Howard is determined to move Indians and stock. If Howard tries to move my stock or troubles me, I shall fight him at once."

When the Indians saw Howard's actions they thought they were bound to fight. Then the Indians concentrated at Camas Prairie to have councils and decide how they should act and what was the best thing for them to do. While camped at Camas Prairie counciling, the three murderers made up their minds what to do.

At this time Looking Glass and Red Owl were camped in another place near Clearwater by themselves. Again and again the Indians were told by their white friends, "You must go; if not, you will be compelled to fight Howard." At the same time the three murderers were told, "The settlers at Camas Prairie were the ones who sent a petition to Washington to get the Indians removed." Looking Glass, on hearing that the soldiers and Indians were at the point of war, sent his brother, Took-alex-see-ma, who is now with Sitting Bull, to tell Joseph and White Bird not to fight. Took-alex-see-ma went from Looking Glass' camp three different times. He was sent by his brother to do the best he could to keep the Indians in peace. He was an influential man.

The murderers, on learning the parties that were trying to get the Indians removed, said "Well, there is nothing dearer than our country and our lives. I, Walitze, was insulted on account of a girl I took for a wife. Now, my friends, let us go and buy arms from the settlers. Some of our friends tell us to buy arms and be prepared for Howard. We might as well start in. Let us kill the parties around Camas Prairie, because they are the ones that sent the petition to Washington. We must make them leave our dear soil before we do. It was bad enough to kill our fathers and they get no punishment, and now they, not satisfied by getting the greatest part of our country and arresting our speaker, must send a petition to Washington to get soldiers to take our country that is dear to us. Let us all die and let somebody else get our country."

While having councils at Camas Prairie, Joseph, Sr., was preparing to go to the buffalo country. The two brothers Joseph started from Camas back towards Wallowa Valley to kill some cattle and dry some meat. Took-alex-see-ma was running around, detailed by his brother Looking Glass to keep the Indians quiet. As Took-alex-see-ma told us once in his tent, "When I reached White Bird's camp the third time my brother sent me, we were in a large lodge and eating dinner, and while I was delivering the message that my brothers sent to the other chiefs, I heard an Indian making a speech on horseback. I recognized him as Big-of-the-Light, mounted on a black horse and with a gun in his hand, saying, 'What are you counciling about? War is commenced. This black horse I am riding is a white man's horse. This gun is a white man's gun. Walitze, Tap-sis-ill-pilp, U-em-till-lilp-cown just got back. They murdered four white men and they brought this horse, gun, saddle, etc.'" At the same time neither Joseph nor Looking Glass was in camp. White Bird was the only chief there.

The insult of Walitze by other Indians and Howard arresting their speaker were their reasons for starting out to murder. Besides, Howard's actions toward them were rather mean, telling them he would move them with bullets or bayonets.

When the tidings that the three Indians mentioned had murdered four white men the night previous reached White Bird's camp, that chief said, "Now, my people, we must do the best we can. It is a great crime to murder white men, especially innocent ones. In time of peace you have no right to kill people, either by night or day. If we are forced to go to war, then you can do as you please, except that you must not kill women. Neither I nor Joseph told you to kill these men."

As stated before, both the Josephs were absent at the time of the murder of these four men. It seems, however, a messenger went speedily across the Salmon River and towards Wallowa Valley searching for the Josephs to tell them the news of the murders committed on Camas Prairie. The two brothers were met by the messenger and were told of the crimes committed by Walitze, Tap-sis-ill-pilp and Um-till-lilp-cown. As soon as the brothers Joseph learned the news they dismounted, cut the ropes by which the loaded meat was lashed to their pack animals, and proceeded with all speed to White Bird's camp. On reaching it Joseph and White Bird ordered camp to be moved towards the camp of Looking Glass and Red Owl, but before reaching it these latter chiefs had heard from Took-aliz-see-na, a brother of Looking Glass, of the crimes committed by White Bird's band. Before reaching the camp of Looking Glass, the three murderers again started out in the dead of night and murdered five or six more men.

Anger is an insufficient expression to convey the feeling of Looking Glass when he saw White Bird's camp moving toward him. He said to Joseph and White Bird, "My hands are clean of white men's blood, and I want you to know they shall so remain. You have acted like fools in murdering white men. I will have no part in these things and have nothing to do with such men. If you are determined to fight, go and fight yourselves and do not attempt to embroil me or my people. Go back to your warriors; I do not want any of your band in my camp. I wish to live in peace."

On hearing these words, Joseph and White Bird made camp a few miles from Looking Glass. They made up their minds not to trouble him because he did not wish to go to war. The next day they moved towards Salmon River in nearly the same direction from which they had come and camped at a place called Camas Prairie. Early in the morning the camp was alarmed by one of the Indians. This Indian had been out nearly all night and about dawn of day he saw some soldiers approaching the camp. (Before the fight with these soldiers, they attacked some freight teams on the road and killed two or three men.) White Bird had only seventy-five warriors in the camp, but they rallied and started out to meet the soldiers and ascertain what they wanted. But before White Bird had a chance to speak, the soldiers opened fire on the Nez Perces. Then the fight opened and there they fought I know not how many hours, but in a short time they surrounded the troops and the Indians charged upon them. White Bird urged his warriors on, saying, "Now is your time to fight. We are attacked. You have been looking for a fight with the white men and now you have got it. Fight now to the last. I want my warriors shot in the breast, not in the back."

They defeated the troops in a short time and killed thirty-five of them. Of the Indians, not one was killed and only four wounded. It is said by some that Joseph was away at the time of this fight. The Nez Perces did not move camp that day. This was the first battle of the campaign and occurred near Salmon River.

(The above presumably refers to Col. Perry's fight with the Nez Perces at the fork of White Bird Canyon about the 15th of June. General Howard reported that Perry had twenty-seven men, including Capt. Theller, killed and wounded in the engagement. The troops numbered one hundred fifty, with some citizens and twenty friendly Indians. The fight lasted three hours and the soldiers were driven sixteen miles. The Indian strength was estimated at one hundred twenty-five.—Ed. N.N.W.)

White Bird did not move camp the day succeeding the defeat of the soldiers, but the next he moved and crossed the Salmon River the same day. Here he went into camp and remained about four days. Their next move was in a southwesterly direction through Joseph's country—that is, Wallowa Valley—and they camped in the mountains. Joseph and White Bird ordered camp to move at daybreak the next morning, and they moved back to and across the Salmon River again. The following day they moved again and reached a large plain where there are some pine trees. Here they camped again.

All this time they were counciling to determine what was best to do—whether they should leave the region which they were in and move toward the Snake country, or go to the Buffalo Plains and join Sitting Bull in the British Possessions. Some wanted to surrender to Howard, but they feared they would be shot or hanged.

All this time Red Owl and Looking Glass were camped on a tributary of Clearwater. Looking Glass believed he was safe from assault, believing he had done that which would commend him to the whites by rejecting the proposals of Joseph and White Bird to go to war and sending them peremptorily away from his camp.

Looking Glass even saved the life of a white man who was captured and who happened to be a friend of theirs. He told his warriors not to molest the man, as he did not wish to see any war between the whites and Indians. At this time he knew a force of soldiers was moving toward his camp. He said to the white man, "Go and tell the whites that I, Looking Glass, am not with the hostiles. I do not wish to fight and will not unless I am compelled to in self-defense. I saved your life because I am a friend of the whites. I do not wish to be regarded or treated as a hostile. I even quarrelled with my relatives who were coming to my camp because they were hostiles. Now, my friend, go and meet the soldiers. Tell them I am camped at this place and wish very much to see the officer in command. I do not want any trouble."

The man started with the message, but instead of meeting it he avoided the command and returned to the camp. He told the chief the soldiers were coming and not far off, and he believed they would attack the camp. Looking Glass ordered some of his men to go and see how far away the soldiers were. This was early in the morning. Two or three of the Indians started in the direction the soldiers were coming, but just as the soldiers reached the bank of the creek, the soldiers charged on the camp.

When the chief saw the soldiers coming, he started toward them with the white man he had tried to send as a messenger. Looking Glass made signs to the soldiers to halt, that he wished to speak to them, but his signs had no effect. Almost immediately the bullets were flying thick. The white man got away from the chief and ran to the soldiers. Looking Glass returned to his camp and told his men to do the best they could. He then had about eleven lodges. The Nez Perces fled in all directions. One woman who tried to swim across the stream with her child in her arms had gotten about half way across when she was shot and drowned. The soldiers captured about twelve hundred head of horses. Most of these animals belonged to the two chiefs. The soldiers burnt everything Looking Glass had in his camp.

Talk about savages being blood-thirsty fiends! If these soldiers were not blood-thirsty fiends, then there is no savage in this world. Even had it been Joseph or White Bird who endeavored to have a talk with the commanding officer of the opposing force, they were entitled to it. There is no law of civilized war that gives a right to shoot a man when he is trying to surrender. Neither Joseph nor White Bird knew of the fight. The soldiers killed no one but the woman who was trying to cross the stream with her child. Is it possible that if a soldier cannot kill a buck Indian that he has a right to shoot at a woman?

Before continuing the narrative succeeding the attack on Looking Glass' camp, I will relate an incident preceding. It seems that at the earliest commencement of the Nez Perce War there were two white women murdered. One of them was murdered by an Indian who was drunk. The other white woman was burned in a house with her child. When her husband and others were murdered by the Nez Perces, she went upstairs. The Indians say they did not see her at the time of killing the men. When the Indians got possession of the house, Joseph, Jr. was present. He was sitting at one side of the place smoking his pipe. He was asked by the warriors what should be done—whether they should set fire to the house or leave without destroying it. All this time the woman and child were upstairs, but the Indians say they did not know it. Young Joseph answered, "You have done worse deeds than burning a house. You never asked our chiefs what was best to be done. You have murdered many men and not asked advice of your chiefs. You can do as you please about the house."

Some of the young men lit a match and set fire to the building. They then went back a little and sat down to watch it burn. They were suddenly startled by the piercing screams of a woman in the second story of the house. Young Joseph ordered them to put out the fire. The young Indians ran down to the water, filled their hats, threw it on the flames, and tried every way they knew to extinguish the fire and to save the woman. But it was too late. She and her child perished.

The same young warriors who were with Joseph, Jr., at the time told me that when he left the place, Joseph held down his head for a long time and, at last looking up, he said they had done very wrong in burning the woman, that he was very sorry, that he had believed the house empty.

The burning of this poor, harmless woman looks very bad for the Indian side. Still there is some blame should attach to the white man. The white man does wrong in allowing the Indian to have whiskey. It is easy to reply that the Indians take the whiskey away from them by force, but there are many whites who are ready to sell whiskey to them in time of Indian wars.

While the Nez Perces were camped in the pine grove, the chiefs sent two spies toward Cottonwood to see if any soldiers were advancing from that direction. While these spies were concealing themselves on their trip to Cottonwood, they discovered and killed two soldiers. The same day the whole Nez Perce camp mounted, but the camp did not move except the horsemen who approached Cottonwood. They knew there were soldiers there and they wanted to attack them. Before reaching Cottonwood they ascended a high ridge on the road from the Lapwai reservation. Here they stopped and were looking through their field glasses to see the soldiers at Cottonwood.

Suddenly they noticed eleven mounted soldiers at some distance, and in another direction saw some Indians. Joseph immediately dispatched two Indians mounted on their swiftest ponies to ascertain what tribe the Indians belonged to. On reaching them they met Looking Glass and Red Owl with their little band of men, women and children, nearly all on foot. It will be remembered that Looking Glass drove Joseph and White Bird from his camp and refused to join them in hostilities. After this he had been attacked by the soldiers, his camp destroyed, his stock taken and one woman killed. When the two envoys from the hostiles now reached him he pressed on and reached Joseph and White Bird, who were preparing to charge on the soldiers and citizens at Cottonwood. Looking Glass approached the chiefs and said, "My relations and friends. I had no idea of fighting the white man. My father had traveled many a mile in time of war. My father's warriors fought many battles as allies of the United States soldiers west of the Rocky Mountains. We had friends and relations killed in fighting along with the United States troops. The Indians the troops fought were more our relations than the white man. Why is it that the Nez Perces, having sided with the soldiers in fighting the Cayuses, Yakimas, Umatillas, Spokanes, and others, that today I am compelled to raise my hand against the white man? Two days ago my camp was attacked by the soldiers. I tried to surrender in every way I could. My horses, lodges, and everything I had was taken away from me by the soldiers we had done so much for. Now, my people, as long as I live I will never make peace with the treacherous Americans. I did everything I knew to preserve their friendship and be friends with the Americans. What more could I have done? It was because I was too good a friend of theirs that I was attacked. The officer may say it was a mistake. It is a lie. He is a dog, and I have been treated worse than a dog by him. He lies if he says he did not know it was my camp. I am ready for war. Come on and let us attack the soldiers at Cottonwood. Many a man dies for his dear native land, and we might as well die in battle as any other way."

During this speech the mounted soldiers who were carrying dispatches were approaching on the Lapwai. Looking Glass, after joining the hostiles, took command and an attack was made on the approaching soldiers. The Indians cut them off from Cottonwood as the soldiers veered off in another direction instead of endeavoring to return to that place, apparently determined to take chances on their horses. Before reaching a high ridge, four of the soldiers dismounted and fought bravely. The four who dismounted were all killed by one Indian, a noted warrior named Wat-zam-yas. The other seven were overtaken on the ridge, the principal murderers being in the advance. The soldiers lasted but a few minutes. I did not ascertain how far this was from Cottonwood. In this fight no Indians were killed or wounded. One horse was shot under Walitze, the warrior who fired the first shot in the war. Another horse was shot under Smoker. White Bird says the soldiers at Cottonwood could have saved this party if they had been brave enough, but they did not even start out from their camp.

That evening the warriors all returned to their camp. The next day Looking Glass ordered camp to move and be made again in a ravine three or four miles distant from Cottonwood, where there are a few pine trees. As soon as camp was pitched, Looking Glass gave orders to the warriors to catch their horses and they would attack the soldiers. Joseph took his Indians and attacked the soldiers, while the rest of the Indians charged on the corral and endeavored to capture the horses. But the corral was well guarded and defended and they only got twenty-four horses. The soldiers held their position. No Indian was killed in this fight, only one horse shot under Way-uch-ti-mamy. On the third day the Indians raised camp. While packing up, Joseph said to the other chiefs it would be a good plan to pass with their whole camp near Cottonwood, but not to attack the soldiers, and thus entice them out of the breastworks and get them to attack the Indians when the Indians could easily whip them. But unfortunately for the success of this plan, some young warriors, without informing the chiefs, had concealed themselves near Cottonwood to attack it.

All this time the Nez Perces believed there was a strong force of soldiers at Cottonwood, and besides, they believed Howard was there. They would rather have him than a hundred soldiers. They wanted Howard badly. The three murderers well knew that whenever the Nez Perces surrendered to Howard they would be the first Indians hanged, and what they wanted was to see "the Indian Herder," as they call Howard, and kill him. In fact the great cry in the

Nez Perce camp was to kill Howard at first sight. He was the one who got the Indians dissatisfied.

The camp moved as suggested by Joseph, but while traveling along and expecting momentarily the Cottonwood garrison to come out and attack them, word was brought that the young warriors who had concealed themselves were already fighting the soldiers. This vexed the chiefs very much and they did not go in that fight. One Indian was killed and two wounded.

The same evening a noted warrior, the same one who killed the four soldiers, took thirty picked warriors, attacked the soldiers in the night and captured forty-five head of horses from them without the loss of a man. Thus ended the Cottonwood battles, only one Indian having been killed and two wounded.

It is a well known fact that when Joseph, White Bird and Looking Glass joined forces they had, all told, just two hundred twenty warriors, twenty-five percent of whom were armed with only bows and arrows, which are poor weapons against needle guns except in close quarters.

The Nez Perces started from Idaho with seventy-seven lodges. They got twelve more lodges in Bitterroot Valley, taking them by force, making eighty-nine lodges in all.

After the fighting in the vicinity of Cottonwood, the Nez Perces moved and made camp near Red Owl's farm. Early in the morning the chiefs were told by one of the peaceable Indians that Howard was approaching them with a strong force of soldiers. But they were prepared all this time for Howard's "traps." The camp was in a little ravine. They put up some breastworks on a ridge between their camp and the approaching soldiers. Howard did the same thing. His breastworks were also on a ridge, and there was a ravine between the two bodies of fighting men. Howard, with all his military ability, did nothing better than to fire across the ravine to where the Indians were lying behind their defenses. He could have taken the whole camp by storm. The Indians think he well knew it was their determination to have his life, even if they had to charge into the midst of his troops and sacrifice themselves to accomplish their purpose. He knew what would be the result if he exposed himself. I have no wish to say offensive things of General Howard, but these are the words White Bird said to me sitting by our campfires in the Sioux camp last summer, "If Howard had been as bold as General Gibbon, we might have been all taken, although we intended to fight to the last."

During the first day's fighting, four Indians killed and four wounded. They fought through the night until daybreak. No Indians were killed in the night fighting. The second day the battle continued the same as the first, but no Indians were killed or wounded. The firing was all at long range. I do not know how many men Howard had in these great battles, but as near as I can ascertain he must have had two or three men to each Indian.

About the middle of the afternoon of the second day's fighting, Looking Glass ordered camp to be moved, and the entire camp was accordingly moved before Howard's eyes. It seems, therefore, that Looking Glass was a better general than Howard, as he withdrew his camp from the front of the enemy and moved away without the loss of either women, children, horses or lodges.

At this time Looking Glass had sole control of the camp, although Joseph ranked as high, or perhaps higher, as chief. Joseph's reason for not leading the camp was that there was more or less discontent and growling among the warriors, and Joseph thought he had best have nothing to do with the camp except to follow the movements ordered by Looking Glass.

After moving camp they reached a creek near Kamiah where they passed another night, expecting to be attacked by Howard at any moment. But no soldiers appeared. The third day they crossed the Clearwater. The river was high. Only about half the camp was across the river when they saw Howard's troops approaching. There was quick work done then. It only took a few minutes to cross the balance of the camp. Shortly after they got across the troops reached the river and tried to cross. But Looking Glass was on the alert and, rallying his warriors, opened fire on the soldiers and compelled them to fall back. This ended the great battles of Idaho. Howard could not cross the

Clearwater, and Looking Glass left the field. It is a well established fact among the Nez Perces that Howard only killed four Nez Perce Indians during his operations in Idaho, and one other killed at Cottonwood foots up the grand total of men killed at five.

After the Idaho battles had ended, the Nez Perce camp moved from near Clearwater to a place called Wyap-p [Weippe]. The second day they made camp at a placed called Sah-wis-nin-mah. The next day Looking Glass took a portion of the warriors back to harass Howard, and the camp moved but a few miles. Looking Glass did not, however, attack or discover himself to Howard, but made a night raid to capture the horses of the "friendly" Indians who were in Howard's service. They captured and drove away sixty-five head. After reaching camp with them, a number of Nez Perce scouts were sent back to look for Howard. They had a very good plan laid to destroy Howard's command, but he did not have nerve to push the Indians. Although they did everything they could to entice him, he was rather shy and took good care not to follow too closely on the Nez Perces after they got on the Lolo Trail, always sending his Nez Perce scouts a few days' march ahead of his command.

While Looking Glass' rear guard scouts were watching the trail one day, they discovered three Indians following it. These three Indians were scouts for Howard. Unfortunately for them they were surrounded before they knew what to do. Looking Glass' scouts were under command of Watz-am-yas, a brave warrior whom I have before mentioned, an honest, good man as ever lived, and who, like Looking Glass, had used every endeavor to preserve peace. When Howard's scouts were captured, Watz-am-yas addressed the prisoners as follows, "We are your relations. Your skins, your hair, your bodies, everything you are or have about you are the same as ours. Your supposed friends, that is, the Americans, have marked our native country with the blood of your relations. The white man has been drawing Nez Perce blood for many years. Our chiefs have put all their nerves between their teeth to keep peace with the white man. And yet you are not satisfied with the way in which we have been treated, but are assisting in working against us. We have captured you before and let you go. We knew you had taken up arms against us, but for relations sake we let you go. You promised us before that you would remain at your homes and not help Howard destroy us. We have kept our promises to you, while your promises have been lies. We have spared your lives many times. We will do so again if you promise me one thing, that when we let you go you will return to your homes and never make another move or step to fight your relations now under Looking Glass."

The prisoners replied, "Yes. We are so glad to be allowed to go unharmed we will never make another attempt to pursue you. You have spared our lives during the battles in our own country and have acted manly with us."

Watz-am-yas said again, "I want you to understand that the next Nez Perce scouts we capture acting under Howard we will kill at once." Watz-am-yas then took all the cartridges they had and two horses, and told them to go home and never make their appearance again during the war.

After the prisoners had been set at liberty, Watz-am-yas moved his band a short distance and they concealed themselves to await the approach of the soldiers. Suddenly they discovered some more Indians moving on their trail. These were more of Howard's scouts. Watz-am-yas quickly formed his men in a horseshoe-shaped line in the brush and encompassing the trail. When Howard's scouts had fairly entered the ambush, Capt. John, the well-known scout of the General's, exclaimed, "Here are some fresh tracks. Let us go back. There is danger around here."

They turned to retreat, but just as they did so Watz-am-yas opened fire. The brush was so dense, however, that all the army scouts, except one that was dangerously wounded, got away. When Watz-am-yas reached the wounded man the latter said, "Spare my life; I am badly wounded and have news to tell you."

"Yes," replied Watz-am-yas "we have spared your lives too often. You can tell your news in the happy hunting grounds." With that he put a bullet through the scout's head.

The Nez Perces were nine days in coming from Clearwater to Lolo.

When the Nez Perce camp reached the Hot Springs on the Lolo Trail, not far from Bitterroot Valley, three Indians met them in their camp. One of these Indians was a Nez Perce, but his home was in the Bitterroot Valley. He told Looking Glass there were some soldiers on the trail watching for them to come.

Looking Glass said he did not want any troubles on this side of the Lolo Range, that he did not want to fight either soldiers or citizens east of the Lolo because they were not the ones who had fought them in Idaho. The idea among the Indians, uneducated as they were, was that the people of Montana had no identity with the people of Idaho, and that they were entirely separate and distinct, having nothing to do with each other. If they had to fight, they believed it was Idaho people they should fight and not Montanans. Looking Glass therefore gave orders to his warriors that in case they should see any white men, either citizens or soldiers, on the Lolo, not to molest them unless, as they had compelled him in Idaho, these citizens or soldiers should compel them to fight in self defense. He said, "We are going to buffalo country. We want to go through the settlements quietly. We do not wish to harm anyone if we can help it."

The chief then sent an Indian called John Hill and two others in advance of his camp while coming down the Lolo. These three came to a post of four or five white men. This was Captain Kinney's camp, and this was the night John Hill was arrested and taken to camp. Hill told Kinney the chiefs had sent him ahead to ascertain if the Nez Perce camp could pass through peaceably. Hill was sent back to invite the chiefs to come to the white man's camp, saying that these white men wished to see the chiefs. This was on Wednesday. Looking Glass immediately started down with a band of warriors to meet Capt. Kinney of the volunteers. When Looking Glass reached Kinney's camp, the chief reiterated to him that he did not wish to harm the whites east of the Lolo mountains, that it was true he had fought the soldiers in Idaho when he was compelled to, that he did not want to fight any more, and that he only wanted permission to go through to buffalo country. At this time the Nez Perces believed that Sitting Bull still retained possession of the Yellowstone country and that if the soldiers still pursued them, they could join Sitting Bull. Kinney replied that he had no authority to treat with them but appointed a council for the next day in the afternoon.

By this time Captain Rawn was preparing in the Lolo a splendid trap for Looking Glass and his band. Looking Glass knew nothing about this trap. He only thought the soldiers were camped in the customary manner, and had no idea of entrenchments being prepared to obstruct the passage of himself and his warriors. Readers, I do not wish my motives misconstrued in giving Looking Glass the leading position in these movements and councils. I am not censuring Joseph when I do not give him preference, nor am I influenced by kinship with Looking Glass. My statements are simply the truth of history. I know it was understood, and probably is yet, by nearly all that Joseph was the commanding chief of the Nez Perce force during the war and that he really is the man who should have credit for the good work in restraining his warriors from excesses in their passage into and through Bitterroot. It is an error. Joseph was a good man but he had nothing to do with the camp after Looking Glass joined it near Cottonwood, only by following it to shelter himself from the retributive hands of the white man. It was Looking Glass who saved many a white man's life during the campaign; he was the commander. As he ordered, camp was moved or remained stationary, and what military credit is due for the conduct of the campaign is due to him. Knowing Looking Glass to be well known to many whites, and that he was entitled to his reputation as a really good, kind-hearted red man, I submit these facts, incidentally, to correct a popular error. White Bird was a fighting cock, but with the exception of an instance on Salmon River, he awaited orders from his superior chiefs.

Capt. Rawn's camp, where he had erected rifle pits in the canyon, was about sixteen miles from Missoula and about four miles above the mouth of Lolo. The mountains on the south side of Lolo are precipitous and densely covered with standing timber, so that escape on that side was impossible. On the north side grassy ridges stretched away from the stream, allowing a passage in almost any direction.

On Thursday Looking Glass and White Bird met Capt. Rawn and a few armed men and shook hands with Rawn. Of course the latter wanted the feather in his hat and told Looking Glass he must give up his arms. Captain Rawn and Looking Glass then appointed another day to have a talk.

Looking Glass returned to his camp and told his warriors the conditions demanded of them. By this time they well knew about "The Corral," as Looking Glass termed Rawn's fortifications. The Indians thought it was ridiculous to give up their arms to their foes. White Bird made a speech and said, "We remember a big war that took place once on the Columbia River. The United States troops fought against the Yakimas, Cayuses, Umatillas, Spokanes and Coeur d'Alenes. Colonel Wright was the big chief of the soldiers. After many battles the Indians were defeated. Colonel Wright told the Indians that if they would surrender, he would treat them well and hurt no one but the murderers. On these conditions the Indians surrendered. Then Col. Wright hanged many innocent Indians. Some of them deserved hanging, but many others' hands were clear of white men's blood. These soldiers camped below us are of the same kind. How do we know but that Joseph, Looking Glass and others will be hanged immediately after we surrender? The officer tells us he does not know who will be hanged, that the government has to decide on that question." There were manifestations of approval when White Bird had spoken.

Looking Glass said, "Yes. We do not want to fight. I tried to surrender in Idaho, but my offer was rejected. The soldiers came upon my camp and the first thing I knew the bullets were flying around my head. The soldiers lie so that I have no more confidence in them. They have had their way for a long time; now we must have ours. We *must* go to buffalo country. If we are not allowed to go peaceably we shall do the best we can. If the officer wishes to build corrals for the Nez Perces he may, but they will not hold us back. We are not horses. The country is large. I think we are as smart as he is and know the roads and mountains as well."

The Nez Perces, however, concluded to have another council and try to make peace without giving up their

arms—the Indian way of making treaties. On Friday Capt.
Rawn made his appearance about a half mile below the
Indian village with about one hundred men and halted. An
Indian by the name of Pierre, a Flathead, was sent forward
by the officer. When Looking Glass saw so many men near
his camp he thought they had certainly come to fight.
Looking Glass returned word by Pierre that he would meet
Captain Rawn, unarmed, half way between the forces. The
council was held and Looking Glass proposed to surrender
all the ammunition of the camp as a guarantee that the
Indians intended to go through the country peaceably. When
told that nothing but an unconditional surrender would be
accepted, he asked for another meeting next day to give him
time to consult with the other chiefs. Captain Rawn told
him that any further communication he had to make must
be made under a flag of truce at the fortified camp.

On considering the matter further, the Indians decided
not to trust themselves under the condition demanded. They
thought perhaps the white man was anxious to make peace,
but still they feared treachery. I remember hearing Delaware
Jim, the acting interpreter, relate that when Rawn met
Looking Glass and demanded the surrender of the Indian
guns, Looking Glass replied through the interpreter, "If you
want my arms so bad you can start in taking them. I made
up my mind before leaving Idaho that we would talk with
the white man only through our guns. When I promise, I fulfill and do not lie as the white man does. When a Chinaman
travels he carries no arms. Do you think I am a Chinaman?
It is foolish to think of a whole camp going to the buffalo
country and not carrying a single gun."

While the Nez Perces were camped on the Lolo and it
was supposed they could not get past "the corral" without
surrendering, Joseph said to Looking Glass, "Let us go on. If
not allowed to pass, we will fight our way through Lolo and
next fight our way through Montana. We want peace, but the
whites want us to be kept in the Lolo Canyon. Let us go
through the best way we can, whether it is by peace or war."

Looking Glass answered, "Did you or did you not, with
other chiefs, elect me for leader through this country
because I knew it and the people, and did you not promise

that I should have the whole command and do as I please? You and the other chiefs told me these words. Now, Joseph, I wish to know if you are going to break your promise. If you are anxious to fight I will withdraw my people and you can fight as pleases you. I fight when I cannot avoid it, but not otherwise. Still I can fight my battles as well as anybody. At the fortifications in our way there are some Flatheads aiding the whites. If we fight the whites we must fight the Flatheads. Some of them are our relations. Now you can make your choice."

Joseph replied, "You are right, Looking Glass. We did elect you head man of the camp. Go ahead and do the best." So Looking Glass remained in supreme command.

On Saturday, Looking Glass ordered camp to be raised and directed the women to travel on the north side of Lolo until they passed the "Nez Perce Corral," then cross the Lolo and turn in a southerly direction up Bitterroot Valley. The warriors were to cover the movement. The camp moved. The soldiers and volunteers got into position in the earthworks, and while they were uselessly standing to arms, the Indians passed deliberately by without any fight whatever.

While the camp was moving in this manner, the Indians captured Henry McFarland, Jack Walsh, and another man. These men were volunteers. Looking Glass told them they could go home and attend to their own business. During the day several white men fell into the hands of the Nez Perces, and to all of them Looking Glass repeated the remark, "Go home and mind your own business; we will harm no man."

It has been discussed whether Rawn acted cowardly or not in permitting the Nez Perces to pass. The Nez Perces gave him credit for wisdom in not opening fire on them. The bravest of their warriors would have done the same. Had he attacked them he would have been severely whipped. It is a well known fact that the biggest "Indian eaters" at Lolo were less courageous than those who professed less.

That evening the Nez Perces made camp on McLain's place, about eight miles above the mouth of Lolo, in Bitterroot Valley.

The same evening W. J. Stephens and about fifty or sixty volunteers reached the camp of Looking Glass. The old chief himself was the first one to meet and speak to them. Some of these volunteers were on their way back to their homes in the Bitterroot Valley and had run into the Nez Perce camp unintentionally. Doubtless some of them thought their lives not very valuable when they found themselves encompassed by the Nez Perces. Looking Glass well knew the facts. He said to them, "You are volunteers; you come over to fight us. I could kill you if I wanted to, but I do not. We have many women and children. I do not care for my own life, but I have pity for them. You can go to your homes. I give you my word of honor that I will harm nobody." After this talk the volunteers dispersed in all directions for their homes.

About this same time three Nez Perces arrived at the Flathead agency. They came direct from the Yellowstone country via Missoula. Eagle-of-the-Light was at that time camped at Flathead agency, and they came here to see him and exchange news. These three Indians had been acting as scouts for General Miles, looking after Sitting Bull's Sioux on the Yellowstone, but while on a scout in that valley they were told by some white men that the Nez Perces had broken out in Idaho, and they deserted Miles to go to their homes in Idaho. The name of the head man of these three was Grizzly Bear Youth. He acted like a grizzly bear in the Big Hole Battle. This man had many engagements with the Sioux and always got away with the white feather. When he learned the hostile Nez Perces were on the Lolo Trail, he remained at the agency waiting for them to pass Missoula County. He was at the agency about one week. The news reached Missoula that these three Indians were at the agency obtaining cartridges from the trader Duncan McDonald, and it caused quite a disturbance of public feeling. But it was an error. These three men had a pack mule, but it was for blankets and cooking utensils and not to pack cartridges. Duncan McDonald knows better than to let hostile Indians have cartridges. During his stay here Grizzly Bear Youth found how near this point is to the National Boundary Line, and he thought he would go over to Lolo and see Looking Glass and tell him. Grizzly Bear Youth was, however, one of Lawyer's Nez Perces, was rich in horses, and desired to get back to the reserve in Idaho. Even before this he tried to go through by the other route, but after reaching Horse Plains, forty-five miles from the agency, he turned back, thinking it was not safe to attempt to get through that way. Duncan McDonald told him he had better go by Lolo Trail and surrender to Howard.

Accordingly, the three Nez Perces started from the agency on Sunday afternoon for the Lolo Trail. Before leaving, Grizzly Bear Youth said here that if he should see Looking Glass, he would try to influence the Nez Perces to go through the Flathead Reservation to Tobacco Plains and not through the settlements of the Territory. When he reached Lolo, he found that the Nez Perce camp was only a few miles above and he concluded he might go over and see his relations, although he did not propose to join the camp. Before dismounting from his horse he told the chiefs they were a band of fools, that it was folly for a handful of Indians to think of fighting the United States government. After dismounting he went to Looking Glass and White Bird and told them what he thought it best for them to do—that was to turn back and go by the Flathead Reservation and Flathead Lake to the British Possessions.

Looking Glass then called a council and told Joseph and the others what Grizzly Bear Youth had said. White Bird and Red Owl agreed; they wanted to go by the reserve. Joseph did not say a word. Looking Glass wanted to go by Big Hole and down the Yellowstone and join the Crows, according to agreement, because the Crows had promised them that whenever the Nez Perces fought the whites they would join them. There was a disagreement, but after quarrelling among themselves they concluded it was best to let Looking Glass have his way. This council was held about a mile or a mile and a half above McLain's ranch on the Bitterroot.

When the Indians were marching past the fortifications and down Lolo, the voice of Looking Glass could be distinctly heard addressing his warriors, "Don't shoot, don't shoot.

Let the white men shoot first." This he repeated over and over. All this time the soldiers and volunteers kept their positions in the breastworks. When the volunteers saw that Captain Rawn would not fire on the Indians, some of them started down the stream to head the Indians off. Looking Glass was on the alert for a movement of this kind and placed his best warriors between the volunteers and his women, children and pack horses—in fact, as they passed down, the women and children were advanced ahead and the warriors held back to act as a rear guard. As they were moving down Lolo, they saw these volunteers dashing down Lolo with the evident purpose of cutting off the women and children. At the sight of this the warriors believed certainly that they were going to have a fight and started with a yell in the direction of the volunteers. Capt. Rawn, seeing the demonstrations of the volunteers and believing a collision was likely to occur between them and the Nez Perces, dispatched a half-breed named A. Matte and a few Flatheads to ascertain whether a fight occurred and to report to him immediately. While Matte and his Flatheads were proceeding down Lolo, they met John Scott riding rapidly back toward Rawn's camp. He had his hat in his hand using it as a whip and his war horse was putting in his best licks. On meeting Matte he told him an engagement was going on—that the volunteers were fighting. He wanted Matte to turn back lest he should be killed. But Matte kept on as he was ordered by Rawn, who desired to reinforce the volunteers if they engaged the Nez Perces. Matte came in sight of the volunteers just as the Nez Perce warriors started for them. The Indian fighters thought sure they had seen their last day and stampeded up Lolo toward Rawn's camp. A few halted when they had gone a little distance or when they had reached Matte and the Flatheads. Looking Glass and his warriors had swift horses and could have intercepted them in their line of retreat, and in case of a fight would have cut them off from Rawn and had the two parties at their mercy. The builders of the Lolo fortifications may have thought they were a shelter, but they were mistaken. The rifle pits were exposed on one side, and on that side there was a steep mountain, covered with trees, fallen timber and rocks, affording excellent cover for the Indian sharpshooters, from which they could have picked off those in the rifle pits at their leisure. It is true that there were a few splendid shots in the force, but two-thirds of them were not, and all the Indians were hunters, experienced fighters and good marksmen.

I remember White Bird said that if war had opened on Lolo, the whole country would have been fired, and many a farmer would have lost his crops and home and perhaps his scalp. It is probable that the Nez Perces would then have moved north through the Flathead Reservation. Whatever the chiefs of the reserve and Bitterroot Valley may have said about the peaceable disposition of their Indians, and that there was no danger of their joining the Nez Perces, such was a mistake. There were Indians on the Bitterroot and Flathead Reserve who had their guns ready for use if a battle occurred at Lolo. Indians had been whispering at these places long before the hostiles reached Lolo. The writer of these papers stated in Missoula before ever Walitze, Tap-sis-il-pip and Um-till-lip-cown raised their hands in Idaho that a Nez Perce war would soon break out in that territory. My prediction was laughed at. Who would believe that the Nez Perces would take to the war path? The situation was but little less threatening with some of the Flatheads and Pend'Oreilles in Missoula County.

After raising camp at McLain's there was still some discussion as to the route to be taken—whether to the British Possessions through the Flathead Reservation, or to the Yellowstone via the Big Hole. If forced to fight, they proposed to join the Sioux or Crows in the Yellowstone country; if not, they designed to return to Idaho the next spring after getting their dried meat. Finally, Looking Glass urged that he wanted to go by Big Hole because he knew the country better, and although this was only a pretext, as they could have found their way just as well northward, his wishes were respected and they started up the Bitterroot Valley.

On reaching the place of Charlos, the Flathead chief, Looking Glass summoned a number of his warriors to accompany him to visit Charlos and inquire of him where the best place to camp was to find good grass. On approaching Charlos' house, Looking Glass thought it would be honorable to extend his hand to Charlos before making his inquiry. But Charlos refused to accept the extended hand, saying, "Why should I shake hands with men whose hands are bloody? My hands are clean of blood." Looking Glass replied, "Your hands are as red with the blood of your enemies as mine are. Why should my hands be clean when I have been forced to fight the white man? Your hands are as bloody as ours. I did not come to talk about blood. I came to ask you the best place to camp." Charlos answered, "Above my house is the best spot to camp," and there they accordingly pitched their tents.

Looking Glass kept close watch of his warriors while camped near Stevensville, in which town they did considerable trading. He sent several to camp for being disorderly. It was very fine for the officers sitting in camp and indulging in strong drink to condemn the people of Stevensville for selling these Indians goods and provisions and allege that they were aiding the Nez Perces to recruit for their march, and that they should be punished therefore. This talk was something like Howard's. Their words have more force than their deeds. These Nez Perces would never stand before a little town like Stevensville and perish of starvation when plenty could be had there. The Nez Perces under Looking Glass offered to buy from the first, but if they had been refused and obliged to resort to that measure they would have plundered. Had as many soldiers as there were men been stationed in Stevensville and a band of starving Nez Perces like these been refused food, the soldiers with all the laws of the United States on their side would have lasted but a short time. It was fortunate for Stevensville that citizens and not soldiers had possession of it. Under the circumstances, the citizens of Stevensville did right.

An incident happened during the time of the encampment near Stevensville that illustrates the indisposition of the Nez Perces to have any conflict with the people of Montana. A citizen wished to visit the Indian camp. He mounted his best riding horse and, accompanied by a half breed who had presented Looking Glass with fifty pounds of flour, rode thereto. It should be remembered that Looking Glass had no lodge nor even cooking utensils. He camped in the open air and received his meals from his warriors. He was so glad to receive as a visitor the half breed who had presented him with the sack of flour that he invited him to have a smoke. He noticed the actions of the citizen and told him there was a certain portion of the camp which it would be best for him not to visit—that some of their relations had been killed in Idaho, and it was not best for him to go near them. The citizen, however, wanted to trade off his horse for a fortune and went charging around the camp promiscuously, making his steed prance and caper, and asking the Nez Perces three of their good horses for his one. He had many good offers to trade, but always refused. In any other camp than the Nez Perces he would have been packed off and that would have been the last of him and his funny horse. In one of his circuits he went to that part of the camp which he had been advised by Looking Glass to avoid. A wounded Nez Perce, some of whose relations had been killed in Idaho, was standing by a log and resting on his gun. On seeing the white man cavorting around in an impudent way, the Indian said in English, "Me give you three horses; my horses very good ones." The white man refused. It seemed that he only wanted to put on style. This made the warrior angry and he exclaimed, "You go home, you d__n white man; you ___." It was a wonder he was not killed. But he left hastily, and if that funny horse of his had a 1:40 gait in him, it was brought out as the citizen lit out for Stevensville.

Not being acquainted with the country above Stevensville, I am unable to designate the other camping places. An incident, however, occurred near the head of Bitterroot Valley, at Lockwood's ranch I believe, which I wish to relate. A certain band of the Nez Perces were under command of T-whool-we-tzoot, the same Indian who was made prisoner by Howard in Idaho when he was elected speaker of the tribe at the council. This was the worst band in the whole camp and a very unruly lot. While passing Lockwood's ranch, some of this band went into the cabin and helped themselves to about two hundred pounds of flour, thirty or forty pounds of coffee, one file, two or three shirts, and some other small articles. On reaching camp they went to Looking Glass and told him what they had done. Looking Glass was very angry and told T-whool-we-tzoot that unless they obeyed his orders they should be put out of the camp. He said he would not permit plundering, and demanded seven head of horses from those Indians as payment for the articles they had stolen. The thieves consented to give up seven head of horses and leave them at the ranch, but Looking Glass would not be satisfied until they branded the horses with Lockwood's brand and left them at his ranch. I understand that Lockwood, not satisfied with the seven horses left him, went on the warpath, joined Gibbon's command, got shot at the Big Hole Battle and lost his brother at the same place.

While traveling slowly toward Big Hole, dragging their lodge poles, White Bird went to Looking Glass and said, "Why do you allow the camp to drag lodge poles? By the way you are acting you seem to anticipate no danger. How do we know but that some of these days or nights we shall be attacked by the whites. We should be prepared for trouble. Let your lodge poles be destroyed and move as rapidly as possible without them to the buffalo plains."

Looking Glass answered, "That is all nonsense and bosh. Who is going to trouble us? What wrong did we do in passing through the Bitterroot settlements? I think that we did very well in going through the country peaceably with a band of hostiles like we have got. We are in no hurry. The little bunch of soldiers from Missoula are not fools enough to attack us. We had best take the world as easily as possible. We are not fighting with the people of this country."

White Bird replied, "Well, it is no harm to be prepared. We know the whites want us to surrender our arms to them. We were told while in the Bitterroot Valley there were soldiers and volunteers all over the country, in front and rear, looking for us. If they want us to surrender our arms to them, they will have to fight for them."

Looking Glass said, "Oh, there is no danger."

Another Indian, well known among themselves as a medicine man, said to the chiefs a day before the battle of Big Hole, "What are we doing here?" After singing his song he continued, "While I slept, my medicine told me to move on, that Death is approaching us. Chief, I only tell you this because it may be of some good to this camp. If you take my advice, we can avoid death, and that advice is to speed through this country. If not, there will be tears in our eyes in a short time."

Now, reader, let me explain about Indian "medicine." The Indians' belief may seem ridiculous to civilized people, but the Indians believe in their medicine as implicitly as Ignatious, Loyola or the Jesuits believed or believe in Christ or a Chinaman believes in Confucius. The Indian medicine man goes to the mountains and starves himself for several days to obtain his medicines. So long as his stomach contains any food whatever he can obtain no medicine. His system must be purified from all edible matter, his body must be made clean by ablutions, and he must have faith that his desires for medicine will be granted. These medicines are chiefly beast, fowls, insects and fishes of all kinds, which come to him and tell him what is going to happen. It seems the Spiritualists have somewhat similar beliefs.

I am not speaking of the semi-civilized tribes, but of the native Indians in their wildest state. Their superstition on this point has cost many a life. The writer of these papers has had many difficulties because he does not choose to believe in what the medicine men say. It is not strange. A man in the South of Ireland who abused a priest might be killed by some devout believer. The Indians are as fixed in their belief in the medicine man. I do not ask readers to believe as they do; I am, however, explaining a matter that has a great deal to do with the actions of Indians.

When the medicine man had advised the chiefs of what to do, Looking Glass, although he protested his inability to see where danger was to come from, ordered camp to be moved forward, and *they camped that night on the Big Hole Battleground*. The Nez Perces say they had seen white men moving down the distant hills. These were some of Bradley's scouts, who have believed they were not discovered by the

Indians. The Indians gave the matter little attention. They thought they were merely scouts watching their movements, a surveillance to which they had become accustomed, and they knew that the little band of soldiers that had tried to bar their passage of the Lolo was following them. They *did not know* this little band had been reinforced by Gibbon's command from Fort Shaw. They had no idea they would be attacked by the Lolo soldiers.

On the night they camped at the battleground most of the warriors were up until a late hour engaged in their war dance. This caused a deep sleep to fall on them after they went to their lodges. Some of them slept so soundly they never awakened. The camp, not apprehending danger, was sleeping soundly, when suddenly the rifles of the soldiers belched forth their deadly fire. The camp was awakened to find their enemies plunging through it dealing death and destruction in every direction. General Gibbon had all the advantage of a complete surprise.

With the soldiers in the midst of their camp before they were even awakened, those who could fled to the brush along a brook. Here it was that White Bird and Looking Glass displayed the valor of true chieftains, rallied their warriors from a rout, and plucked a victory from the very jaws of defeat. White Bird was the first to rally his warriors to a charge upon the soldiers. "Why are we retreating?" he shouted in Nez Perce. "Since the world was made, brave men fight for their women and children. Are we going to run to the mountains and let the whites kill our women and children before our eyes? It is better we should be killed fighting. Now is our time; fight! These soldiers cannot fight harder than the ones we defeated on Salmon River and in White Bird Canyon. Fight! Shoot them down. We can shoot as well as any of these soldiers." At these words the warriors wheeled around and started back to fight the soldiers in their camp.

Looking Glass was at the other end of the camp. His voice was heard calling out, "Walitze! Tap-sis-ill-pilp! Um-til-lilp-cown! This is a battle! These men are not asleep as were those you murdered in Idaho! These soldiers mean battle. You tried to break my promise at Lolo. You wanted to fire at the fortified place. Now is the time to show your courage and fight. You can kill right and left. I would rather see you killed than the rest of the warriors, for you commenced the war. Now, go ahead and fight." The warriors addressed were so angered and aroused they did not care for their lives and rallied to the charge with those led by White Bird. Some of them said they had heard the white man was a good fighter, but he seemed to fight best when his enemy was asleep.

Many women and children were killed before getting out of their beds. In one lodge there were five children. One soldier went into it and killed every one of them. When the warriors rallied and opened fire, they poured their shot into the soldiers so rapidly and effectively that the soldiers suffered considerable loss and soon retreated to a point of timber near the trail. In the midst of the hottest of the fight Tap-sis-ill-pilp was killed. Walitze, on being told his companion was dead, ran right into the soldiers and was shot down dead in his tracks. Thus did two of the three murderers who brought on the war expiate their offense, and it is due to them to say that they died as brave as the bravest.

Before these two men were killed an episode of interest occurred at the lodges. In a fight between an officer and a warrior, the warrior was shot down dead. The warrior's sister was standing by him when he fell, and as he lay there his six-shooter lay by his side. The woman, seeing her brother dying and the blood running from his mouth, seized the six-shooter, leveled it at the officer, fired, shot him through the head and killed him. From all the information I can obtain, I believe the officer was Captain Logan.

While the soldiers were retreating across to the timber, Grizzly Bear Youth followed them and was doing rapid work with his Henry rifle. If I remember correctly the description, there was a crossing or slough the soldiers had to go over that impeded them. While the soldiers were at this place, a volunteer turned around and commenced damning the Indians lustily. He is described as a tall, ugly looking man, and I will describe the incident following as it was related to me by Grizzly Bear Youth last summer at the Sioux camp near Fort Walsh.

"When I was following the soldiers, trying to kill as many of them as possible, a big, ugly volunteer turned around swearing and made for me. I suppose he had no time to load his needle gun, so he swung it over his head by the barrel and rushed at me to strike me over the head with the butt end. I did the same thing. We both struck and each received a blow on the head. The volunteer's gun put a brand on my forehead that will be seen as long as I live. My blow on his head made him fall on his back. I jumped on him and tried to hold him down. The volunteer was a powerful man. He turned me over and got on top. He got his hand on my throat and commenced choking me. I was almost gone and had just strength left to make signs to a warrior who was coming up to shoot him. This was Red Owl's son, who ran up, put his needle gun to the volunteer's side and fired. The ball passed through him and killed him. But I had my arm around the waist of the man when the shot was fired, and the ball, after going through the volunteer, broke my arm."

This was the second scuffle Grizzly Bear Youth had in the Big Hole Battle. The other man was a soldier, but he did not last long.

I dissent from the plea that the women had to be shot because they fought as well as the men. It was shameful the way women and children were shot down in that fight. The five children I mentioned were sleeping when they were killed. It was reported Sergeant Wilson killed nine Indians. Yes, nine women and children. I understand he received a medal from the Government for his bravery at Big Hole. Instead of receiving a medal, he should have been court-martialed. It is a well-known fact that the command wasted more powder and lead on the women and children than on the warriors. There were seventy-eight Indians, all told, killed in the Big Hole battle. Of these only thirty were warriors. The others were women and children. About forty women and children were piled up in one little ravine where they had run for shelter. Many women, with from one to three children in their arms, were found dead in that ravine. Some of the children had their mother's breasts in their mouths when both were found there dead. What reason could the soldiers have had to kill them? Had the warriors been with them we might have believed the soldiers could not help it. A daughter of Looking Glass, now north of the line, had hundreds of bullets whiz past her while crawling with a child in her arms to find shelter. The gallant Seventh Infantry! It should be called the Cursed Seventh! They were not satisfied in killing Indians whom they found asleep. They must kill women and children too. Why, if they wanted to kill women, did they not kill the woman who killed Capt. Logan? It is said she was killed on the spot. It is a lie. I do not even blame her. Any woman would have done the same. There was her brother dying at her feet, his loaded revolver lying by his side. What sister would not have seized it and avenged her brother's death?

While the fight was going on in the morning, some of the Nez Perces noticed the howitzer approaching the battle ground. They charged upon the squad with it, killing, I believe, the man in command. After capturing the howitzer, they damaged it so that, as they believed, it could not be used. A few minutes later an Indian reached the gun and expressed great regrets that it was rendered useless. He said, "It is a great pity. I know how to use this kind of gun. I learned when I was with Col. Wright fighting Cayuses and Yakimas."

According to White Bird's statement, Gibbon's command retreated to a high point and entrenched itself. It was thereby saved temporarily, but White Bird did not deem the place impregnable. It was another circumstance that saved Gibbon—the Indians were informed Howard's command was close up on their trail and that volunteers were coming from the eastern part of the Territory. They continued to harass Gibbon and would have stayed with him till they wore him out had they not been apprehensive of his receiving reinforcements. They got their news in this way: About the time the main fight was over and the warriors were examining their dead, they discovered a white man, a citizen, breathing, with his eyes closed and pretending to be dead, although he was not even wounded. When they found he was playing 'possum, they took hold of his arms and raised him up. Finding the Indians were too smart to let him get away, he jumped to his feet. Looking Glass ordered the warriors not to kill him, saying that he was a citizen and they might obtain information from him concerning Howard. They then questioned him, and in reply he said Howard would be there in a short time and that plenty of volunteers were coming from Virginia to head them off. While he was telling the news, a woman who had lost her brother and some of her children in the fight came up. She was crying at the time and on seeing the citizen, slapped him in the face. He instantly gave her a vigorous kick with his boot. He had not more than kicked her when some of the warriors killed him. He would not have been killed had he refrained from kicking her. His statement decided them to raise camp and move on to a more secure place.

White Bird says the volunteers fought better than the regular soldiers, but it was a shame for the Bitterroot volunteers, after the Nez Perces had treated them so well, to join Gibbon and fight them. A white man must have no respect for himself. It makes no difference how well he is treated by the Indians, he will take the advantage. The Nez Perces felt that they behaved themselves while passing through the Bitterroot, and now feel sorer toward the people of that valley than they do toward the soldiers.

The officer remembered as having acted most manly in the Big Hole fight is Capt. Browning. He stopped his soldiers from killing two women in front of him.

The Nez Perces were crippled more in the Big Hole Battle by General Gibbon than in any battle before or after. It was in this fight they lost their best warriors.

And here I wish to make a correction. In my article last week I stated that the woman who shot Captain Logan escaped unharmed. In this I was mistaken. She was killed on the spot by a soldier.

The particulars of the killing of the murderers of the Hayden party and the ranchmen at Horse Prairie and Birch Creek are not generally known to the Nez Perces. After numerous inquiries, I find there were two men killed at one place. One of them was murdered in his cabin and the other while endeavoring to escape from the cabin. It must be remembered the Nez Perces were actuated at this time to commit murders by a spirit of revenge. They had just met with a considerable loss in the battle of the Big Hole and felt that every white man in their path was their enemy, and by taking his life they could thereby avenge the death of their comrades. After the battle with Gibbon's command the march was resumed. The Indians first came in contact with a party in which there were several white men and two Chinamen. The exact number of whites is not known, but it is thought the number did not exceed six. The party had wagons and a lot of mules, and the Indians came upon them while they were in camp; the Indian camp was made near the train. The whites had in their possession some whiskey which they proposed trading to the Indians for articles of which they stood in need. While the trade was in progress, it began to grow dark. This suited the young and reckless Indians and, as soon as it was dark, they proceeded to help themselves. Under the influence and stimulated by copious draughts of the intoxicant, their hatred for the white race was intensified and they fired their guns into the train. As soon as the firing was begun, the whites and Chinamen beat a retreat. I say they beat a retreat. The Indians did not make an examination to find whether or not they had killed any of the party, but after the volley they approached and rifled the train, taking all the articles in the wagons and camp. They also took the animals. This ended the fight at this place.

The place at which this occurred is not known to either the Indians or the writer. As has been stated, the route was new and unknown to the Indians. Following is the language of my informant: "We did not ask the whites under whose command they were. The fact that they were under command of Hayden was of no interest to us. All we wanted was the whiskey in their possession. Once that was obtained, the appropriation of the rest of the possessions was merely a question of time. An Indian under the influence of whiskey has no more sense than a white man when drunk and is not any more responsible for his actions. When an Indian is drunk, he will commit crimes he would not think of when sober. As an evidence of the truth of this statement, I have only to say that while under the influence of the whiskey captured from the train, one of the bravest and best warriors in the Nez Perce band was killed and another narrowly escaped death at the hands of their comrades."

While the Nez Perce camp was moving beyond Camas Meadow, two days ahead of Howard's command, Grizzly Bear Youth lay in his tent suffering from the wounds received in the Big Hole fight. Here a great bird, that never alights on the earth or trees but rests only in the clouds, appeared to the sufferer in his lodge. In regard to this bird, it is claimed by the Nez Perces to live in their country, that it is never seen except by those wishing it for their medicine. They also say it is much larger and far superior to the eagle and will pick up game of any kind and fly with it. This bird was the medicine of Grizzly Bear Youth, who was awakened from a troubled sleep into which he had fallen by the voice of the bird, which said, "I see you have tears in your eyes, caused by grieving over the loss of your relatives, your country, and your arm. Why do you cry? Look behind about two days' travel and you will see two creeks. These creeks are at Camas Meadow. The big chief of the Idaho soldiers, 'Cut Arm,' and his force are camped there. It is rather a strong force, but fear them not. The Nez Perces will kill some of his men and get possession of his animals. There are two kinds of animals in the camp. I can tell you the name of only one kind. This kind is horses. The other differ from the horse in many ways. Now I must leave you. You may rely on what I have told you. Good luck to you." The bird then disappeared.

It is customary for Indians, when they have received news from their medicine, to summon all their brethren and inform them of what they have been told. Grizzly Bear Youth sent for the warriors, who came to his lodge. After singing his medicine song, he told the Indians of the news he had received from his medicine, the Air Bird. He told them that next night Cut Arm's (Howard's) animals would be in their possession. One-half of the animals were horses; the other half he could not describe. He further said, "I want all the warriors to go back to Camas Meadow tomorrow evening."

When the talk at Grizzly Bear Youth's lodge was over, the warriors retired and the camp was soon quiet. While they slept, two scouts who had been sent to look for Howard's command returned to the camp. They immediately went to Looking Glass and told him that Howard would camp next day at Camas Meadow and that he had with him a large pack train. Looking Glass at once summoned the Nez Perces and told them that he wanted the warriors, with the exception of twenty-five who were to remain under charge of White Bird to guard the camp, to get ready to go and attack Howard. Accordingly, about two hundred and twenty-five warriors, under command of Looking Glass and Joseph, left the camp next morning. They sent scouts all over the country, and traveling slowly, reached Howard's camp about midnight. The Indians were told not to approach the camp until so ordered by Looking Glass, who first sent spies to examine the location. The report made to the camp showed that there were two creeks about three hundred yards apart. Howard's command crossed both creeks and went into camp. The Virginia volunteers made their camp before crossing the second creek. The night was so dark the spies had not discovered the volunteer camp, and they were under the impression that their enemies were all with Howard. It was very lucky indeed for the volunteers that their presence was not known.

On learning the situation, Looking Glass thought it best to have no fight. He told the warriors he only wanted to capture the stock, and that they were to make no move until so ordered by him. A short time before daybreak he gave the order to approach the camp. In obeying, a death-like stillness was observed. The Indians made their way on their hands and knees. Howard's pickets could be heard conversing in a low tone of voice. The Indians afterward said they could have captured all the cavalry horses if they had only known where they were, but the night was so dark that they feared the reports of the spies might be incorrect, and they were consequently in doubt as to the real position of the soldiers. After getting close to the camp, Looking Glass ordered his men to prepare for a charge, and told them if they could capture the animals without fighting it would be the better way, as he only wanted the animals. He also said, "We know American horses are afraid of Indians; make all the noise you possibly can, as by so doing we may be able to stampede the whole herd at once."

The order to charge was given, and the work of stampeding the stock commenced. Ever and anon the voice of Looking Glass could be heard, calling on the Indians to pay no heed to the soldiers, but secure the horses. His men obeyed his commands and rent the air with the most hideous yells. They succeeded in capturing over two hundred head of animals—one-half of which were mules. (These latter were the ones which the Medicine Bird could not describe.) While driving the herd a short distance from the scene of attack, some soldiers were discovered in pursuit. The first thought was that Howard's command was after them, but it subsequently proved to be only a small body of cavalry. These were the troops which were subjected to the whitewashing process in the newspapers—Captain Norwood's command, I believe. Looking Glass ordered the stolen animals to be left in charge of three warriors and the rest of his force to conceal themselves. He said, "Let the fool in command of the soldiers come up to us. Does he think he can take these animals from us with the force he has? Make haste and hide yourselves." The Indian force was divided and two lines formed, the warriors concealing themselves behind trees, rocks, etc. Looking Glass wanted Norwood to advance between the lines formed, but the officer was too wary to be drawn into the trap. He stationed his men some distance away and commenced firing. Looking Glass ordered his men not to fire; he thought the soldiers had not yet seen them and were only firing by guesswork. The troops failing to advance, orders were given to the Indians to fire, and the fight commenced. The Indians endeavored to get the soldiers between the lines formed, and had they succeeded, there would have been a massacre similar to that when Custer's command were killed by Sitting Bull and his warriors. The Indians finally made a charge and the troops retreated to a point of timber. While here the Nez Perces became uneasy lest Howard's command should have heard the firing and reinforce the troops under Norwood. Joseph and Looking Glass held a consultation, and as they had suffered no loss whatever, they started back to their camp.

This ended the great battle of Camas Meadow. About noon the Indians halted and Looking Glass divided the stolen animals among his warriors.

When the Nez Perces were camped at Bear Paw Mountains, Poker Joe grew dissatisfied with the other chiefs for not making their way into the British Possessions. Poker Joe had a good deal of influence over the Indians, but after a discussion with the chiefs, and they not agreeing to his plans, he declined having anything further to do with their future movements. Howard's whereabouts were known to the Indians. They knew his animals were worn out, while their own were in splendid condition. As a consequence, they were in no hurry to move their camp and spent their time in making merry, as they then had no doubt but they would effect their escape without difficulty. They had no intimation of the approach of the troops under General Miles.

While resting in fancied security on the morning of the attack, the scouts being all in camp, an alarm was suddenly given. The cry was "Prepare for a fight; there is a large body of soldiers close on us." White Bird ordered his warriors to prepare for a defense and said, "What a pity we did not have scouts out. Had we known this half an hour ago, how differently might we now have been situated. Had I known then of the approach of the soldiers we would not have to fight. Our horses are fresh and we could have made our escape. But it is too late now. Escape is impossible— fight we must."

About the battle of Bear Paw, I have not much to write, as the Indian version is but a repetition of the published accounts. The Indians got worsted in the engagement, as is well known, and the white man's version was the true one. I propose relating, however, the conversation between Looking Glass and White Bird, some facts in relation to the officer who was taken prisoner, and the promises made Joseph by the commanding officer in charge of the soldiers in case the Indians would surrender.

General Miles, like many others, supposed Joseph to be the leader of the hostiles and wanted his surrender in place of the real leader—Looking Glass. This suited the Indians exactly and they allowed Joseph to go to the camp of the soldiers. That night he remained in the tent of Gen. Miles. During the truce the Indians were engaged in fortifying their position, and some soldiers under command of Lieut. Irvine who ventured into the Indian camp were taken prisoners and held as hostages for the return of Joseph. The fight was renewed at this time. In the afternoon of the second day an exchange was effected, the soldiers returning to their command and Joseph to the Indian camp. Before the exchange, while the fight was in progress, one of the warriors was in need of some needle-gun cartridges. He went to the officer who was yet a prisoner and told him what he wanted. He asked for two cartridges and was given five by the officer, whose name I was told was Lieut. Irvine. A few such men as him in the Indian camp would have made more trouble for the soldiers.

While the fight was in progress, many of the Indian women and a few children made their escape. A large part of the camp believed that Sitting Bull was near at hand and that he would come to their rescue. One of the women had escaped at the first appearance of the soldiers and it was thought she had gone to the Sioux camp. But such was not the case, as the woman went but a short distance and remained until the fight was over.

On the evening of the fourth day a flag of truce was raised for the third time. Gen. Miles told the Indians that if they surrendered he would treat them well, that he would take them to Tongue River that winter and in the spring would send them back to Idaho. He furthermore said that any promises he might make to them would be fulfilled. Joseph wanted to surrender, but the other chiefs kept him from doing so. They feared that in case they were to surrender to Gen. Miles, they would be treated similarly to the Indians who surrendered to Col. Wright on the Columbia in 1858. After surrendering, the principals were all hanged by command of the officer to whom they surrendered. Joseph endeavored to persuade the chiefs that the best thing they could do was to accede to the demands made by Gen. Miles. Looking Glass and White Bird then said, "Joseph, you do not know the Americans as well as we do. Never in the world will they fulfill the promises made the Indians. The commanding officer speaks sweet, but it is doubtful whether he will send the Indians back to their country." Next morning Joseph told Looking Glass he had concluded to surrender to Gen. Miles. The latter chief then went to White Bird, told him the conclusion arrived at by Joseph and said, "We will leave here tonight. I know we will never see our country again."

Near the Indian camp was a ridge on which some of the warriors lay watching the movements of the soldiers. Looking Glass, his brother and the other chiefs were in the camp talking over the proposed flight in the evening. Looking Glass requested his brother to get him his pipe, saying he wanted a smoke. While his brother had gone for the pipe, Looking Glass had his attention attracted by the movements of the warriors on the ridge. He started towards them. He was asked to remain where he was, but the chief replied that he would return shortly, that he wanted to see what the warriors on the ridge were doing. He reached the place where the warriors were. It was some five or six hundred yards from the soldiers' position. He raised himself up to view the surroundings. As he did so a volley from the guns of the soldiers was directed towards him and one of the bullets entered his forehead, throwing him some distance down the hill and killing him instantly. Poker Joe, the friend of the lady prisoners taken in the National Park, was also killed in the Bear Paw fight.

White Bird and his warriors escaped that night. In the escaping party were one hundred three warriors, sixty women, eight children and about two hundred head of horses. One remarkable feature of the party was that there were no dogs with them. An Indian procession is usually considered incomplete unless there are in it a number of these latter animals. In a residence of thirty years in the Indian country, I have not heard of a parallel case.

Joseph could have escaped as well as White Bird, but the conditions promised him by Gen. Miles influenced him to surrender. If he had endeavored to escape, he would have had on his hands his wounded warriors and helpless women and children. He thought it the better plan to rely on the word of the officer to whom he surrendered—the representative of a nation of forty million people.

After White Bird made his escape from the U. S. troops at Bear Paw and before he reached Sitting Bull's camp, he lost seven warriors by the Assiniboins and Gros Ventres. One of the killed was Umti-lilp-cown, the third and last of the Nez Perces who committed the murders in Idaho which brought on the war.

White Bird did not know whether or not it would be safe for him to go to Sitting Bull's camp, but after a consultation with his followers they came to the conclusion they might as well be killed by Indian enemies as by the whites. Coming to a half-breed camp near Milk River, they hired one of the party to guide them to Sitting Bull. As they were proceeding toward the Sioux camp, they came upon an Indian skinning a buffalo. The hunter appeared rather shy, but after considerable parley told White Bird that he was a Sioux and that he had come from Sitting Bull's camp. White Bird told him to go to Sitting Bull and tell him the Nez Perces were anxious to see him, that they were refugees, fleeing for protection from the U. S. troops. The buffalo hunter started on his mission and the Nez Perce camp moved slowly in the direction he had gone. After marching a few miles they discovered a large body of mounted Indians coming toward them. They numbered nearly three thousand warriors and were coming at full speed. A short distance in advance of the main body rode an Indian warrior on a magnificent war horse. When within hailing distance of the Nez Perces the command halted. The warrior in advance asked White Bird, by signs, to what tribe he belonged. White Bird made answer, saying he was a Nez Perce. The other then said, "I am Sitting Bull, and these," pointing to his followers, "are my warriors." Sitting Bull then came up and shook hands with White Bird and his warriors. After bidding them welcome, he said, "I am sorry indeed that your skin is like mine, that your hair is like mine, and that every one around you is a pure red man like myself. We, too, have lost our country by falsehood and theft."

Although the Indians were now north of the line, they expected to be followed and attacked by U. S. soldiers. The Sioux had not thus far been attacked, but they did not know but now that so many soldiers were near them they would follow the Indians and give them battle. Sitting Bull, after hearing of the Bear Paw fight, said, "If I had known you were surrounded by soldiers at Bear Paw Mountains, I certainly would have helped you. What a pity that I was not there with my warriors. But now you are here, and as long as you are with me, I will not allow the Americans to take even a child from you without fighting for it." Sitting Bull received a present of seven horses from White Bird. The Nez Perces were welcomed in the Sioux camp and received from Sitting Bull and his followers nothing but the kindest of treatment.

Part III

In-mut-too-yah-lat-lat Speaks
Chief Joseph Shows His Heart

by
Chief Joseph

Part III

The Inexhaustible Book
Chief Joseph Shows His Heart

Chief Joseph

Introduction

"Our chiefs are killed. Looking Glass is dead. The old men [the council] are all killed. He who led the young men [Ollicut] is dead." These excerpts from Joseph's message to General Howard at the Bear Paw Battlefield describe the conditions that resulted in the emergence of Joseph as the primary leader of the non-treaty Nez Perces and confirmed the widely held view of U.S. Army personnel of Joseph as the brilliant military strategist. Indian victories or stand-offs in a total of thirteen battles and skirmishes against ten different military commands over a period of almost four months and a distance of thirteen hundred miles did call for extraordinary explanation. In reality, emerging from the ravines of Snake Creek on October 6, 1877, was simply the last of the Nez Perce chiefs, in his words "tired...sick and sad," who wanted time to look for his freezing children.

More accurately, Joseph had been caught up in a series of events he could not control—the original murders on the Salmon River while he was away from camp, the decision to recross the Salmon River at Billy Creek and later to strike out on the Lolo Trail rather than surrender at Kamiah, the fateful choice of traveling up the Bitterroot Valley rather than heading north from Lolo to the British Possessions. For much of the campaign he played an insignificant leadership role and was clearly not the military commander he was portrayed to be. As a caretaker of his people, however, Joseph was unsurpassed and deserves history's recognition for his leadership in peace.

Joseph made two trips to Washington, D. C., during early 1879, pleading for the relocation of his people to a land that would permit their survival—and for their return to Idaho as was promised at the time of their surrender. He met with congressmen, cabinet members, and even with President Hayes. While he was always well received and given much encouragement, and his activities were favorably reported by a friendly press, he found that the white man's "good words" resulted in no action.

During Joseph's second Washington visit he granted an interview to a reporter of the *North American Review*. When the interview appeared in print, Joseph's message had been filtered through his interpreter (most likely Arthur Chapman) as well as through the reporter and perhaps the journal's editor. However, the message seems characteristically Joseph's. It is an appropriate message with which to end this brief saga in the story of the American West. It speaks as well to today's Native Americans and the dominant society with which they are still attempting to cope.

In-mut-too-yah-lat-lat Speaks

My friends, I have been asked to show you my heart. I am glad to have a chance to do so. I want the white people to understand my people. Some of you think an Indian is like a wild animal. This is a great mistake. I will tell you all about our people, and then you can judge whether an Indian is a man or not. I believe much trouble and blood would be saved if we opened our hearts more. I will tell you in my way how the Indian sees things. The white man has more words to tell you how they look at him, but it does not require many words to speak the truth. What I have to say will come from my heart, and I will speak with a straight tongue. Ah-cum-kin-i-ma-me-hut (the Great Spirit) is looking at me and will hear me.

My name is In-mut-too-yah-lat-lat (Thunder-Traveling-over-the-Mountains). I am chief of the Wal-lam-wat-kin band of Chute-pa-lu, or Nez Perces (nose-pierced Indians). I was born in eastern Oregon, thirty-eight winters ago. My father was chief before me. When a young man he was called Joseph by Mr. Spalding, a missionary. He died a few years ago. There was no stain on his hands of the blood of a white man. He left a good name on the earth. He advised me well for my people.

Our fathers gave us many laws, which they had learned from their fathers. These laws were good. They told us to treat all men as they treated us; that we should never be the first to break a bargain; that it was a disgrace to tell a lie; that we should speak only the truth; that it was a shame for one man to take from another his wife, or his property, without paying for it. We were taught to believe that the Great Spirit sees and hears everything, and that He never forgets; that hereafter He will give every man a spirit-home according to his deserts; if he has been a good man, he will have a good home; if he has been a bad man, he will have a bad home. This I believe, and all my people believe the same.

We did not know there were other people besides the Indian until about one hundred winters ago, when some men with white faces came to our country. They brought many things with them to trade for furs and skins. They brought tobacco, which was new to us. They brought guns with flintstones on them, which frightened our women and children. Our people could not talk with these white-faced men, but they used signs which all people understood. These men were Frenchmen, and they called our people "Nez Perces," because we wore rings in our noses for ornaments. Although very few of our people wear them now, we are still called by the same name. These French trappers said a great many things to our fathers, which have been planted in our hearts. Some were good for us, but some were bad. Our people were divided in opinion about these men. Some thought they taught more bad than good. An Indian respects a brave man, but he despises a coward. He loves a straight tongue, but he hates a forked tongue. The French trappers told us some truths and some lies.

The first white men of your people who came to our country were named Lewis and Clark. They also brought many things that our people had never seen. They talked straight, and our people gave them a great feast as proof that our hearts were friendly. These men were very kind. They made presents to our chiefs, and our people made presents to them. We had a great many horses, of which we gave them what they needed, and they gave us guns and tobacco in return. All the Nez Perces made friends with Lewis and Clark and agreed to let them pass through their country and never to make war on white men. This promise the Nez Perces have never broken. No white man can accuse us of bad faith and speak with a straight tongue. It has always been the pride of the Nez Perces that they were the friends of the white men.

When my father was a young man, there came to our country a white man (Rev. Mr. Spalding) who talked spirit law. He won the affections of our people because he spoke good things to them. At first he did not say anything about white men wanting to settle on our lands. Nothing was said about that until about twenty winters ago when a number of white people came into our country and built houses and made farms. At first our people made no complaint. They thought there was room enough for all to live in peace, and they were learning many things from the white men that seemed to be good. But we soon found that the white men were growing rich very fast and were greedy to possess everything the Indian had. My father was the first to see through the schemes of the white men, and he warned his tribe to be careful about trading with them. He had a suspicion of men who seemed so anxious to make money. I was a boy then, but I remember well my father's caution. He had sharper eyes than the rest of our people.

Next there came a white officer (Governor Stevens) who invited all the Nez Perces to a treaty council. After the council was opened he made known his heart. He said there were a great many white people in the country, and many more would come, and that he wanted the land marked out so that the Indians and white men could be separated. If they were to live in peace, it was necessary, he said, that the Indians should have a country set apart for them, and in that country they must stay. My father, who represented his band, refused to have anything to do with the council because he wished to be a free man. He claimed that no man owned any part of the earth, and a man could not sell what was not his own.

Mr. Spalding took hold of my father's arm and said, "Come and sign the treaty." My father pushed him away and said, "Why do you ask me to sign away my country? It is your business to talk to us about spirit matters, and not to talk to us about parting with our land." Governor Stevens urged my father to sign his treaty, but my father refused. "I will not sign your paper," he said. "You go where you please, so do I; you are not a child, I am no child. I can think for myself. No man can think for me. I have no other home than this. I will not give it up to any man. My people would have no home. Take away your paper. I will not touch it with my hand."

My father left the council. Some of the chiefs of the other bands of the Nez Perces signed the treaty, and then Governor Stevens gave them presents of blankets. My father cautioned his people to take no presents, for "after awhile," he said, "they will claim that you accepted pay for your country." Since that time four bands of the Nez Perces have received annuities from the United States. My father was invited to many councils, and they tried hard to make him sign the treaty, but he was firm as the rock and would not sign away his home. His refusal caused a difference among the Nez Perces.

Eight years later (1863) was the next treaty council. A chief called Lawyer, because he was a great talker, took the lead in this council, and sold nearly all of the Nez Perces' country. My father was not there. He said to me, "When you go into council with the white man, always remember your country. Do not give it away. The white man will cheat you out of your home. I have taken no pay from the United States. I have never sold our land." In this treaty Lawyer acted without authority from our band. He had no right to sell the Wallowa country. That had always belonged to my father's own people, and the other bands had never disputed our right to it. No other Indians ever claimed Wallowa.

In order to have all people understand how much land we owned, my father planted poles around it and said, "Inside is the home of my people—the white man may take the land outside. Inside this boundary all our people were born. It circles around the graves of our fathers, and we will never give up these graves to any man."

The United States claimed they had bought all the Nez Perces' country outside the Lapwai Reservation from Lawyer and other chiefs, but we continued to live on this land in peace until eight years ago, when white men began to come inside the bounds my father had set. We warned them against this great wrong, but they would not leave our land, and some bad blood was raised. The white man represented that we were going upon the warpath. They reported many things that were false.

The United States Government again asked for a treaty council. My father had become blind and feeble. He could no longer speak for his people. It was then I took my father's place as chief. In this council I made my first speech to white men. I said to the agent who held the council, "I did not want to come to this council, but I came hoping that we could save blood. The white man has no right to come here and take our country. We have never accepted presents from the Government. Neither Lawyer nor any other chief had authority to sell this land. It has always belonged to my people. It came unclouded to them from our fathers, and we will defend this land as long as a drop of Indian blood warms the hearts of our men."

The agent said he had orders from the Great White Chief at Washington for us to go upon the Lapwai Reservation, and that if we obeyed, he would help us in many ways. "You must move to the agency," he said. I answered him, "I will not. I do not need your help; we have plenty, and we are contented and happy if the white man will let us alone. The reservation is too small for so many people with all their stock. You can keep your presents; we can go to your towns and pay for all we need; we have plenty of horses and cattle to sell, and we won't have any help from you. We are free now; we can go where we please. Our fathers were born here. Here they lived, here they died, here are their graves. We will never leave them." The agent went away, and we had peace for awhile.

Soon after this my father sent for me. I saw he was dying. I took his hand in mine. He said, "My son, my body is returning to my mother earth, and my spirit is going very soon to see the Great Spirit Chief. When I am gone, think of your country. You are the chief of these people. They look to you to guide them. Always remember that your father never sold his country. You must stop your ears whenever you are asked to sign a treaty selling your home. A few years more, and white men will be all around you. They have their eyes on this land. My son, never forget my dying words. This country holds your father's body. Never sell the bones of your father and your mother." I pressed my father's hand and told him that I would protect his grave with my life. My father smiled and passed away to the spirit-land.

I buried him in that beautiful valley of winding waters. I love that land more than all the rest of the world. A man who would not love his father's grave is worse than a wild animal.

For a short time we lived quietly. But this could not last. White men had found gold in the mountains around the land of the winding water. They stole a great many horses from us, and we could not get them back because we were Indians. The white men told lies for each other. They drove off a great many of our cattle. Some white men branded our young cattle so they could claim them. We had no friend who would plead our cause before the law councils. It seemed to me that some of the white men in Wallowa were doing these things on purpose to get up a war. They knew that we were not strong enough to fight them. I labored hard to avoid trouble and bloodshed. We gave up some of our country to the white men, thinking that then we could have peace. We were mistaken. The white man would not let us alone. We could have avenged our wrongs many times, but we did not. Whenever the Government has asked us to help them against other Indians, we have never refused. When the white men were few and we were strong, we could have killed them off, but the Nez Perces wish to live at peace.

If we have not done so, we have not been to blame. I believe that the old treaty has never been correctly reported. If we ever owned the land, we own it still, for we never sold it. In the treaty councils the commissioners have claimed that our country had been sold to the Government. Suppose a white man should come to me and say, "Joseph, I like your horses, and I want to buy them." I say to him, "No, my horses suit me, I will not sell them." Then he goes to my neighbor, and says to him, "Joseph has some good horses. I want to buy them, but he refuses to sell." My neighbor answers, "Pay me the money, and I will sell you Joseph's horses." The white man returns to me and says, "Joseph, I have bought your horses, and you must let me have them." If we sold our lands to the Government, this is the way they were bought.

On account of the treaty made by the other bands of Nez Perces, the white men claimed my lands. We were troubled greatly by white men crowding over the line. Some of these were good men, and we lived on peaceful terms with them, but they were not all good.

Nearly every year the agent came over from Lapwai and ordered us onto the reservation. We always replied that we were satisfied to live in Wallowa. We were careful to refuse the presents or annuities which he offered.

Through all the years since the white man came to Wallowa, we have been threatened and taunted by them and the treaty Nez Perces. They have given us no rest. We have had a few good friends among white men, and they have always advised my people to bear these taunts without fighting. Our young men were quick-tempered, and I have had great trouble in keeping them from doing rash things. I have carried a heavy load on my back ever since I was a boy. I learned then that we were but few, while the white men were many, and that we could not hold our own with them. We were like deer. They were like grizzly bears. We had a small country. Their country was large. We were contented to let things remain as the Great Spirit Chief made them. They were not and would change the rivers and mountains if they did not suit them.

Year after year we have been threatened, but no war was made upon my people until General Howard came to our country two years ago and told us that he was the white war-chief of all that country. He said, "I have a great many soldiers at my back. I am going to bring them up here, and then I will talk to you again. I will not let white men laugh at me the next time I come. The country belongs to the Government, and I intend to make you go upon the reservation."

I remonstrated with him against bringing more soldiers to the Nez Perces' country. He had one house full of troops all the time at Fort Lapwai.

The next spring the agent at Umatilla Agency sent an Indian runner to tell me to meet General Howard at Walla Walla. I could not go myself, but I sent my brother and five other head men to meet him, and they had a long talk.

General Howard said, "You have talked straight, and it is all right. You can stay at Wallowa." He insisted that my

brother and his company should go with him to Fort
Lapwai. When the party arrived there General Howard
sent out runners and called all the Indians to a grand
council. I was in that council. I said to General Howard,
"We are ready to listen." He answered that he would not
talk then, but would hold a council next day, when he
would talk plainly. I said to General Howard, "I am ready
to talk today. I have been in a great many councils, but I
am no wiser. We are all sprung from a woman, although
we are unlike in many things. We cannot be made over
again. You are as you were made, and as you were made
you can remain. We are just as we were made by the Great
Spirit, and you cannot change us; then why should children of one mother and one father quarrel?—why should
one try to cheat the other? I do not believe that the Great
Spirit Chief gave one kind of men the right to tell another
kind of men what they must do."

General Howard replied, "You deny my authority, do
you? You want to dictate to me, do you?"

Then one of my chiefs—Too-hool-hool-suit—rose in the
council and said to General Howard, "The Great Spirit Chief
made the world as it is, and as He wanted it, and He made a
part of it for us to live upon. I do not see where you get
authority to say that we shall not live where He placed us."

General Howard lost his temper and said, "Shut up! I
don't want to hear any more of such talk. The law says you
shall go upon the reservation to live, and I want you to do
so, but you persist in disobeying the law. If you do not
move, I will take the matter into my own hand and make
you suffer for your disobedience."

Too-hool-hool-suit answered, "Who are you, that you ask
us to talk and then tell me I shan't talk? Are you the Great
Spirit? Did you make the world? Did you make the sun?
Did you make the rivers to run for us to drink? Did you
make the grass to grow? Did you make all these things that
you talk to us as though we were boys? If you did, then you
have the right to talk as you do."

General Howard replied, "You are an impudent fellow,
and I will put you in the guardhouse," and then ordered a
soldier to arrest him.

Too-hool-hool-suit made no resistance. He asked General Howard, "Is this your order? I don't care. I have expressed my heart to you. I have nothing to take back. I have spoken for my country. You can arrest me, but you cannot change me or make me take back what I have said."

The soldiers came forward and seized my friend and took him to the guardhouse. My men whispered among themselves whether they would let this thing be done. I counseled them to submit. I knew if we resisted that all the white men present, including General Howard, would be killed in a moment, and we would be blamed. If I had said nothing, General Howard would never have given an unjust order against my men. I saw the danger and while they dragged Too-hool-hool-suit to prison, I arose and said, "I am going to talk now. I don't care whether you arrest me or not." I turned to my people and said, "The arrest of Too-hool-hool-suit was wrong, but we will not resent the insult. We were invited to this council to express our hearts, and we have done so." Too-hool-hool-suit was prisoner for five days before he was released.

The council broke up that day. On the next morning General Howard came to my lodge and invited me to go with him and White Bird and Looking Glass to look for land for my people. As we rode along we came to some good land that was already occupied by Indians and white people. General Howard, pointing to this land, said, "If you will come onto the reservation, I will give you these lands and move these people off."

I replied, "No. It would be wrong to disturb these people. I have no right to take their homes. I have never taken what did not belong to me. I will not now."

We rode all day upon the reservation and found no good land unoccupied. I have been informed by men who do not lie that General Howard sent a letter that night telling the soldiers at Walla Walla to go to Wallowa Valley and drive us out upon our return home.

In the council next day General Howard informed us in a haughty spirit that he would give my people thirty days to go back home, collect all our stock, and move onto the reservation, saying, "If you are not here in that time, I shall consider that you want to fight and will send my soldiers to drive you on."

I said, "War can be avoided and it ought to be avoided. I want no war. My people have always been the friends of the white man. Why are you in such a hurry? I cannot get ready to move in thirty days. Our stock is scattered, and Snake River is very high. Let us wait until fall, then the river will be low. We want time to hunt our stock and gather our supplies for the winter."

General Howard replied, "If you let the time run over one day, the soldiers will be there to drive you onto the reservation, and all your cattle and horses outside of the reservation at that time will fall into the hands of the white men."

I knew I had never sold my country, and that I had no land in Lapwai, but I did not want bloodshed. I did not want my people killed. I did not want anybody killed. Some of my people had been murdered by white men, and the white murderers were never punished for it. I told General Howard about this, and again said I wanted no war. I wanted the people who live upon the lands I was to occupy at Lapwai to have time to gather their harvest.

I said in my heart that, rather than have war, I would give up my country. I would rather give up my father's grave. I would give up everything rather than have the blood of white men upon the hands of my people.

General Howard refused to allow me more than thirty days to move my people and their stock. I am sure that he began to prepare for war at once.

When I returned to Wallowa, I found my people very much excited upon discovering that the soldiers were already in the Wallowa Valley. We held a council and decided to move immediately to avoid bloodshed.

Too-hool-hool-suit, who felt outraged by his imprisonment, talked for war and made many of my young men willing to fight rather than be driven like dogs from the land where they were born. He declared that blood alone would wash out the disgrace General Howard had put upon him. It required a strong heart to stand up against such talk, but I urged my people to be quiet and not to begin a war.

We gathered all the stock we could find and made an attempt to move. We left many of our horses and cattle in Wallowa, and we lost several hundred in crossing the river. All my people succeeded in getting across in safety. Many of the Nez Perces came together in Rocky Canyon to hold a grand council. I went with all my people. This council lasted ten days. There was a great deal of war talk and a great deal of excitement. There was one young brave present whose father had been killed by a white man five years before. This man's blood was bad against white men, and he left the council calling for revenge.

Again I counseled peace, and I thought the danger was past. We had not complied with General Howard's order because we could not, but we intended to do so as soon as possible. I was leaving the council to kill beef for my family when news came that the young man whose father had been killed had gone out with several hot-blooded young braves and killed four white men. He rode up to the council and shouted, "Why do you sit here like women? The war has begun already." I was deeply grieved. All the lodges were moved except my brother's and my own. I saw clearly that the war was upon us when I learned that my young men had been secretly buying ammunition. I heard then that Too-hool-hool-suit, who had been imprisoned by General Howard, had succeeded in organizing a war party. I knew that their acts would involve all my people. I saw that the war could not then be prevented. The time had passed. I had counseled peace from the beginning. I knew that we were too weak to fight the United States. We had many grievances, but I knew that war would bring more. We had good white friends, who advised us against taking the warpath. My friend and brother, Mr. Chapman, who has been with us since the surrender, told us just how the war would end. Mr. Chapman took sides against us and helped General Howard. I do not blame him for doing so. He tried hard to prevent bloodshed. We hoped the white settlers would not join the soldiers. Before the war commenced, we had discussed this matter all over, and many of my people were in favor of warning them that if they took no part against us, they should not be molested in the event of war being begun by General Howard. This plan was voted down in the war council.

There were bad men among my people who had quarreled with white men, and they talked of their wrongs until they roused all the bad hearts in the council. Still I could not believe that they would begin the war. I know that my young men did a great wrong, but I ask, who was first to blame? They had been insulted a thousand times. Their fathers and brothers had been killed; their mothers and wives had been disgraced; they had been driven to madness by the whiskey sold to them by the white men; they had been told by General Howard that all their horses and cattle which they had been unable to drive out of Wallowa were to fall into the hands of white men; and, added to all this, they were homeless and desperate.

I would have given my own life if I could have undone the killing of white men by my people. I blame my young men and I blame the white men. I blame General Howard for not giving my people time to get their stock away from Wallowa. I do not acknowledge that he had the right to order me to leave Wallowa at any time. I deny that either my father or I ever sold that land. It is still our land. It may never again be our home, but my father sleeps there, and I love it as I love my mother. I left there hoping to avoid bloodshed.

If General Howard had given me plenty of time to gather up my stock and treated Too-hool-hool-suit as a man should be treated, there would have been no war. My friends among white men have blamed me for the war. I am not to blame. When my young men began the killing, my heart was hurt. Although I did not justify them, I remembered all the insults I had endured, and my blood was on fire. Still I would have taken my people to the buffalo country without fighting, if possible.

I could see no other way to avoid a war. We moved over to White Bird Creek, sixteen miles away, and there encamped, intending to collect our stock before leaving but the soldiers attacked us and the first battle was fought. We numbered in that battle sixty men, and the soldiers a hundred. The fight lasted but a few minutes when the soldiers retreated before us for twelve miles. They lost thirty-three killed and had seven wounded. When an Indian fights, he only shoots to kill, but soldiers shoot at random. None of the soldiers were scalped. We do not believe in scalping, nor in killing wounded men. Soldiers do not kill many Indians unless they are wounded and left upon the battlefield. Then they kill Indians.

Seven days after the first battle General Howard arrived in the Nez Perces' country, bringing seven hundred more soldiers. It was now war in earnest. We crossed over Salmon River, hoping General Howard would follow. We were not disappointed. He did follow us, and we got between him and his supplies and cut him off for three days. He sent out two companies to open the way. We attacked them, killing one officer, two guides, and ten men.

We withdrew, hoping the soldiers would follow, but they had had fighting enough for that day. They entrenched themselves, and next day we attacked again. The battle [at Cottonwood] lasted all day, and was renewed next morning. We killed four and wounded seven or eight.

About this time General Howard found out that we were in his rear. Five days later he attacked us with three hundred and fifty soldiers and settlers. We had two hundred and fifty warriors. The fight [at Cottonwood Creek] lasted twenty-seven hours. We lost four killed and several wounded. General Howard's loss was twenty-nine killed and sixty wounded.

The following day the soldiers charged upon us, and we retreated with our families and stock a few miles [to Kamiah], leaving eighty lodges to fall into General Howard's hands.

Finding that we were outnumbered, we retreated to Bitterroot Valley [in Montana]. Here another body of soldiers came upon us and demanded our surrender. We refused. They said, "You cannot get by us." We answered, "We are going by you without fighting if you will let us, but we are going by you anyhow." We then made a treaty with these soldiers. We agreed not to molest anyone and they agreed that we might pass through the Bitterroot country in peace. We bought provisions and traded stock with white men there.

We understood that there was to be no war. We intended to go peaceably to the buffalo country and leave the question of returning to our country to be settled afterward. With this understanding, we traveled on for four days, and thinking that the trouble was all over, we stopped and prepared tentpoles to take with us. We started again, and at the end of two days we saw three white men passing our camp. Thinking that peace had been made, we did not molest them. We could have killed them or taken them prisoners, but we did not suspect them of being spies, which they were.

That night the soldiers surrounded our camp. About daybreak one of my men went out to look after his horses. The soldiers saw him and shot him down like a coyote. I have since learned that these soldiers were not those we had left behind. They had come upon us from another direction. The new white war-chief's name was Gibbon. He charged upon us while some of my people were still asleep. We had a hard fight. Some of my men crept around and attacked the soldiers from the rear. In this battle [at the Big Hole] we lost nearly all our lodges, but we finally drove General Gibbon back.

Finding that he was not able to capture us, he sent to his camp a few miles away for his big guns (cannons), but my men had captured them and all the ammunition. We damaged the big guns all we could and carried away the powder and lead. In the fight with General Gibbon we lost fifty women and children and thirty fighting men. We remained long enough to bury our dead.

The Nez Perces never make war on women and children; we could have killed a great many women and children while the war lasted, but we would feel ashamed to do so cowardly an act. We never scalp our enemies, but when General Howard came up and joined General Gibbon, their Indian scouts dug up our dead and scalped them. I have been told that General Howard did not order this great shame to be done.

We retreated as rapidly as we could toward the buffalo country. After six days General Howard came close to us, and we went out and attacked him and captured nearly all his horses and mules (about two-hundred and fifty head). We then marched on to the Yellowstone Basin.

On the way we captured one white man and two white women. We released them at the end of three days. They were treated kindly. The women were not insulted. Can the white soldiers tell me of one time when Indian women were taken prisoners and held three days and then released without being insulted? Were the Nez Perce women who fell into the hands of General Howard's soldiers treated with as much respect? I deny that a Nez Perce was ever guilty of such a crime.

A few days later we captured two more white men. One of them stole a horse and escaped. We gave the other a poor horse and told him that he was free.

Nine days' march brought us to the mouth of Clark's Fork of the Yellowstone. We did not know what had become of General Howard, but we supposed that he had sent for more horses and mules. He did not come up, but another new war-chief (General Sturgis) attacked us. We held him in check while we moved all our women and children and stock out of danger, leaving a few men to cover our retreat.

Several days passed, and we heard nothing of General Howard, or Gibbon, or Sturgis. We had repulsed each in turn and began to feel secure when another army, under General Miles, struck us. This was the fourth army, each of which outnumbered our fighting force, that we had encountered within sixty days.

We had no knowledge of General Miles' army until a short time before he made a charge upon us, cutting our camp in two and capturing nearly all of our horses. About seventy men, myself among them, were cut off. My little daughter, twelve years of age, was with me. I gave her a rope and told her to catch a horse and join the others who were cut off from the camp. I have not seen her since, but I have learned that she is alive and well.

I thought of my wife and children, now surrounded by soldiers, and I resolved to go to them or die. With a prayer to the Great Spirit Chief who rules above, I dashed unarmed through the line of soldiers. It seemed to me that there were guns on every side, before and behind me. My clothes were cut to pieces and my horse was wounded, but I was not hurt. As I reached the door of my lodge, my wife handed me my rifle, saying, "Here's your gun. Fight!"

The soldiers kept up a continuous fire. Six of my men were killed in one spot near me. Ten or twelve soldiers charged into our camp and got possession of two lodges, killing three Nez Perces and losing three of their men, who fell inside our lines. I called my men to drive them back. We fought at close range, not more than twenty steps apart, and drove the soldiers back upon their main line, leaving their dead in our hands. We secured their arms and ammunition. The first day and night we lost eighteen men and three women. General Miles lost twenty-six killed and forty wounded. The following day General Miles sent a messenger into my camp under protection of a white flag. I sent my friend Yellow Bull to meet him.

Yellow Bull understood the messenger to say that General Miles wished me to consider the situation, that he did not want to kill my people unnecessarily. Yellow Bull understood this to be a demand for me to surrender and save blood. Upon reporting this message to me, Yellow Bull said he wondered whether General Miles was in earnest. I sent him back with my answer, that I had not made up my mind, but would think about it and send word soon. A little later he sent some Cheyenne scouts with another message. I went out to meet them. They said they believed that General Miles was sincere and really wanted peace. I walked on to General Miles' tent. He met me and we shook hands. He said, "Come, let us sit down by the fire and talk this matter over." I remained with him all night. Next morning, Yellow Bull came over to see if I was alive and why I did not return. General Miles would not let me leave the tent to see my friend alone.

Yellow Bull said to me, "They have got you in their power, and I am afraid they will never let you go. I have an officer in our camp, and I will hold him until they let you go free."

I said, "I do not know what they mean to do with me, but if they kill me, you must not kill the officer. It will do no good to avenge my death by killing him."

Yellow Bull returned to my camp. I did not make any agreement that day with General Miles. The battle was renewed while I was with him. I was very anxious about my people. I knew that we were near Sitting Bull's camp in King George's land, and I thought maybe the Nez Perces who had escaped would return with assistance. No great damage was done to either party during the night.

On the following morning I returned to my camp by agreement, meeting the officer who had been held a prisoner in my camp at the flag of truce. My people were divided about surrendering. We could have escaped from Bear Paw Mountain if we had left our wounded, old women, and children behind. We were unwilling to do this. We had never heard of a wounded Indian recovering while in the hands of white men.

On the evening of the fourth day, General Howard came in with a small escort, together with my friend Chapman. We could now talk understandingly. General Miles said to me in plain words, "If you will come out and give up your arms, I will spare your lives and send you back to the reservation." I do not know what passed between General Miles and General Howard.

I could not bear to see my wounded men and women suffer any longer; we had lost enough already. General Miles had promised that we might return to our country with what stock we had left. I thought we could start again. I believed General Miles, or I never would have surrendered. I have heard that he has been censured for making the promise to return us to Lapwai. He could not have made any other terms with me at that time. I would have held him in check until my friends came to my assistance, and then neither of the generals nor their soldiers would have ever left Bear Paw Mountain alive.

On the fifth day I went to General Miles and gave up my gun and said, "From where the sun now stands I will fight no more." My people needed rest—we wanted peace.

I was told we could go with General Miles to Tongue River and stay there until spring, when we would be sent back to our country. Finally it was decided that we were to be taken to Tongue River. We had nothing to say about it.

After our arrival at Tongue River, General Miles received orders to take us to Bismarck [North Dakota]. The reason given was that subsistence would be cheaper there.

General Miles was opposed to this order. He said, "You must not blame me. I have endeavored to keep my word, but the chief who is over me has given the order, and I must obey it or resign. That would do you no good. Some other officer would carry out the order."

I believe General Miles would have kept his word if he could have done so. I do not blame him for what we have suffered since the surrender. I do not know who is to blame. We gave up all our horses—over eleven hundred—and all our saddles—over one hundred—and we have not heard of them since. Somebody has got our horses.

General Miles turned my people over to another soldier, and we were taken to Bismarck. Captain Johnson, who now had charge of us, received an order to take us to Fort Leavenworth [Kansas]. At Leavenworth we were placed on a low river bottom, with no water except river water to drink and cook with. We had always lived in a healthy country, where the mountains were high and the water was cold and clear. Many of our people sickened and died, and we buried them in this strange land. I cannot tell how much my heart suffered for my people while at Leavenworth. The Great Spirit Chief who rules above seemed to be looking some other way and did not see what was being done to my people.

During the hot days (July, 1878) we received notice that we were to be moved farther away from our own country. We were not asked if we were willing to go. We were ordered to get into the railroad cars. Three of my people died on the way to Baxter Springs [Kansas]. It was worse to die there than to die fighting in the mountains.

We were moved from Baxter Springs to the Indian Territory and set down without our lodges. We had but little medicine and we were nearly all sick. Seventy of my people have died since we moved there.

We have had a great many visitors who have talked many ways. Some of the chiefs (General Fish and Colonel Stickney) from Washington came to see us and selected land for us to live upon. We have not moved to that land, for it is not a good place to live.

The Commissioner Chief (E. A. Hayt) came to see us. I told him, as I told everyone, that I expected General Miles' word would be carried out. He said it "could not be done, that white men now lived in my country and all the land was taken up; that if I returned to Wallowa, I could not live in peace; that law papers were out against my young men who began the war, and that the government could not protect my people." This talk fell like a heavy stone upon my heart. I saw that I could not gain anything by talking to him. Other law chiefs (Congressional Committee) then came to see us and said they would help me to get a healthy country. I did not know whom to believe. The white people have too many chiefs. They do not understand each other. They do not talk alike.

The Commissioner Chief (Mr. Hayt) invited me to go with him and hunt for a better home than we have now. I like the land we found (west of the Osage Reservation) better than any place I have seen in that country but it is not a healthy land. There are no mountains and rivers. The water is warm. It is not a good country for stock. I do not believe my people can live there. I am afraid they will all die. The Indians who occupy that country are dying off. I promised Chief Hayt to go there, and do the best I could until the Government got ready to make good General Miles' word. I was not satisfied, but I could not help myself.

Then the Inspector General (McNeill) came to my camp and we had a long talk. He said I ought to have a home in the mountain country north and that he would write a letter to the Great Chief in Washington. Again the hope of seeing the mountains of Idaho and Oregon grew up in my heart.

At last I was granted permission to come to Washington and bring my friend Yellow Bull and our interpreter with me. I am glad we came. I have shaken hands with a great many friends, but there are some things I want to know which no one seems able to explain. I cannot understand how the Government sends a man out to fight us, as it did General Miles, and then breaks his word.

Such a government has something wrong about it. I cannot understand why so many chiefs are allowed to talk so many different ways and promise so many different things. I have seen the Great Father Chief (the President), the next Great Chief (Secretary of the Interior), the Commissioner Chief (Hayt), the Law Chief (General Butler), and many other law chiefs (Congressmen), and they all say they are my friends, and that I shall have justice, but while their mouths all talk right, I do not understand why nothing is done for my people. I have heard talk and talk, but nothing is done. Good words do not last long until they amount to something. Words do not pay for my dead people. They do not pay for my land, now overrun by white men. They do not protect my father's grave. They do not pay for my horses and cattle. Good words will not give me back my children. Good words will not make good the promise of your War Chief, General Miles. Good words will not give my people good health and stop them from dying. Good words will not get my people a home where they can live in peace and take care of themselves. I am tired of talk that comes to nothing. It makes my heart sick when I remember all the good words and all the broken promises. There has been too much talking by men who had no right to talk. Too many misrepresentations have been made, too many misunderstandings have come up between the white men about the Indians.

If the white man wants to live in peace with the Indian, he can live in peace. There need be no trouble. Treat all men alike. Give them all the same law. Give them all an even chance to live and grow. All men were made by the same Great Spirit Chief. They are all brothers. The earth is the mother of all people, and all people should have equal rights upon it. You might as well expect the rivers to run backward as that any man who was born a free man should be contented while penned up and denied liberty to go where he pleases. If you tie a horse to a stake, do you expect he will grow fat? If you pen an Indian up on a small spot of earth and compel him to stay there, he will not be contented nor will he grow and prosper. I have asked some of the great white chiefs where they get their authority to say to the Indian that he shall stay in one place, while he sees white men going where they please. They cannot tell me.

I only ask of the Government to be treated as all other men are treated. If I cannot go to my own home, let me have a home in some country where my people will not die so fast. I would like to go to Bitterroot Valley. There my people would be healthy; where they are now, they are dying. Three have died since I left my camp to come to Washington.

When I think of our condition, my heart is heavy. I see men of my race treated as outlaws and driven from country to country, or shot down like animals.

I know that my race must change. We cannot hold our own with the white men as we are. We only ask an even chance to live as other men live. We ask to be recognized as men. We ask that the same law shall work alike on all men. If the Indian breaks the law, punish him by the law. If the white man breaks the law, punish him also.

Let me be a free man—free to travel, free to stop, free to work, free to trade where I choose, free to choose my own teachers, free to follow the religion of my fathers, free to think and talk and act for myself—and I will obey every law or submit to the penalty.

Whenever the white man treats the Indian as they treat each other, then we shall have no more wars. We shall be all alike—brothers of one father and one mother, with one sky above us and one country around us and one government for all. Then the Great Spirit Chief who rules above will smile upon this land and send rain to wash out the bloody spots made by brothers' hands upon the face of the earth. For this time the Indian race are waiting and praying. I hope that no more groans of wounded men and women will ever go to the ear of the Great Spirit Chief above, and that all people may be one people.

In-mut-too-yah-lat-lat has spoken for his people.

Joseph

Index